the art of friction

the art of fRiction

where [*non*]fictions come together

EDITED BY CHARLES BLACKSTONE AND JILL TALBOT

university of texas press, austin

Requests for permission to reproduce material from this work should be sent to:
Permissions
University of Texas Press
P.O. Box 7819
Austin, TX 78713-7819
www.utexas.edu/utpress/about/bpermission.html

♾ The paper used in this book meets the minimum requirements of ANSI/NISO Z39.48-1992 (R1997) (Permanence of Paper).

LIBRARY OF CONGRESS CATALOGING-IN-PUBLICATION DATA

The art of friction : where (non)fictions come together / edited by Charles Blackstone and Jill Talbot. — 1st ed.
  p.   cm.
ISBN 978-0-292-71879-1 (cl. : alk. paper) — ISBN 978-0-292-71891-3 (pbk. : alk. paper)
  1. American literature. 2. United States—Literary collections. 3. American literature—21st century—History and criticism. I. Blackstone, Charles, 1977– II. Talbot, Jill Lynn.
  PS507.A78   2008
  810.8—dc22   2008026880

Contents

ACHY OBEJAS
achy obejas

When my first book, *We Came All the Way from Cuba So You Could Dress Like This?*, was released in 1994, my publishers were ecstatic at the starred review it received in *Publishers Weekly.*

But though I appreciated the applause, I was a bit dismayed. The review referred to the seven pieces that comprise the book as "autobiographical essays." I found this particularly alarming, since six of the seven stories were first-person narrations, mostly Puerto Rican and Mexican voices, while I am Cuban, and one was from the point of view of a white gay man named Tommy who is dying of AIDS.

I'd have thought that the reviewer might have noticed that nationality, race, and gender seemed to shift from story to story—and that is what they were, stories, not essays; fiction, not memoir—but perhaps that reviewer, like many others who followed, felt more comforted in believing that the stories were not products of the imagination but lived experiences.

The imagination is a very powerful, mysterious, and intimidating force. It's the secret sauce in the recipe for Art, the code in the magic decoder ring. Art—unlike science or the nonfiction practices that pretend to be based in "real life" or on "facts"—is rather borderless; it's a place of mayhem and disorder. In the very best cases, Art—literature being an essential example—is also utterly lawless.

This makes people really nervous.

Two years later, *PW* still couldn't let go of the autobiographical angle, only it was more subtle. "With prose so crisp it could read as biography . . . ," it raved about my first novel, *Memory Mambo.*

From the start, my publishers kept telling me this was all a good thing: My writing rang true, my writing felt real.

But I knew there was more to it than that. This fiction-nonfiction, I was convinced, was going to come back to bite me.

I remember when I went out on tour for *We Came All the Way from Cuba So You Could Dress Like This?* that readers would frequently come up to me and tell me how sorry they were about my father. This threw me off at first until I realized they had confused me with the narrator of the title story, whose father dies in a car accident about halfway through the tale.

What was most fascinating to me was people's reactions when I explained that, in fact, my own father was very much alive.

They felt cheated. They felt deceived. One person told me, "That's a pretty big thing to lie about."

"Well," I tried to explain, "it's not a lie. I just made that up."

"That's what I mean," she insisted. "You can't just make that up."

But of course you can—we can—writers make stuff up all the time.

This resistance to the imagination, I discovered, was not limited to complete strangers.

My mother, who rarely reads my work because, as she puts it, she doesn't know how much she can take, once picked up a draft of *Memory Mambo*. In that novel, the Las Casas family, like my own, escapes from Cuba by boat.

But my mother, upon reading just the first few lines, quickly thrust down the pages and declared her verdict: "That's not how it happened."

"I know, Mami," I said, "but that's fiction."

"Well," she said, "that may be how you remember it but that's not how it was."

In 1996, after *Memory Mambo* came out, I noticed I began to get invitations to speak at domestic abuse conferences. At the end of that novel, there's a particularly horrific and violent scene.

And whenever friends would introduce me to a potential date, they'd say: "She's very gentle. Really." When I'd say, "That was fiction, I've never been abused," I'd get these blank stares and the distinct feeling that they thought I was just trying to cover up.

After *Days of Awe*, each and every one of my friends in Cuba was convinced I'd been having an affair with a driver I routinely hired when I was on the island. People were advising my then-girlfriend to not let me get away with that kind of humiliation.

But something peculiar happened with *Days of Awe* too: Often, the stuff that was "true," i.e., based on facts, was not always believed.

"That was pretty ingenious," a critic suggested at a panel discussion in Mexico City, "to make Fidel Castro's grandfather a Turkish Jew."

Except that I didn't. He really was a Turkish Jew.

"That was great, that the CIA tried to kill Fidel 637 times—that was so wonderfully over the top," an American friend who is also a so-called Cuba expert—and a leftist—said with a laugh at a dinner party. "Where did you get a silly number like that?"

Er, from the CIA. From former CIA agents. From Fidel quoting CIA reports.

Some stuff you really can't make up: That the CIA tried to kill Fidel with an exploding cigar, that it actually thought it could drive him to suicide by developing a cream that would make his beard fall off and cause such humiliation that he'd want to off himself.

I thought about using that but decided that, you know, it just didn't sound real enough.

At a panel at the Jewish Museum in New York, a man in the audience stood up and flatly told me he didn't believe anything I'd said about contemporary crypto-Jews. "C'mon, it's been five hundred years since the Inquisition," he said. "How can people still be afraid? Where in Latin America are Jews banned from doing anything?"

Well . . . in 2003, in the Tucumán Province of Argentina, with a population of more than a million people, José Alperovich, then a federal senator, was almost denied the right to run for governor because he was Jewish. A clause in the province's Constitution, held over from Inquisitional times but affirmed again in the 1990s, required the governor to swear allegiance to "God, the Fatherland, and the Christian saints."

Imagine writing that. Imagine bringing that in to workshop.

Earlier in my career and long before book publication, I'd already experienced reality trumping fiction with its absurdity.

A couple of friends and I wrote a play, *Carniceria Rodriguez,* a political satire in the middle of the 1983 Chicago mayoral campaign, when Harold Washington, the city's first black mayor, would be elected. *Carniceria,* which became the longest-running Spanish-language play in the city at nine months, was rollicking good fun.

We wrote, facetiously, of a precinct captain who'd forged 230 votes. After the elections, a precinct captain was indicted for forging 315 votes.

In our play, we had a character who'd set a shrimp peeling record of forty-seven a minute. We were later contacted by a woman who worked in a cannery in Maryland who claimed more than sixty a minute.

Then there's the stuff I thought was fiction and later discovered wasn't.

In *Memory Mambo*, I portray a large family that owns and works in a Laundromat. My own family has had a varied work experience: Upon arrival in the United States, my parents were migrant workers, picking tomatoes in South Florida. My father pumped gas. My dad also sold fruits and vegetables from the back of his station wagon. He was a waiter at a Chinese restaurant and even worked as a dog groomer.

But to my knowledge, we had never gone near a Laundromat.

Leave it to my mother to ruin my pride in imagining it. It turns out that my Aunt Juana briefly owned a Laundromat somewhere in Gary, Indiana, and my dad helped out.

I thought I'd constructed, in *Memory Mambo*, a character with a sweet but inflated sense of self. In the book, the father thinks he invented duct tape and that Dupont Corporation stole the formula.

Really, how could that be vaguely true?

My mother tsk-tsked.

"Making fun of your father like that," she said.

"What?" I exclaimed. "There's no way you're going to tell me Papi invented duct tape!"

"Well, no, he didn't 'invent' it," she said, and I was almost relieved. "But he perfected it. Don't you remember all those men in the courtyard of our house in Havana rolling the tape onto spools? What did you think they were doing?"

And of course, I did remember—except I thought I'd imagined it. I'd given myself tremendous credit for inventing something that really happened.

What, exactly, is my father's real relationship to duct tape? I have no idea. He never said. When he died in 2002 he took that secret—and a million others—to his grave.

This just forces me to imagine myriad scenarios about my father and duct tape. Maybe he did invent it. Maybe he just thought he did. Maybe he did improve on it in some way. What the hell were those guys doing spooling that tape in our Havana home?

How much is fact and how much is fiction? Given the persistent problem, I thought I'd just take a minute to clear some things up about my work.

Unlike Enrique in *Days of Awe,* my father was not a highly regarded translator, but a retired high school Spanish teacher and forlorn former lawyer. Actually, we're not sure about the lawyer part. He said he was a lawyer in Cuba, but doubts have been raised. A cousin in Cuba remembers his dropping out of law school to spite my grandfather.

My mother is not nearly as patient or generous of spirit as her counterpart in the book. She claims that she has never put a glass of water under the bed as an offering to the gods and has no idea where I picked up such crazy ideas.

I have never made love at the side of a country road in Cuba with dogs howling in the background. I want to make this perfectly clear: There were NO dogs howling.

ACHY OBEJAS was born in Havana and came to the United States as a young child. She is a cultural writer for the *Chicago Tribune*. Her articles have appeared in *Vogue, The Nation,* the *Los Angeles Times, Chicago Reader, Girlfriend, High Performance, New City,* and the *Chicago Reporter.* She is the author of the novels *Days of Awe* and *Memory Mambo,* and *We Came All the Way from Cuba So You Could Dress Like This?,* a collection of short stories. She is a frequent speaker at universities and community centers across the country and in Cuba.

Acknowledgments

We'd like to thank our creative writing professors for showing us the way; our publisher, the University of Texas Press, and editor-in-chief Theresa May, for believing in us and this project; and our students, friends, and families, especially Alpana and Indie, for the experiences that have made us writers time and again.

the art of fRiction

Introduction

jill talbot

While I was teaching an advanced creative nonfiction course one recent spring, Sherman Alexie blasted Nasdijj in *Time* for stealing his story. As several major newspapers and journals got in the line of shame-on-you-ers, my students and I were discussing *The Blood Runs Like a River through My Dreams.* Nasdijj's memoir was vilified for its falsified Navajo persona created by author Tim Barrus. Blurb on cover: "An authentic, important book . . . unfailingly honest and very nearly perfect." Oops. I let my students get through the entirety of the memoir before I told them the truth, actually offered them a link to Alexie's article, along with one from the *Navajo Times,* through the class blog and asked for comments. Posts and comments came in quickly, and most were negative: all shock and scorn. However, many came to the writer's defense. "I don't care if he's a liar; we all are," wrote one young man. Of course, I used the articles as a critical exercise in order to foment debate and various critical responses about the genre they were writing, exemplified by the work they had just read. I assured them, and perhaps myself, that I assigned the memoir for the writing, and I'll stand by my claim that it's still writing worth reading, though the reading experience will no doubt now be completely different, each word shadowed by scandal. I was surprised one day to find a posting from "Nasdijj" himself on the class blog, his response to a discussion about persona, following the students' discovery that Tim Barrus had, at one time, been an advice columnist for *Genesis,* a gay male pornography publication. Commenting on this discussion, I had posted the following question:

> Question: So if Nasdijj writes as a Navajo when he's not, why are some jumping to the conclusion that he's gay? Just a question. Is Nasdijj/Tim Barrus/writer of a 1,000 personas (when does persona cross a line?) just writing a litany of the most lucrative personas?

Nasdijj commented:

> Good question re: SEXUALITY. For years, I wrote/ghosted an advice

column for a men's magazine where "real" men were supposedly writing to a PORN STAR about their sexual problems. Of course, if they had known it was me they were writing to . . .

Anyway . . .

Does that make me a porn star?

No.

It makes me a struggling writer trying to raise children and pay the rent. I'd write porn again in a minute if I could get away with it and get paid for it. For all the screaming that goes on on the Internet, I make less than ten thousand dollars a year.

So. I wrote porn for the ADVOCATE. They pay on acceptance.

Does that make me gay?

Oh, please.

If I write about dogs does it make me a veterinarian?

And this is where I led my students in class the next day: How far do we, can we, go in creating a persona? How is persona like character? What truths do you find in this work? For the latter, I had them write on the board the truths they found in the book. Truths, as we defined it, being "ideas, thoughts, feelings that you can identify with or have learned through experience to be valid." The whiteboard filled quickly with various quotes, allusions, and one-word responses. Still, some of the students weren't willing to accept a truth if that truth had been presented under false pretenses. We didn't come to a consensus. I didn't intend, or even desire, such an outcome. I wanted them to consider the questions in relation to their own writing, their responsibility, their proximity to facts and the truth and how close or far they were willing to go. Another scandal, involving James Frey's book *A Million Little Pieces,* published as a memoir, became the focus of a media indictment, with Oprah, who had initially revered Frey's book on her show, shaking the brightest accusatory torch.

The summer before the media mêlée, Charles Blackstone and I sat on my front porch one afternoon positing the disarming of the divide between fiction and nonfiction by discussing our own writings, his stories, my essays, and eventually, we arrived at the conclusion that an anthology placing these essays/

stories side by side would create a cogent dialogue between the two genres. Whatever genre you write, whether it be creative nonfiction, fiction, or both, tells, I believe, its own story.

In the home where I grew up in Mesquite, Texas, we had a front bedroom. Here my mother kept the albums my parents had long stopped listening to: the Eagles, the Four Seasons, the one with that great song about December, Carole King's *Tapestry*. I'd pull these records off the shelf and consider them the words and music that had at one time captured my parents' earlier lives, wondering why they had abandoned them; after all, we still had a record player. I had one in my room. Though I was too young to recall this, my older brother by sixteen years kept his own set of records, some of which were now in this pile, and on afternoons while he still lived at home, he'd move a speaker to an open window and listen as he worked outside, mowing the yard perhaps, or just hanging out. I don't remember; I was four when he left home for college in his red VW bug. There was so much about this family I did not know or did not remember. I can only imagine that's why I resurrected the lyrics and melodies of these silenced songs and played them in my own room, becoming an aficionado of Seventies music. Though it wasn't the Seventies I was trying to relive in my room, it was what I could not possibly be a part of: the past I was there for but did not recall. The years before me when my parents had dreams, and when those dreams failed, they found new ones, or at least settled for the things that came along.

Also in that front room, my mother kept a typewriter. I'm not sure she ever used it, but I can remember pulling a chair up to the desk regularly and typing. I even had a typewriting book, one of the large ones that would fold over so that you could balance it on the desk next to the typewriter and practice: bbjjffvv. But I wasn't just typing, I was writing a book, what I would later learn was called a memoir. Its title clear in my head, *The Coach's Daughter,* my book was to detail the life I led in Texas as the daughter of a head football coach. Even though I loved going to the field house with my father on Saturdays, envisioned those high school boys as grown men mysteries, and in later years developed a crush on one or two a season, I can recall feeling that I had a unique window into a life, a world, that I wanted to let others see through. I'd go into the front room daily, a writer's persistence already instilled within me, and write, much to my mother's protests that I should be playing outside. Though when I played outside, it involved sitting under a tree with my dog Skeeter, narrating my thoughts and feelings at length. *Too much in your head,* a phrase a man once used to describe me. In those early years, the only way that internalization found any air was in writing. Of course, I didn't conceptualize it that way at the time, I just felt a need to write, as if it was something I did, like the way I sing or hum all the time without noticing until someone points it out to me. Bottom line: I suspect I write stories that have never been told. If I make anything up, it's still true.

A student of mine had come back from Christmas break after a stint in rehab. When James Frey's memoir *A Million Little Pieces* was shot down by thesmokinggun.com, my student came to my office after a discussion in my nonfiction class of the ramifications of the media maelstrom. "I actually read Frey's book while I was in rehab," he told me, something I'm sure he didn't want to share in class, which was unfortunate, though fair. After all, wouldn't an addict in a rehabilitation facility be an expert on the truth of Frey's foray into the addict mind? My student told me that the book had been kind of a passed-around contraband in rehab, because Frey so vehemently disparages the program of Alcoholics Anonymous, the foundation of most rehabilitation facilities. My student told how he'd borrowed the book from a fellow drunk, read it in two days, and passed it on—and so on it went. He said, "My counselor said that all the AA old-timers say Frey's gonna go back to drinking. He's gonna crash." To me, well to all of us the student told, this was the debate about Frey's book. "I mean here we all were locked up for twenty-eight days, and Frey essentially says that you have a choice: drink or don't. And he hasn't. At least that's what he claims in the book. But none of that matters to me. What I took from it was I had a choice, too."

Charles sent me an e-mail during the Frey frenzy: "The only truth is in fiction."

Please. Let's not simplify the distinction between fiction and nonfiction with the adage "Truth is stranger than fiction." First, creative nonfiction has a difficult time defining itself. Now, set it down for cocktails with its etymologically opposing genre, and we're going to be here long past happy hour. First, how are we to define truth? I had a professor who once demanded that all terms in a literary analysis be defined for clarification and limitation purposes. Should we begin by defining fiction? Nonfiction? This anthology presumes to race beyond that starting gate to consider where the genres intersect, commingle, challenge genre lines. We wish to problematize the distinctions, in the debate that follows, through authors' selected works and their respective commentaries. If you want to join the debate, begin by completing the following statements:

Fiction is _____.

Nonfiction is _____.

Now, alternate your answers. Do they still work? If your answer is yes, where might you find meanings in order to distinguish? If your answer is no, you have already completed this section of the program. However, if, like us, you find that taking a stance foils the opportunity for exploration and debate, read on. We have purposely not identified the pieces in this anthology by genre so that readers might be able to discuss the merits of each piece without labeling while also proving that putting a label on some of these is more like the Gilbert family trying to identify that final, elusive answer from the survey on *Family Feud*, or for you younger readers, a viewer accurately picking out the top twelve of *American Idol* at the beginning of the season.

So there I was, a student, spending my afternoons in that front room on Grubb Street, typing what it was like to be me. I felt against the world, or that my world was against me. I wanted to put it down, imagined a film being made of my story, my struggles. What those struggles were at the age of nine, I cannot recount, but I have an idea. Even though the situations and persons involved have changed, I still have something within me that feels the same way it did when I sat in Mrs. Hopkins's fourth-grade class. Eventually, I abandoned the book-length project for cheerleading and light blue letter jackets in middle school. From that point through high school, my writing turned to poetry, where I confessed my secret loves and longings in easy, rhymed verse. One thing that did not change, however, was my penchant for listening to only Seventies music. By the time I was in college, I had collected all of the Eagles CDs and kept the *On the Border* album that I had rescued from that front room as a showpiece in my various apartments and duplexes through graduate school. I liked showing everyone that the original price sticker remained: thirty-three cents. Eagles at a bargain, simpler times that I wasn't trying to get back in my writing, but get *at*.

———

Some of you may be reading this anthology as part of an introductory creative writing course. During one of my own intro courses, after the class had studied and written both fiction and creative nonfiction, I put the two genres on the board and asked students to tell me the basic elements of each, beginning with fiction. We had studied craft by reading John Gardner's *The Art of Fiction*. We began our list: plot, character, dialogue, narrator, description, detail, setting. Now, I said, let's do creative nonfiction. One student from the back suggested we could list the same items we had included for fiction. I wrote the same characteristics under the CNF column and waited for the inevitable question: What's the difference? Indeed. As we pondered, students added the following to CNF: persona, voice, memory, truth. Next question: Can't those go under fiction as well? Sure they can. An interesting discussion, whether you're in an introductory class or a graduate seminar, or talking about the genres with fellow writers over coffee, would be: Where do we go from here? What might we add to each column to differentiate the two genres?

———

For many years, I didn't write anything but poetry; in fact, I entered the University of Colorado's Masters Program in Creative Writing for poetry, until my final semester when I took a creative nonfiction course and read the introduction to Phillip Lopate's *The Art of the Personal Essay*. Reading his descriptions of the essayist—"the desire for contact," "world-weary personae," "candor," and "self-disclosure"—I thought, *This is me.* Just as Pablo Neruda claimed to have been found by poetry, I knew the essay had found me, and I felt myself open up the poems I had been writing to expose the emotions and ruminations that hid between their lines. The essay comes naturally to me—its purpose, its patterns, its persona, *my* persona. The first essay I ever wrote, "On Longing," captured my capacity to miss, to long, for desiring never to be fulfilled. I continue to write about distances, the "betweenness" of my existence, but I've always felt that when I write essays, what I'm truly embarking upon is an exploration of answers I cannot possibly know, the conversations never allowed, the words unwilling to be shared. I dig down into the unknown, though Lopate says it better: "Personal essayists are adept at interrogating . . . they ask . . . what it is they don't know—and why." In other words, I write what I don't know, have never known, and probably never will.

A couple of years ago, I sent a piece that I had written as an essay, then later revised into a story, to a journal. The editors' response: "This appears to be creative nonfiction rather than short fiction though we do welcome nonfiction submissions." Clearly, I hadn't fooled anyone. A year later, when I had a creative nonfiction piece that I thought worked quite well for the journal, I sent it to the nonfiction editor. Response: "Thank you for your fiction submission. We felt the characters weren't really developed and thought you might move the part of the husband leaving to the opening of the story."

With each essay that I write, I sit down to interrogate absences, those "misses" in memory or in reality. I write my grandmother, a woman I understood but didn't know very well. I write my father's story, one I've only heard a portion of. I write the distance between my mother and my self, and while my words are not meant to create a solution or even a catharsis (though sometimes they do offer closure), they are a means of communicating, a luxury not privileged in my family. I tell my students that perhaps the reason I write essays is because I was raised in a family that did not talk about things.

When I was teaching in Utah, my department was fortunate enough to have Bernard Cooper, whose work appears in this anthology, and Erika Krouse, author of *Come Up and See Me Sometime,* a collection of stories, give both readings and master classes. First, Cooper. The morning after his delightful reading, he came to my creative nonfiction class after agreeing to listen to some of the students' pieces and offer feedback. One young man read a piece that "sounded like fiction": there was no I, rather two characters named Juan and Marie; there was no young college student in the story, rather a young boy who showed his father his math homework; no ruminations, rather a story about the missed equations. Cooper encouraged the young man to continue what the young man had introduced as a "short story," though I knew that the student had written the piece as a metaphor about his own missed opportunity between him (middle name John) and a young woman in the class (middle name Marie). Exercise: Call a short story an essay. Call an essay a short story. What ensues? Next, Krouse. During her reading, she spoke about how many readers mistake her female voices for her own. She's one of those writers who is often bombarded with the "Did that really happen?" question. In her master class, she explained that while some people collect stamps, others books, she collects people, as she held up a small black notebook in which she writes down stories she hears about people or impressions she has of people she meets. In fact, at dinner one night, the fiction writer in our program told a story about his childhood, and she quickly inquired, "Can I have that?" We all borrow, it seems, from (for?) ourselves or from (for?) others in order to write the works we need to write.

———

There are essays I am not ready to write, because I cannot access the emotion necessary to write them. Perhaps I am not ready to explore the truth of them. Truth in the essay, as I write it, is how the persona interprets it. Yet there are essays I've written a dozen times in various forms in order to approach my questions from as many possible doorways as I can, and until I find one that truly allows me into the house of my longing's end, I imagine I'll keep writing it.

———

When I teach Pam Houston's title piece from *Cowboys Are Not My Weakness,* I call it an essay. To me, it is.

———

My father raised me to appreciate all kinds of music, from Waylon Jennings and Elvis to classical and Eighties pop. But he and I share an understanding about certain songs, though we don't share what it is we know about the feelings contained in certain lyrics. I loved those songs at nine; I love them now. For Father's Day in 1992, I gave my father a mix tape entitled *Our Favorites*. Cliff Richard's "We Don't Talk Anymore" comes in at number one on that tape, and when it was released in 1979, my father was a grown man who I now know had some history to go with that song, though what connection could I have made at the age of nine when I was twirling to it in my baton class? Though the single was labeled a dance hit, I rotated my wrists and did toss-turnarounds thinking: *This is sad.* I could recognize the longing in that man's voice. Thus, I assume I must have been born with a distance within me and an ability to recognize the distance within others, though I don't write to close any of those emotional avenues; I write to wander through them.

———————

Recently, I received an e-mail rejection from a nonfiction journal. Reason: "Your piece reads like fiction, and our readers would read it as such. We do not accept unsolicited fiction." I thought I had submitted to a creative nonfiction journal. And while the piece was indeed a personal essay, I had employed the third person "She" in order to examine my own actions from a few years back. Experimental, sure, but (1) I wanted to evoke some kind of distancing, my persona's refusal to claim her own actions' effect, and (2) I wasn't anticipating any discrimination for what the editors assumed was subversive genre swapping. These editors proclaimed what they represented as a protection of their readership. As if to say, we can't have our readers out there reading a piece in our journal as if it's fiction. Even if we tell them it's CNF, they'll read it as fiction. Thanks for submitting.

———————

In my late thirties, I still listen to Bread, the Allman Brothers, Ambrosia, America, though the music is now imbued with my own memories: the lover who played Bob Seeger to wake me one morning, the guy who brought America on our road trips because it was "good conversation music," the jukeboxes on afternoons in my favorite bars, when I can play every Seventies selection without annoying a crowd. Yet something within me craves my own song, and something within me craves to sing the songs that those I love abandoned to a front room in Texas, never to be played again. And so I write for them. I write myself.

In Charles Blackstone's novel *The Week You Weren't Here,* Hunter Flanagan tells a female character that he's writing a "fictionalized personal narrative." As a personal essayist and one privy to the facts of Charles's undergrad days (University of Illinois at Chicago, writing center tutor, graduate school applicant who'd eventually move to Boulder), I asked my students, given this data, how far away we were from memoir? And on that summer afternoon on the porch, I directed the same question to Charles. At CU, we took a fiction workshop together, and each class period sitting next to him, I felt like a poser. I knew nothing about creating characters and plots from thin air. After all, my life had given me enough characters and plots to sort through as a writer. I knew nothing of writing this thing called fiction. It wouldn't be until I began teaching fiction in Introduction classes that I would discover ideas like literary versus literal and writing the stories that tell the truth you want to tell. Charles and I began asking each other about our respective genres, and I wondered if he saw mine the way I saw his: a murky mystery that I cannot get to on my own, like the little boy who watches the high school football games from the sidelines. He loves the game, but he's more enraptured with the mystique of the bigger boys who know what it feels like, what it smells like, to crouch down at the line of scrimmage. He *watches* the game; I *read* fiction.

Most of the writers in this anthology, unlike Charles and me, do write both, and they write both well. Others, however, are monogamous writers; they stick to stories or they write only essays. I wanted to understand how much genre-space there is between a scenario I created in an essay about my grandmother in order to add to her tragedy, her missed opportunities, and the lines in which Hunter Flanagan goes to the same school, does the same things, even thinks the way my friend does. I suspected Charles of cheating, maybe we both were. We knew we were onto something, and we knew we'd hit upon something that would take more time, more voices, to unravel.

I.

When I was twenty-eight, I found myself on a train, headed to Ann Arbor, Michigan, to give a reading at a famous town bookstore. I'd published a novel about two months before and was now going through the rigors of promoting it. Publishing a book is, by most accounts, an extremely confusing, off-putting, uncomfortable, surreal sort of endeavor. So many obstacles leading up to this point, so many people pointing out just how unlikely you ever realizing your dream would be but then, pretty much by accident, serendipity, or bad luck, there you are on a train to Michigan to read before an audience of two or twenty.

As the train slogged through the cornfields, I thought about where I was, this published book and concomitant promotional tour, and in the strangeness of it all, was reminded of when I was first starting out, when I first began to write seriously. As much as we think we've eluded our pasts, they're always there, lurking in the background like a stray cat, or a conscience, aren't they?

Long before I was first drafting Hunter Flanagan's interior monologues—his Flanalogues—I was a precocious teenaged novelist. And, yes, it should be known that I spent little time during my teens writing short fiction—I wrote *books*. Most of them featured the same three characters (two of whom make their public debut in *The Week You Weren't Here*), and I recall one sequence I sketched out then. Trey, the dissolute in the triad, the dreamer, decides the only way to get on with his life is to run away from his past, confronting him literally in the Chicago neighborhood in which he grew up, the summer after his sophomore year of college on the East Coast. Trey was probably twenty at that point. First writing him, I was a high school junior, seventeen years old, and had never been to college. Sure, I'd known college, or thought I did—having been raised on the University of Chicago campus, in Hyde Park—from the restaurants and posters and the math-tutoring undergrads I occasionally interacted with when my eighth-grade algebra equations became rigorously parenthetical, but that was the extent of it. I'd never lived in a dorm, I'd never been away from home, come back, and tried to figure out how everything disparate and fragmented could magically cohere, if only for a summer. I certainly had no empirical evidence gathered on what it was like when everybody could come home, family dynamics restored, the natural order returned, and the rest. Even now, as a college graduate who has resided for several years in a different state, I wouldn't say I understand it any better than I did as a teenager.

And, most glaringly absent in my experience up to that point, I'd never, in any context, ridden a train. Then, I'd probably only been on the subway a handful of times. But I wrote this scene where Trey flees, gets on a train (a cross-country Amtrak), drinks at the bar, picks up a teenager, takes her back to his room, and has sex with her. Years later, when revising this scene for a chapter in my grad school master's thesis (hey, I still thought it was a good story), equipped with all the knowledge and acute awareness of realism that one can't help thinking about after years of ubiquitous reminders—workshop members jumping up to point out errors of logic and fact in fiction (and, curiously, usually only in those workshops and not the nonfiction ones) and the like from peers and friends ("You could never find someone drinking shots of scotch in Mexico"), I asked myself, how could I really write convincingly about a character on a train if I'd never been on one? I could put myself into the emotions okay, but was there actually a bar car? Did it matter? Would the story be any richer if I knew the "truth" about bar cars? If they didn't exist, was the answer to just give Trey a suitcase of beer? (I would never have thought of that at the time, having not had occasion to smuggle beer in luggage yet.)

These questions (issues) are, to my mind, at the heart of the debate over what constitutes fiction, what nonfiction, to what degree may the imagination be relied upon, and to what extent must we remain in thrall to the tired edict "Write what you know." I'd always figured I could get away with writing characters with experiences I didn't have firsthand knowledge of if I were writing what *they* knew. Trey knew the bar car existed, and, at the time, that seemed to be enough.

Still, though, I felt a certain measure of relief when I discovered my train actually had a bar car. I'd found myself restless in hour three of the seemingly interminable rail journey and went off in search of something to drink. Other passengers, maybe those who'd taken many trips on Amtrak, had already made their way behind the curtain for cookies and small cups of coffee and orange juice and bottles of soda and ice cream bars. The bartender, an older gentleman in full rail regalia, complete with boxy conductor hat, was busy with difficult customers in front of me, and the time allowed for an opportunity to familiarize myself with the menu. Yes, there were cocktails. There was beer. These things were somewhat outrageously priced, but still—trains did, in fact, serve booze. So Trey could have purchased a drink or two (suspending disbelief for the moment and allowing for the possibility that he wouldn't have been carded, or would have had the cash).

Fiction, like nonfiction, is really about the possibility of something. Often we're way too literal, want a story to do more things for us than it's supposed to. I've always stressed, when defining verisimilitude for students, that it's *like* life. *Like*. It's not life, but it's damn near close. Yes, we believe our characters are real and have lives of their own, that they're not just products of our imagination, just as ardently as essayists claim that their characters (including themselves) really do exist beyond the page. (I maintain that both sets of players do and don't exist in equal proportion.) I like Ernest Hemingway's bit of advice, which I recently came across moving some books, and couldn't believe I'd almost forgotten: *Don't describe the world, make the world.* Is this concept at odds with verisimilitude, with the tenets of realism? I don't think so. I think it dovetails nicely with the others. Maybe describing the world is to rely too heavily on what we all know too well. Maybe the *like* part of verisimilitude is the *making*: It's only *like* life because we haven't experienced it yet. Not that I'm advocating we should do everything we read in fiction just so that we can say the prose has transcended realism and has become real; if you must, please don't start with my coke-snorting, beer-drinking, ripped-jean-sporting band of sophomores— you'll no doubt blame me for the injurious effects on your sleep, your psyche, your liver, and your wallet.

Also, I think people forget about how quote-unquote real life is a fiction. Many long hours after I'd begun my journey that early June morning, I'd reached Ann Arbor and I was sitting in the front seat of a very strange gypsyesque taxi.

The first sign of trouble was that there were two drivers in the car. (One sat in the back and I rode in the front.) The second sign was, after I'd explained I was in town for the night to do a book reading (and withdrew my reading copy of the novel to substantiate this claim), that the front-seat driver within a matter of moments declared himself my regional tour manager and began to plan my evening itinerary, with little regard for what I wanted to do. He started working out a schedule, asking me a litany of questions I had no strength or presence of mind to answer: "What do you want to eat tonight?" "I don't know . . . I'll probably just pick something up—" "Well, what do you like? Japanese? Italian?" "Those sound fine, but, to be honest, I don't usually eat before I read. I like to have a drink and—" "Well, if I pick you up at seven, that would give you forty-five minutes to eat. Do you think that's long enough? And what time is your train in the morning? It takes twenty minutes to get from your hotel to the station and you should allow at least a half hour to check in and—" I was at a loss. I kept looking behind me for some kind of assistance or at least empathy from the silent trainee in the backseat. Were all guests this guy picked up shown such cloying hospitality? Was there a meter in the cab? Was I going to be abducted? What street were we on? Where was this Motel 6? Eventually, we did reach the hotel. I thanked the drivers profusely, overtipped, and promised that I would give them a call in a few hours. After I unpacked and got dressed for the reading, I called the front desk and asked them for the number of the local Yellow Cab company. When a sane driver came to pick me up, I relaxed in the backseat, watched the digits of the meter begin to scroll, breathed in the air-conditioning, and asked how long the driver thought I should allow to get to the station in the morning. "There's usually traffic," he said. "So at least a half hour." To get two, two and a half miles in Ann Arbor, Michigan? In the morning, I ended up at the station a good hour and a half before the train departed. The traffic was nonexistent and Amtraks were notorious for being at least an hour late in departing. So maybe all the cab drivers were a little crazy, or maybe they weren't, but the reading went well, and I had the beginnings of an interesting story to use at a later date. I wasn't sure how meaningful this episode would be for my fiction, though I certainly didn't rule anything out. Maybe it was something I could use as an anecdote for a future book tour. When something went wrong, when a microphone wasn't ready or there wasn't ample stock or even pens to sign arms and T-shirts and children, I could tell the story of when in Ann Arbor, I briefly feared for my life in the front seat of a taxi. Or maybe I'd just know better for the future. Any way I'd spin it, I always ended up better off with what I'd had—not just in terms of experience but also in terms of reflection, projection, imagination. And trust me, as I don't doubt you'll quickly realize once you begin reading this anthology, to be good, to be really good, you need just about everything you can get.

II.

This anthology raises some interesting questions about experimental fiction— really about any fiction, literature, art of any kind, anything we create that makes people think and feel and react and inspires discussion. A painting is a glimpse, a fragment, a story, but not the whole story, and neither is prose. To put it simply, in writing fiction (and creative nonfiction), anytime you, as writer, make a choice to have a character do something or have something or want something (choices ranging from wanting a new pair of shoes to having a specific need to tell a story using a certain narrative device, like, say, an epistolary novel), there are always going to be some things that you're able to explore through the writing that you otherwise wouldn't have been able to, and, of course, there are going to be certain things that your choices will necessarily exclude.

This is not a bad thing. Another good question we should consider is the all-time favorite—who is the writer writing the essay or story for? For whom does anybody writing any sort of narrative write that narrative? Likely the answer we'd hear from the writers in this collection would be "I wrote this for people who read these sorts of narratives, people that get this, and the hell with everyone else," and I think that's a good answer. One piece of writing, or one novel, or one memoir, or one stage play, is not for everyone. Once writers let go of trying to please every imaginable reader, they discover there is actually more freedom for them linguistically, artistically, not less, and they're freed from having to consider the implications of certain abstract concepts that, again, less informed readers like to grab up and champion, like, say, the generic and uncontextualized

charles blackstone

sense of "love" or "understanding." Sophisticated readers, or sophisticated livers of life, aren't that impressed by oversimplification, and fortunately narrative resists being reduced. Good narrative, anyway.

I think that whether the story is putatively "fiction" or "creative nonfiction," whatever those terms actually mean, the same thing is going on in both worlds. We're telling a story, letting the characters–slash–narratized "real" people tell their stories. That's the most important thing we can do. That's the only thing we can do. When writers stop seeing the world through their characters' eyes, stop experiencing events as the character would experience them, and start answering to external exigencies, their writing ceases to be consequent. Writers have agendas. Readers have agendas. I don't give a shit about either. Because it's when we become sixteen again, and write the hell out of an idea, paying little attention to form and implication and social issue and who's holding the latest pen of contention, that the writing—fiction and nonfiction alike—comes alive, really starts to happen, and runs the risk of actually meaning something to readers and to the world. The unfortunate part is that writers can't make this happen. Sure, we're at the reins of the carriage, but we're just the anonymous drivers. As Cris Mazza would say, "I shouldn't see the author's hand" when reading prose. If something isn't important to the character, or, for the CNF fans, narrator (an entity, in my mind, as separate as the former from the writer), why should it be significant to the author? If the author is concerned with things the characters aren't, we have an excellent claim for a heavy-handedness charge. Flannery O'Connor said it best: "You can write anything you can get away with, but nobody has ever gotten away with much." This is true. The story has to be able to justify choices. In *The Week You Weren't Here*, I make some pretty strong choices, and those choices have really resonated with some readers. And have really pissed off others. I think what I did, how I wrote the book, what I included, what I excluded were all very much part of the story itself (as any good narrative structure should be). I wanted the narrative to interact with the story, be the story, not just be a means for conveying it. And I'm also interested in really messed-up characters. Some people get this. But these are not issues particular to fiction. Creative nonfiction has to deal with them all as well, even if essayists don't always want to admit it.

And the reason for that is simple: as humans, we all think (and fallaciously, I might add) our thought processes are flawless. Good thing we don't go through life alone. It takes other people, other perspectives, or other situations, obstacles, and the rest to make us realize that we are actually terribly flawed, and our flawed logic is what gets us into trouble. And that's how we are able to have interesting, relevant narratives. So instead of creating more trouble for each other by claiming there are profound differences between fiction and creative nonfiction, let's just shut up and write. (Or, since we're sitting here with books open, read what the contributors have written.) Trust me. We'll all be better off that way.

It was Friday night and Alex lay on his mother's bed, watching television with glassy eyes while his mother sat in the kitchen reading, or talking on the phone, or doing whatever it was she did in the kitchen while he watched television. He secretly suspected that what she was doing was giving him the privacy to watch television alone, which made the use he put this privacy to even more unsettling. As eleven-thirty approached, his pulse began to quicken. When it arrived he turned down the volume and changed the channel.

It was at the age of thirteen, when cable television was installed in his home and Bar Mitzvah season commenced, that Alex was hit by the twin lightning bolts of sex and religion, two previously unrelated subjects that came crashing into his life simultaneously, as though holding hands.

Eleven-thirty on Friday night was when a program called *Ugly George* aired for half an hour on Channel J. *Ugly George* was a television show about the adventures of a man named Ugly George. The plot was very simple and yet never lost its suspense from one show to the next. The opening scene would invariably be a shot of a busy street somewhere in the city. The camera was mounted on Ugly George's shoulder as he strolled along, pointing his camera this way and that while he described the scene for his viewers in the singsong voice one might use to read a bedtime story. This introductory segment was equivalent to a magician's showing the audience that the top hat was empty, before reaching in and producing a rabbit. Ugly George was showing his viewers that this was the real world, the same sort of crowded street they might have walked down the other day, looking at faces, making tiny judgments about people, having fleeting moments of lust, and proceeding on without anything eventful happening. Ugly George, on the other hand, possessed the ability to make things happen.

Alex did not. He had experimented with petty forms of vandalism and theft, as well as belligerent wisecracks at school that left him stunned and amazed at his own audacity moments after he made them, as though he had been momentarily possessed by some strange demon. Yet everyday circumstances continued to sweep him along, diverting his plans and wishes, impervious to his efforts to change his own life. He had been planning to do something about his crush on Tania Vincent, for example, and yet had hardly been able to meet her eyes. He felt like a captain who drew up elaborate navigational plans for his ship, only to discover anew that the wind and waves would dictate his path, and nothing else.

For Ugly George, the sailing was not smooth, but the direction was clear. If a young woman walked by, Ugly George would point his camera at her and begin talking. He was cordial and polite, but he got to the point fairly quickly. The point was: would the woman care to duck into an alley, or a restroom, or some nook and cranny of the city that Ugly George was always able to find, and show him, and his camera, and a large portion of the subscribers to Manhattan Cable, her breasts.

Ugly George was an anthology of rejection. The styles were as varied as the women. But every now and then a woman said yes. The amateurism of the footage and the awkwardness with which the whole thing progressed added to its intensity and its immediacy. There was no airbrushing here, no poses and props as in dirty magazines, just this strange voluntary gesture of a woman exposing herself to a man with a camera, usually after considerable coaxing.

Alex watched *Ugly George* in a state of extreme excitement and agitation, because all this visual delight had to be experienced with his mother sitting in the kitchen at the end of the hallway, in her slippers and robe. His Friday-night bedtime was midnight. The floor of the hallway was carpeted. And though Alex had developed a hypersensitive device in his ear to detect his mother's footsteps in the hall, all the erotic stimulation of *Ugly George* had to coexist with an intense vigilance for her arrival.

He watched now crouched in the small space between the television and the foot of her bed, arm outstretched, with his hand on the cable-box dial, ready to spin to another channel at the first sound of her steps. This was the position he maintained for the entire half-hour duration of the show.

Ugly George had gone to the auto show to see what he could find. He found the latest cars from Detroit and Japan, as well as hot rods, and drag racers, and men demonstrating incredibly sharp kitchen knives that would stay sharp no matter what you did to them. Scantily clad women stood on platforms next to the cars like gigantic live hood ornaments. Ugly George approached one after the other.

"Excuse me!" he called out pathetically. "Excuse me, ma'am, can I talk to you a moment?" He was ignored. Or he was told, "I'm busy." Or "Go away." Men in suits approached him. Representatives of Ford, Chrysler, and General Motors told Ugly George to get lost. There had never been an entirely fruitless *Ugly George* program, but now it was eleven-fifty, ten minutes until his bedtime, and things were looking bleak. Then an attractive woman standing next to a car with a lot of chrome started paying attention to what Ugly George had to say. She listened to him with a serious expression.

"I'll talk to you on my break," she said.

Suddenly she was standing on a dark staircase and talking about her modeling career. The bright light on top of the camera gave her face a pale washed-out quality. Ugly George told her that many women had their careers launched on his show. While she spoke, a hand appeared in the lower corner of the screen and tugged gently at her spandex top. "Could you pull this down a little?" he asked.

She pulled it down, showing more cleavage, and said, "Is this good?" She was quite young and looked a little confused by the bright light.

"Yes, that's great," said Ugly George. "Great." Then the hand reappeared at the bottom of the screen. Ugly George was persistent. His hand was like a pale moth that kept flitting back to the bright light of her breast. "You know what would be ideal?" he said.

Her face responded coolly to the suggestion. "You want me to take it *all* the way off?" The hand reached out and gave a gentle tug. She cooperated. Two breasts popped out. Alex and half the adolescent male population of Manhattan let out a silent, heart-thumping cheer. Unfortunately the palpitations of his heart were echoed by his mother's footsteps thudding gently in the hall. He spun the television dial and threw himself back onto her bed. The spin was as arbitrary as roulette.

Alex's mother often walked in on her son watching strange programs. Cooking shows. News specials. And now she found a preacher extolling to his congregation the merits of God and the perils of sin. He made exaggerated gestures with his arms and punctuated his sentences with long meaningful stares into the camera. Alex stared at him with the same blank rapt expression he always had when he watched television. She watched this for a while, standing next to the bed. Finally she turned to him and asked, "Does this interest you?"

"Sort of," he mumbled. "It was just on."

This exchange depressed him far more than abandoning the beautiful woman and her breasts. The real business of his life was, more and more, conducted on a subterranean level, out of his mother's sight, and he felt a pang of sadness and pity for her now, as she puzzled over this strange new fragment like an archaeologist who has just found yet another incongruous item on her dig.

"This is a mistake," he wanted to explain. "The guy talking about Jesus is a fluke. It doesn't accurately reflect my interests and you shouldn't draw any conclusions from it." But this explanation would have to lead to other, impossible explanations, and so he just kept quiet, and suffered through five minutes of the preacher vehemently insisting that Jesus Christ loves you, and that if you love Jesus he will save you, but only if you let him into your heart. Then it was time for bed.

The next morning Alex stood still while his mother helped him with his tie. She tugged at the knot, tightening it, and he pretended to be having an out-of-body experience, so as not to be so close to her face. His father had not lived long enough to teach Alex how to knot a tie, and his mother wasn't too good at it either, so they made it a perennial joint enterprise, a shared task of pulling and tugging until they got it right. Alex felt he could do it on his own at this point, but wasn't quite ready to deprive his mother of the task.

He was on his way to Phil Singer's Bar Mitzvah. It was a cold blustery day in April, and Singer's Bar Mitzvah was the grand finale of a yearlong circuit of Bar Mitzvahs. Under his arm was a gift-wrapped copy of *Great Jews in Sports*. In a rare moment of foresight last fall, Alex had fished ten copies of this book out of a discount bin and had them gift-wrapped, thereby resolving the Bar Mitzvah gift problem. They sat in an ever-shrinking stack in his room.

"It's cold," his mother said as he headed for the door. "Let me get your scarf." He stood in the doorway while she went and got his scarf. He could picture all her movements through the apartment by the sounds of her footsteps, reced-

thomas beller

ing and then approaching again, hurried and purposeful. She handed him the scarf. "Have a wonderful time," she said.

He glared at her because of the word "wonderful," which was a typical word for his mother. It was impractical and romantic and strange. Furthermore it was too dignified. There was something barbaric about these Bar Mitzvahs. Without the context of either school or home, whatever humanity existed within each individual eighth grader was submerged, and they became one pulsating headless group of stimulation seekers, constantly seeking out new life forms to devour. Bar Mitzvahs were like petri dishes in which the germs that composed his class were allowed to commingle and multiply.

Today's Bar Mitzvah boy, Phil Singer, was the coolest person in the grade and, amazingly, someone Alex felt close to, but he did not think "wonderful" was the word for what lay in store.

"I'm not going to have a wonderful time," said Alex stoically. "I may have a good time. And that's a maybe."

"All right," she said. "Then have a good time. Have whatever time you want to have."

He stood in the small vestibule outside their apartment, and she stood in the doorway while the elevator came.

"You look very handsome," she said, smiling, as though she knew she should refrain from this sort of comment, but couldn't resist.

There she goes again, he thought. *Handsome.* What kind of word was that? When a girl at school liked a boy, she called him *cute.* But then did he want his mother to call him cute? The thought was disturbing. He was rescued by the elevator.

"Goodbye," he said. The elevator door closed. There was a small window in the elevator door through which they could see each other for one last second. It was only at this moment, as his mother stood framed by that little window, smiling at him and meeting his gaze, that his feelings of contempt and disgust for her abated, and were replaced by a wrenching and overwhelming sensation of love. Then the elevator dropped, the picture disappeared, and he was descending in what he had come to feel was the world's slowest elevator, a tiny decompression chamber between his home and the real world.

He took a taxi to the Park Avenue Synagogue, which in spite of its name was located on Madison Avenue. There was a group of boys on the sidewalk standing around talking in their gray three-piece suits. Gerstein, Conroy, Fluss, Edelman, and Cohen. They sounded like a law firm, and all except for Gerstein would eventually graduate from law school. Gerstein was a cynical and manipulative creep who had been popular and attractive ever since he stood up in the sandbox. These waning months of eighth grade would be the last uncomplicated and happy months of his life; soon the world would get complicated, and he would be unable to get complicated with it.

Someone racing up Madison in a taxi might have mistaken the group for a bunch of brash young executives, but Alex recognized them as a bunch of leering and belligerent adolescents, spoiled brats, and, he had to admit, the sorry group of humans he spent a lot of his time with. Alex had by now witnessed rabbis of all shapes and sizes explain that the Bar Mitzvah was the ceremony that celebrated a boy's passage to manhood. Gerstein, Edelman, and Fluss had already had theirs. The transformation was not evident.

Alex joined the group.

"Nice jacket, Fader," said Gerstein, his good friend. "Do you wear the same underwear to every Bar Mitzvah too?"

"Nice face," Alex replied, and immediately marveled at his inability to say anything insulting to anyone else, while, on the other hand, every insult directed at him was like a radioactive thorn that leaked poison into his system for hours if not weeks after it was inserted. Already he felt a tiny vibration of hatred toward his mother for having bought him this stupid blue blazer and gray slacks. At least, he reflected, Gerstein had not called him fat. He wasn't even that fat anymore, but he had been when he first arrived at the school in fourth grade, and had continued to be for several years, and now he was like a character actor who is not allowed to change his character—Fat.

"Today is going to be good," said Cohen. "The Plaza."

"Singer is a maniac," said Fluss.

"I hope we get a good gift," said Gerstein.

"I hope it's better than a little cup that says 'Arnold's Bar Mitzvah' on it," said Fluss, referring to Gerstein's Bar Mitzvah gift a month earlier.

"I wonder if Singer will be wasted when he reads from the Torah," said Cohen.

"Scott would be so pissed if Singer messed up," said Fluss. Scott was Phil Singer's father.

"Scott!" said Edelman.

"Scott!" replied Fluss, as though responding to a mating call. "Scott Scott Scott Scott!" he continued. All the boys started bleating the name "Scott." They sounded like honking geese. Alex joined in meekly. It was the strange custom of all of Alex's classmates to refer to their own and everyone else's father by their first names. The mention of one of these names sent all his friends into peals of ecstatic laughter, as though it were the most ridiculous thing they had ever heard. Were his father still alive, Alex could not imagine taking any pleasure in referring to him as Sol and to chanting his name derisively with them.

When the chanting subsided, the boys turned to go inside. The Park Avenue Synagogue, at Eighty-eighth and Madison, was just three blocks south of Alex's barbershop, Michael's, and Alex suddenly thought of it. Michael specialized in children. It had been founded sometime during the Kennedy administration, and its interior design had not been revised since. The walls were covered with the Kennedy kids sporting a haircut called the John-John. The chairs were large imperial contraptions made of white porcelain and red leather that went up and down, and some of them had little toy cars, orange and green, built around them, for the youngest children, which gave the place a carnival atmosphere. Every kid got a Tootsie Pop while his hair was cut. There was a small room in the back where partially distressed children were taken, so their screams and wails would not disturb everyone else. Alex had been a frequent visitor to this back room when he was very young. He remembered the cooing sounds of the barber, his mother's hand caressing him, and the shrill snip snip of the scissors next to his ear. Above all, as he entered the cool interior of the Park Avenue Synagogue, he remembered his own screams. A bloody corpse would not have provoked more hysterical cries of distress.

Why had he screamed like that? Now, at age thirteen, it was a mystery to him. Already a small pool of his own humanity had slipped forever beyond his reach, locked under a pane of glass through which he could only peer, as though looking at an exhibit in a museum. He no longer cried in Michael's barbershop. But then, it occurred to him, he rarely went. His hair was long and unruly. There had been a palace coup on the subject of hairstyles a couple of years ago, and the John-John had been deposed. He took his seat amidst the pre-service hum of conversation and took out a Bible from the rack in front of him, not to read, just to hold, like an amulet. He too, in his own small way, had taken steps away from being a boy and toward being a man, although there had been no ceremony to commemorate it. He wasn't even sure it was an event worth celebrating.

The idea of a Bar Mitzvah had never been discussed between Alex and his mother, and he had never given it any thought until the beginning of the eighth-grade school year, when the invitations began to arrive. He remembered the first one, which he and his mother had puzzled over with the unabashed awe of primitives who have found a functioning matchbook. It was a large square envelope, cream-colored and made of a paper stock less flexible than certain kinds of wood. The type on the enclosed invitation was thick enough to read by touch. There were copious amounts of gauzy tissue paper in there as well, and other envelopes, already stamped, with RSVP cards asking for commitments to far-off dates. The slightly askew stamp was the only evidence that a human being had had anything to do with this assemblage of objects.

"What I don't understand," said Alex at the time, "is that I don't think Richard Edelman even likes me. Why is he inviting me to his Bar Mitzvah?"

"Maybe he does like you," his mother, ever the optimist, had replied.

"No, that's not an issue, okay? That's not possible. Maybe he just invited the whole grade." He was making a joke.

Edelman had in fact invited the whole grade. Six weeks after the invitation arrived, Alex had been stuffed into a jacket and tie and sent off to attend a service in which Edelman, a nervous boy who, at the age of thirteen, had a body that suggested that not one single pubic hair had yet sprouted on it, stood robed in strange garments and read Hebrew for an interminably long period of time. Alex sat there in the synagogue along with the rest of his class. The boys sat in one section and the girls in another. Afterward there was a bus that took everyone down to the World Trade Center. The invitation had said: "Reception at Windows on the World."

Windows on the World was a restaurant on the top floor of one of the World Trade Center towers. Therefore it had a view. Everyone was very excited about the view, and for the first ten minutes the whole class flocked to the windows and pressed their faces against them, peering out at New Jersey or the Atlantic Ocean, depending on which way they were facing. Windows on the World was a distinguished restaurant that served very good food at exorbitant prices, and the presence of fifty screaming kids would have depressed and angered many of the lunch patrons, had they been there. But no one was there, because, for a fee equal to about two years' school tuition for their son, the Edelmans had rented the place out.

Alex was one of those whose face was pressed eagerly to the glass 101 stories above the ground. But in a short while he unstuck his nose and began walking around the tables, looking at the name cards that were written out in neat script and sat on every plate.

He lingered among the tables, feeling intimidated by the array of silverware and the fancy lettering on the name cards. He had sat through that lunch with a stiff posture, had spoken hardly at all, and had made a point of keeping his elbows off the table. For some reason he was under the impression that his mother was going to be judged by his behavior here, and he wanted to make a good showing.

His classmates did not feel the same compulsion. Specifically, the gang of boys, led by Phil Singer, who more or less ran the grade, and to whom Alex had tangentially attached himself, discovered that Mr. Edward Edelman, who was presiding over this celebration of his son's Bar Mitzvah with evident pride, smoked a pipe. To correspond with his son having invited his whole eighth-grade class, Edward Edelman had invited the entire executive staff of the electronics firm of which he was vice president, and was busy greeting them and making jokes and spotting small intrigues of conversation and affiliation that were bubbling around the room. So he was very surprised when a rumor welled up among the younger generation that the stuff in his pipe was not tobacco, but marijuana. He reassured himself that no one actually believed he was smoking pot, but Edward Edelman was, on some deep and partially buried level, a nice man, and furthermore he was genuinely moved by his son's

the art of friction

Bar Mitzvah, and proud of the event he was putting on, and all these genuine human emotions made him vulnerable. Alex's classmates had a desire to attack vulnerability that was as natural and innate as their ability to detect its presence.

And so from the depths of the party came the chant "Eddie is stoned! Eddie is stoned!" And soon kids were running around laughing hysterically and screaming, "Crazy Eddie! He's in*sane!*"

Soon Mr. Edelman's expression became strained. One of his colleagues sidled up to him and said, "What's up, Crazy Eddie?" Mr. Edelman had the nauseating premonition that it was a name that would stick around the office for years. The sight of a gang of thirteen-year-olds running around calling him Eddie was not part of the fantasy he had long nurtured for how this day would unfold. He put his pipe away. He stopped milling around the party and hung back in a corner, looking a bit tired and aggrieved. Eventually he was discarded as the favored object of scorn because the troublesome group of boys were distracted by a more interesting target. They began harassing a group of girls. One girl in particular seemed to be the object of their scorn and desire. From across the room he could see that she looked genuinely frightened by the group of boys that encircled her. An hour earlier Mr. Edelman would have intervened, but he had been mauled into submission and simply turned his gaze elsewhere, back to the real world of adults and serious business.

What Crazy Edward Edelman had looked away from was a heated discussion between a group of girls and a group of boys. Greg Neuman, who did double duty as class clown and class pervert, had tried to grab Marcy Goldblum's breast. Marcy—who was still two years away from the nose job she already fantasized about, who was popular, and who didn't have much of a breast to grab—knocked his hands away with an aristocratic slap. A conversation, or rather an inarticulate screaming match, followed, in which the girls more or less tried to explain that the boys couldn't just grab, they had to at least try and talk to them. After a minute of this, Greg, who was crashing from the initial sugar rush of euphoria he experienced whenever he touched a girl, walked over to Tania Vincent and grabbed her breast.

Tania had wavy golden hair, pale skin, and a pretty nose. Her claim to fame in the eighth grade was that she had breasts. Her breasts made it impossible for most of the boys in the grade to interact with her in a civilized manner.

Now, everyone watched Greg's knotty little fingers sink into Tania's right breast. She screamed. The girls shrieked and the boys let out a yell as though someone had just hit a home run, and in one short instant the essential architecture of Bar Mitzvah socializing for the remainder of the year had been established. It was a peculiar form of flirtation that mixed elements of tag and rape. There was a weird element of status involved as well, since only the more popular boys did the grabbing, and only the more popular girls had to run around with their hands over their breasts.

In the midst of all the screaming, Alex looked across the room and was amazed to see Mr. Edelman off in the distance, watching the proceedings, but standing immobile. He had been beaten into submission by the eighth grade. Years later Alex would still think about the Bar Mitzvahs of that year and wonder that such behavior was allowed by the adults. But by then Alex would know that adults were full of their own fears and anxieties, and were as mortal and prone to error as any eighth grader, if not more so.

Edelman's Bar Mitzvah was just the beginning. A few months later, Alex was a veteran of Windows on the World, which seemed to be the destination of choice for Bar Mitzvah parties, although there were other opulent destinations as well. He had seen adults get drunk, and had stolen half-finished drinks off the adult tables to drink himself. He had watched classmates anxiously sing Hebrew words, be praised by rabbis, and later receive envelope after envelope from friends and relatives, each containing a check of biblical proportions.

He had been barraged by clowns and magicians and enthusiastic disc jockeys who played "Ring My Bell" and "Push Push in the Bush" when they wanted to get people dancing, and who then played the soundtrack to *Saturday Night Fever* once they were. He possessed, along with a closetful of stupid door prizes, the more abstract but lasting memory of himself jumping around spastically on the dance floor in a rare moment free of inhibition, while simultaneously puzzling over whether what the Bee Gees said about the *New York Times*'s effect on man was true.

And now it was spring. The stack of *Great Jews in Sports* was down to one, and it made sense that Phil Singer should get the last book. Phil was good at sports, the fastest kid in the grade, but the connection went beyond that; he had the special grace of great athletes, a kind of magic that infuses their every gesture with possibility. He would change things. He already had, in the small scale of the eighth grade. He was the grade's leading mystic and delinquent. And he was Alex's friend.

Singer's Bar Mitzvah promised to be different from all the others, and at first glance it was—it was even fancier. After Phil had done his duties at the Park Avenue Synagogue, they were all loaded onto a pair of buses and shipped down Fifth Avenue to the Plaza Hotel ballroom. Bouquets of flowers sat on each table, above which hung clusters of white helium balloons. Already Alex could sense a weird panic in the eyes of his friends. There had been such a buildup to this Bar Mitzvah that something had to happen. A big brass band played quietly, though ominously, as though they were just limbering up, and would start to seriously swing once people had a chance to digest.

The boys wore their suits and exulted in the discovery that the bartenders scattered around the Plaza ballroom were willing to serve them drinks. The Singer myth expanded another notch. The girls, meanwhile, continued to refine their adultlike behavior. They wore dresses and elegant suits, they had had their hair done, they wore makeup and jewelry, and they carried it all off with a kind of ease, as though they dressed this way all the time.

Alex was seated at the same table as Tania. She looked assured and womanly as she engaged in conversation with Marcy Goldblum.

"And then she got up to go to the bathroom and missed the backseat scene," Tania was saying now, "and when I told her about it later she was so pissed."

"That was the most intense scene of the movie," replied Marcy.

"What backseat scene?" said John Goldman, who was sitting next to Alex. "Why is it that I never understand what the hell anyone is talking about?"

"They're talking about a dirty scene in a movie," said Alex.

"We're talking about *Saturday Night Fever*," said Marcy from across the table, in a loud aggressive voice that seemed to scold the two boys for trying to have a conversation of their own.

Tania didn't even look over. She just tossed her hair a little. She nodded knowingly as she spoke and elegantly brought her fork to her mouth. She was quite womanly, Alex thought. She was wearing a pretty dress with lace frills around the collar and sleeves; a provocative pink ribbon tied together the two pieces of fabric holding her breasts, as though it were a shoelace. Alex stared intently at her hands as she used her silverware, as though for tips, and occasionally he stared at the space between her breasts, covered but not entirely obscured by the ribbon. He imagined Ugly George's hand reaching out and gently tugging at that ribbon until it came apart.

"I didn't see *Saturday Night Fever*," said John. "My mother wouldn't let me."

Alex stared at him incredulously, torn between hating him passionately for being a geek and admiring him for having the audacity to say the truth, which, as it happened, was the same truth that applied to Alex. He would have seen the movie anyway had it not been for the fact that the *Jaws 2* experience still lurked, with accompanying soundtrack, in the back of his mind. He had been forbidden from seeing *Jaws 2* but had snuck in on his own one afternoon a few days before leaving for sailing camp. He returned from sailing camp with awards in riflery, archery, and tennis, but the only water that had touched his skin either came out of a shower or was heavily chlorinated, and every time someone touched his leg in the pool he became hysterical.

Something about the way Tania moved, the way she talked, the way she brought her fork to her mouth, made her seem much too good for the bacterial fungus that composed eighth-grade society. Alex was intent on interacting with her in a civilized manner, but could not seem to manage it. She liked art, and spent time after school in the art studio painting, and once Alex had seen her all by herself after school, walking with a canvas wrapped up under her arm. He was by himself as well. This was the perfect opportunity for him to express his admiration for her, to show he was interested in art, and to generally distance himself from the baboonlike behavior of his classmates. Practically hyperventilating with effort, he had made himself call out to her as she walked by.

"Let me see it!" he said.

He was referring to the canvas, but Tania hurried past without looking up. He stood there amazed at this misunderstanding, but unable to correct it.

Now he tried to glance at her surreptitiously, but his glances kept devolving into stares, which would only be broken when her eyes raked briefly across his face and he immediately looked down. Unwilling and also unable to muster the grabby aggressive prerogative of his classmates, or Ugly George for that matter, he had no strategy except to be so passive and pathetic and conspicuously inept that she would be forced to take pity on him, approach him, talk to him, get to know him really well, and then, on her own volition, for no real reason—and here Alex's thoughts became vague and possessed of the illogic of dreams—she would take off her shirt, and let him see, just because she felt like it.

He understood that this was an unrealistic scenario, but was at a loss for anything to replace it.

Eventually the party became wild and dispersed. The grownups got drunk and danced. The kids got drunk and danced. The usual ritual of boys grabbing girls was played out. The swing band was replaced by a disc jockey. Phil Singer made out very publicly with Audrey Stevens, and then they both disappeared, and a joke made the rounds that they had rented a room. Then Audrey reappeared and said Phil had passed out on one of the couches outside.

Gradually all the kids came out to view the body. He lay there looking very peaceful, with envelopes bulging out of all his pockets. The only thing askew was his feet, which were not really in a comfortable position, but turned in toward each other.

"Oh jeez, Phil becomes a man," said Mrs. Singer when she saw her son. She stroked his face and put a pillow under his head and then went and got a shoe box and put all the envelopes in it. An older lady came out and looked down at Phil and then at the assembled youth who were standing around.

"Who did this?" she demanded of the crowd, as though someone had forced Phil to get drunk, or had perhaps hit him over the head and robbed him. "Who did this to Philly?"

She was, Alex surmised from the "Philly," the grandmother. He wanted very much to explain to this woman that no one had done anything to Phil Singer, quite the contrary, this was yet another small bit of philanthropy that Phil had doled out to the rest of the class in a moment of generosity. He wanted to explain that her grandson was a great guy because he had single-handedly changed the definition of cool in the eighth grade—he had written the word

thomas beller

TULL on the back of his down jacket, instantly catapulting Jethro Tull into the front rank of popular bands in the grade, and had then, once this happened, drawn a single canceling line through the word. This in a class where the most popular boys had previously been neat fastidious creeps like Arnold Gerstein, who didn't even want his down jacket to get *wet*. Phil did bong hits before the morning bus and once brought a bottle of vodka into school, which he shared with a large group of boys during lunch, leading to Allen Fluss's infamous vomit in geometry episode. Phil was a rebel who understood that things were fucked up and was willing to do something about it. If what he was willing to do was pass out at his own Bar Mitzvah, then so be it!

All this raced through Alex's mind, which the woman seemed to read like a ticker tape, for she turned toward him and said, with a quivering accusatory finger raised in his direction, "You! What have you done to Philly?"

"Me?" said Alex, more a croak than a statement.

"You! The ringleader!"

This was perhaps the least accurate description of himself that Alex had ever heard. He couldn't face this hysterical woman, and he suddenly couldn't face the mirth of the Bar Mitzvah party. He saw that a number of people were drifting off into an adjoining room, and he followed them.

He walked into the cream-and-candy-colored sitting area which was adjacent to the ladies' room. Couches and easy chairs and throw pillows were placed elegantly here and there, and the beige carpet gave the strange piece of theater unfolding before his eyes a hushed, unreal quality.

Greg Neuman and Jack Gold were struggling with Tania Vincent, who was strangely quiet while she tried to get them off. After occupying the huge cathedral of the ballroom for so long, this small, pretty, enclosed space seemed illicit and private. The room was filling up with kids, as though some accident had just occurred, and they were gathering around to rubberneck. Except the accident was in progress.

"Stop it!" Tania finally gasped. "Stop it!" She kept saying that over and over again. What was so strange was rather than performing a hit-and-run attack, which was the normal mode of operation, Greg Neuman and Jack Gold were struggling with Tania as though she were a running back in football whom they were trying to tackle. Then there was a ripping sound. Jack Gold had managed to get his hand into that space where the pink ribbon was, and had torn the dress, and just then Arnold Gerstein came running over and grabbed both of Tania's arms and held them behind her back, and for one split second Tania's dress was pulled all the way down to her waist and her breasts fell forward, completely exposed, jiggling and awkward. Every person in the room screamed. The girls screamed in horror and the boys screamed as though they were at a sporting event and the home team had just scored. Alex started laughing with hysterical glee, and within his own laughter he heard hoarse yelps of panic and fear. Everyone was yelling and running around, and he just stood there watching it unfold, amazed at the momentum of events. Tania was crying now, her hands cupping her breasts, while several pairs of hands tried to pry them off or squeeze the parts that were not covered. Her friends came to the rescue. There were shrieks and screams. Ellen Levine was pounding Jack Gold in the face, and Tania broke away and ran for the ladies' room.

Every boy in the room followed in hot pursuit. There was no context to their actions, just wild giddiness, the chase, the yelling, the brief glimpse of that which had been imagined for so long. Alex, swept up in the momentum of what was happening, ran with them.

Tania pushed through the door to the ladies' room, and it had hardly closed before eight more boys were clamoring to get through the same door. The cream-colored hues of the sitting room had given way to the harsh reality of the fluorescent light. Tania ran into one of the stalls, slammed the door shut, and locked it. The boys leapt over its sides like braying animals. Tania shrank back in tears. Alex was among the first to leap onto that flimsy metal partition. He looked down at Tania. The first thing he saw was her braces. Tania didn't have the kind of mouth that showed her teeth, but now her mouth was configured in the figure eight of sobs, and they gleamed in the light. She clutched her torn dress to herself.

She was crying real sobs. Under the bright fluorescent lights, all that womanliness was gone. Alex could see thin blue veins on her chest and neck and face; her whole body seemed pale and bluish in that light, except for her flushed cheeks; her tears streaked mascara and her hair was a mess.

For one brief moment, as he vaulted up onto the edge of the bathroom stall,

Alex had felt ecstatic. For the first time he felt part of his group, part of his class, and his world. Then, when he saw Tania, the feeling abated. He hung there, feet dangling, eyes bulging from the strain of the thin metal wall pressing into his stomach, looking down at her. He wanted very much to say something. He wanted to apologize. But this was not a good time for apologies. His pride at finally having done something vied with his shame at what he had done.

Eventually he was herded into the group of boys that the Plaza Hotel security staff, who had burst onto the scene in their uniforms, walkie-talkies cackling, identified as the criminal element. The criminal element stood there unworried.

Phil Singer's grandmother appeared on the scene and again became hysterical at the sight of Alex. "It's him!" she cried. Alex was amazed to note that he felt flattered by this misunderstanding.

"What are you going to do?" Gerstein said to one of the men with walkie-talkies. "You're just security guards. We pay you guys." They were kept in the room just long enough for the truth of this statement to dissipate a little. Tania, for her part, had rearranged her dress and seemed amazingly composed. She walked out without saying a word, her chin held high, flanked by all her friends, who called the boys assholes over their shoulders.

Soon afterward the party began to disperse. Alex walked through the Plaza's glittering lobby, his knees loose and bouncy with nervous energy, the plush springy carpet making him feel as though he might float up toward the ceiling. None of the guests in the lobby knew of the events that had just occurred in the ladies' room, yet it seemed as though they could fathom them, understand their context, grasp the dreamlike quality of their sequence, and perhaps forgive them with a knowing wink.

The same could not be said for the world beyond the Plaza's heavy front door, the real world. He pushed through it and was greeted by a slap of cold moist air. It was dusk, and cloudy, and the city looked a bit blue, as though it weren't getting enough oxygen. He had moved through the ballroom, and that small warmly lit sitting room, and the bright fluorescent bathroom, like a Super Ball racing through the air for longer than seemed natural. But now gravity reasserted itself, and time returned to its normal pace.

the art of friction

He walked up Central Park South to Sixth Avenue, shivering a little in the cold air. He took his scarf out of his pocket and tied it tightly around his neck. He had cab fare but decided, as some kind of penance, to take the Number 5 bus. He waited for the Number 5 until the sky was black and his teeth were chattering, and then decided to come up with some other form of penance and took a cab.

When he got into his apartment he felt its warmth envelop him as though a blanket had been thrown over his shoulders. His mother was sitting at the kitchen table, reading. He fled past her to his room.

"Did you have a nice time?" his mother called after him.

"Yes!" he said, more a yelp than a comment. He stepped into his room and pulled the door shut.

author's commentary

"Great Jews in Sports" had, as its origin, an image that did not in the end make it into the story—two boys throwing an orange Super Ball back and forth across an enormous open space with white floors and glass walls that looked out over the city. It was an image taken from life. When I was a kid, I had this weird adventure in the World Trade Center, when it was already built, but long before they had rented out all the floors. Somehow a friend and I wandered into an elevator we should not have been on, or got off on a floor we should not have been on, and ended up on—I think—floor seventy-something of one of the World Trade Center towers, which had no walls, but was one huge expanse, except for the elevators. By some twist of kid magic, we had a Super Ball, and so went to opposite ends of the floor and threw it back and forth. That was the original image, and I built around it for a while, worked it in as a flashback to this later scene at Windows on the World during a Bar Mitzvah, and then another Bar Mitzvah scene got in there, and the story took shape around these two Bar Mitzvahs, and then the Ugly George stuff at the start came in toward the end. But even after many drafts the Super Ball was still in there, as a flashback to when Alex Fader arrives at the Windows on the World, which is itself a flashback. Finally it just seemed too extraneous, a flashback within a flashback, so I took it out, but right

35

until the end it persisted in the title, which was "Super Ball." When you have one working title for a long time, it feels weird to give it up. There was some temptation to keep it, since I love that name, but the story had nothing to do with Super Balls, or vice versa. So I changed it to the more relevant though still pretty obscure title.

The last trace of that Super Ball was the World Trade Center itself, which seemed like a minor thing until 9/11. Then, about a year after that event, I read the story in public, in Boston, and when I got to that part that mentioned Windows on the World, I really wanted to change the venue in midstride. The story has nothing at all to do with 9/11. Why bring that in? But then I thought that would be cowardly. So I plowed through with the setting as it is written, and the effect was that the previously boisterous crowd—the series was called Books 'n' Brews—became a bit somber.

I realize I am edging toward one of the all-time absurd laments concerning 9/11—it sucked because it makes my story less funny when I read it out loud!

But there is an odd resonance between the story and that event. There is so much libidinal rage, hostility, energy, and this weird teenage myopia that, for whatever reason, gets focused into laserlike intensity by the Bar Mitzvahs. And there was something oddly oblivious and also innocent about that period of time. If you think about the setting, American Jews in New York in the late Seventies, my God, they had it good! And the kids are on a rampage, totally oblivious. Compare those kids' lives to those of even their own parents, who had spent their own Bar Mitzvah years in Europe, only to evacuate under duress. My parents. So even if the story is all about these interpersonal dynamics, the gurgle of potential disaster on some level was already present as well, somehow.

THOMAS BELLER is the author of *Seduction Theory, The Sleep-Over Artist,* and *How to Be a Man.* He is also the founder of www.mrbellersneighborhood.com.

In the early 1990s I found myself, as a cure for depression, undergoing hypnosis to recover repressed memories. The severity of my depression seemed out of proportion to its presumed causes: a difficult separation from my husband, followed by his death; overwork; and a brief fling with an old flame that had ended badly. I had reached that state, frightening and incomprehensible for anyone observing it, where I could focus on little but the pain of being the person I was, and I think the hypnosis was the therapist's last resort.

He had begun a carefully worded suggestion that I should agree to be hospitalized when he interrupted himself.

"Let's try one thing," he said.

He began by asking me to imagine myself descending a staircase that led deeper and deeper underground. I could stop at any time; I could climb back up the stairs if I felt anxious. But I should remember that I was absolutely safe as I took one step and then another, down and down. The sound of his voice was relaxing. I was aware of myself in my usual chair in his cheerful office of posters and children's toys even as I allowed myself to be coaxed gradually downward. The sensation was mildly pleasant, even in my miserable state. The session came to an end before I knew it, and I went home feeling—the first feeling I had had in weeks, other than pain—a mild curiosity about what I would find at the bottom of those stairs.

It took several more sessions before I arrived at the bottom of the staircase and was asked to imagine a screen on which I could view images of myself as a young child. "What do you see?" the therapist would ask, and I would hear my voice answering in a child's pitch, with a child's vocabulary: "She's in the tall grass." As the images grew more horrific, I would begin to tremble, and the therapist would warn, "Keep it on the screen!"

"What does she see?"

"The tops of the tall grass. Sun in her eyes."

"What does she smell?"

"The—from Sam's old car. The puffs."

"The exhaust from his car?"

"Yes."

"What else does she see?"

"She sees—Sam."

Twelve years later, I finally risk an e-mail to my sister. *Do you remember a man named Sam, who may have worked for our dad at the ranch on Spring Creek, probably in the late 1940s?*

I had forgotten about Sam, she e-mailed back. *I remember Dad liked him because he was a hard worker. It seems like Dad just picked him up in town one day. Wasn't he the one who every so often went to town and got drunk? I think Dad didn't mind because it apparently never affected his work. I remember he was an interesting person. I wish I could remember more because there was something of interest about his past.*

So there really was a Sam.

What I remember about him—what I seem to remember—is that he was short-legged and wide, with powerful forearms that my dad explained were a legacy of his years with an axe. He was French-Canadian; he had worked as a lumberjack in Canada. Perhaps this is the "something of interest" about his past that my sister recalls. It is amazing that she recalls anything at all about him, because she would have been only four years old during the summer and fall of 1947, if that's when he worked for us, or five if it was the summer and fall of 1948, and I would have been seven or eight. What ranch work Sam had been hired to do, I have no idea, and I don't recall that we ever had another hired man while we lived on the Spring Creek ranch.

I do have two specific memories of Sam, the kind of snapshot memories that illuminate a face or a scrap of conversation as fragments out of context. In one of these fragments, Sam is boasting to someone outside the frame about the way he teases my sister. "She has two kittens, and she has a turtle about the size of a quarter, and I'm all the time telling her I'm going to feed them kittens to her turtle." In the other fragment, he is laughing and talking loudly, and I think it must be late evening around the supper table, because the scene seems to be lamp-lit. "So the fella says to me, better have another, the Old Crow can't fly on one wing!"

Sometimes it seems to me that I can see Sam's face. Quick dark eyes in a broad face, a thick shock of graying hair and grizzled stubble over heavy jowls. But is this really what he looked like? As a writer of fiction, I can invent a face, endow it with stubble and jowls (or not), and provide the character who wears that face with a backstory, provide him with grievances and perhaps an ingrown desire. How much have I invented about Sam?

Did he tell the story about the Old Crow that couldn't fly on one wing? Did my sister have a turtle?

My therapist recommended Ellen Bach's and Laura Davis's *The Courage to Heal,* which he called a useful reference book, with an index to symptoms, case studies, and current research. That I could read at all is a testament to how much better I was feeling. Whether as a result of the therapy I was undergoing, the patient lifeline of my therapist's voice and presence, the antidepressants (I had begun to take Zoloft), or nothing more profound than the passing of time, I was beginning to deal with day-to-day tasks that once seemed beyond my strength, and I was able to concentrate and focus on a page, and I read *The Courage to Heal* and, for a while, everything else on repressed memories that I could get my hands on.

As a label, a "useful reference book" suggests a certain dry dependability. *The Courage to Heal,* however, turned out to contain a harrowing set of narratives about woman after woman who, as children, suffered horrific sexual abuse, repressed all memory of that abuse, and consequently, as adults, endure symptoms ranging from failed relationships, depression, anxiety, and addictions to career struggles and eating disorders. To overcome these symptoms, according to Bach and Davis, the victim must gather her courage and confront her trauma, usually by overcoming her "denial" of her memories or by "retrieving" her repressed memories through a form of the hypnosis I had undergone.

My initial reaction to the whole topic was distaste for the language of the various theorists and sufferers. I had already puzzled my therapist with my embarrassment at his suggestion that my inner child was in need of nurturing. But if my life depended on it—and there were times when I feared that my life *did* depend on it—I could not take seriously an "inner child" that was the subject of *New Yorker* jokes. The *New Yorker* had not, so far as I knew at that time, taken to satirizing repressed memories, but I cringed whenever I read a sentence that seemed to invite me into a warm bath of self-indulgence and secondhand compassion.

Even the appearance of these books suggested the commercially sentimental. As I write, I have before me one of the books that I probably bought in 1992, when it was published. Its cover is a pale violet, its title—*Repressed Memories: A Journey to Recovery from Sexual Abuse*—is written in a dark violet italic script. Its contents promise "healing" through "overcoming denial," "self-empowerment," and "closure"—the language and style of a greeting card, or worse, the language and style of those pamphlets that used to be passed out to girls when I was an adolescent, promising us that menstruation was a wonderful confirmation of our womanhood and offering to sell us the accoutrements. I am reminded of the old full-page advertisement in women's magazines that pictured a lovely woman in evening dress with a single line of script: *Modess . . . because.*

Still, what was I to make of the images that had illuminated the imaginary screen I had found at the foot of an imaginary staircase? Out of the dark appeared Sam's curious old car—a car converted into a truck by having a plank box hammered into the space where its rear seat and trunk had been blowtorched out—sitting in the dirt track along the edge of the meadow and chugging out its exhaust. Was there ever such a vehicle, and why would I remember it, or forget it, or recover a memory of it?

Or Sam himself, braking his car/truck to a halt, yanking open the door and striding through the grass with purposeful face toward the momentarily startled child. Had he slammed on his brakes because she stuck out her tongue at him, or did he simply stop because she was there, and he saw his chance? Before she knows it, she's flat on her back and looking up as his burly dark silhouette blots out the sunlight falling through the tops of tall meadow grasses. Then the inexplicable pain.

And then. He's gone. She's alone in the grass with nothing but the lingering odor of exhaust.

The busy imagination is only too ready to gather the flashing images into a narrative. Details the child could not have known. *He'd come back to the ranch drunk once too often. Her dad had fired him that very morning. He'd packed his gear, everything he owned, in the rough-carpentered box on the back of his altered vehicle. Was on his way, angry to the brim with this most recent resentment in a lifetime of accumulated resentments, when there on the verge of the road, screened from the house and barn by the grove of chokecherries between the corrals and the hay meadow, stood the brat. And not the cute little one, but the long-legged mouthy one. Would serve her right. He saw his chance, slammed on his brakes.*

Afterward she picks herself up, pulls down her dress, limps to the house. Doesn't register the thin line of blood running down her leg, doesn't exactly know what has happened to her, wouldn't have the words to tell it if she did. But knows from the expression on her mother's face that it was something awful.

"What would your mother have done?" asked the therapist.

She would have patched me up and hidden the evidence as well as she could. What else would she have done, in that Montana ranch country just after World War II, a time and place when so much that is spoken openly today would have been whispered, if at all? Girls who were raped were ruined. I would have been ruined in my mother's eyes, but not in anyone else's eyes if she could help it.

The therapist, I think, was puzzled at my lack of anger. He spoke of confronting, not just the perpetrator, but those who had protected the perpetrator. He spoke of taking the next step, of "healing." But whom would I have confronted? My father had been dead for years. My mother was still living, but her mind had faded. As for Sam, there was no telling what had become of him. If he was alive, he surely would have been in his nineties.

The truth was, I was too detached from what I had seen on the imaginary screen to feel anger, or indeed anything stronger than curiosity. The assault, if it had happened, might explain my mother's dislike of me. Or it might explain that aspect of myself that I thought of as the outcome of my no-nonsense, stoical ranch upbringing, but which others often saw as a lack of emotion, a flatness of feeling. Was this the "dissociation" the recovery books described?

If it had happened.

The therapist was matter-of-fact about it. Yes, the assault had happened. I had not forgotten it, but I had buried, or "repressed," the memory as too painful and bewildering to admit. All these years later, the memory was struggling to resurface, and my increasingly desperate efforts to suppress it were draining my energy and causing my depression. No, repressed memories were not rare or unusual. He came upon such cases all the time in his practice.

"How do your recovered memories seem different from any of your other memories?" he said, when I pressed him.

That was a good question, one I thought about for a long time. So many of my memories, particularly the earliest, are abbreviated motion pictures. The toddler named Mary staggers out of a glare of sunlight, scent of alkali and sagebrush, with her bottom on fire. Family story provides a frame, keeps the picture alive: out by the barbed-wire fence that separated the sagebrush from the dry grass around the house, she'd found an anthill. Sat on it.

Take away the family story and what remains is burning sun and burning bottom. Odors? She couldn't have named them. Barbed-wire fence? Well, there must have been a fence, and the busy mind is all too willing to create a context.

When I set the memory of toddler Mary and the anthill beside the memory (if it is a memory) of seven-year-old Mary and the assault in the meadow grass, what strikes me in each are sensations I intuitively feel certain I have experienced. In the first, the burning sun and the burning bottom. In the second, the waving tops of grasses and the smell of exhaust. Especially the smell of exhaust—to this day, I cannot bear the smell of exhaust. But all the rest, whether the anthill by the barbed-wire fence or the outraged face of the man as he jumps out of his car/truck and grabs the startled child by the wrist, feels secondhand.

Early in my reading about recovered memories, I came across the Franklin case, which was still very recent. In California in 1990, a George Franklin had been tried and convicted of the rape and murder of an eight-year-old girl. The crime had been committed in 1969. The only witness to testify against Franklin was his grown daughter, Eileen, who claimed to remember that she had seen her father assaulting her playmate and smashing her skull with a rock. According to her psychologist, Eileen had been so traumatized by the experience that she had repressed the memory for twenty years until, gazing into her own daughter's eyes, she had spontaneously recovered it and gone to the authorities.

Public opinion, at first, enthusiastically supported Eileen Franklin and the phenomenon of repressed memory as a miraculous window into the past. State legislators in California proposed new laws in which the statute of limitations on crimes would begin its countdown not from the time of the crime, but from the time of the recovered memory of the crime. Guests on television talk shows told of their recovered memories of horrific sexual abuse, often by fathers or other family members. Popular magazine articles provided more testimonials, ever more lurid. *If your memories are unusually grisly or bizarre,* advised one writer on repressed memories, *you may be a survivor of ritual abuse.* Law enforcement officials sponsored workshops on uncovering and investigating satanic cults. Fields were dug up in search of the bodies of babies murdered during these rituals; individuals were prosecuted and convicted. Families were wrenched apart, whole communities traumatized. Even more bizarre: therapists began to report clients who were recovering memories of being abducted and sexually abused by extraterrestrials.

In retrospect, I wonder if it was the exhaustion of excess that changed the direction of public opinion. I had hardly finished reading about the Franklin case when I came across the backlash. Now the talk-show hosts were full of derision, their guests the "wrongly accused" victims of something called False Memory Syndrome. *Of course* there had been no rape of a child in the meadow grass, any more than there had been satanic rituals or abductions by extraterrestrials. So-called recovered memories actually were monstrously spun fictions implanted through hypnotic suggestion by unscrupulous therapists. The fathers and grandfathers, the uncles, the brothers, in some cases the mothers and grandmothers, had been themselves the victims of witch hunts. Out in California, state legislators lost their enthusiasm for new laws. George Franklin's murder conviction was overturned, and prosecutors decided not to retry him.

"I have little doubt that Eileen Franklin believes with every cell of her being that her father murdered Susan Nason," wrote Elizabeth Loftus, distinguished professor of psychology and law at the University of California, Irvine, who had become the best-known and most cogent opponent of recovered memory theory.

But I believe there is a very real possibility that the whole concoction was spun not from solid facts but from the vaporous breezes of wishes, dreams, fears, desires. Eileen's mind, operating independently of reality, went about its business of collecting ambiguities and inconsistencies and wrapping them in a sensible package, revealing to her in one blinding moment of insight a coherent picture of the past that was nevertheless completely and utterly false.

Distressed, I read and reread this passage, analyzing every word and phrase. Did "very real possibility" allow any hope that Eileen Franklin's "memories" (and by extension, mine) were based in reality? But then, "concoction," or, "the business of collecting ambiguities and inconsistencies and wrapping them in a sensible package." Were all recovered memories "completely and utterly false"?

In the years since the phenomenon of recovered memories has faded from public interest, I still haven't uncovered the answer to that question. Maybe. Probably. Almost certainly, most recovered memories are completely and utterly false. This conclusion was a blow to me, and it did not strike me as perverse that I preferred to believe that I had been raped as a child than that I had, through hypnotic suggestion, imagined that I had been raped. The fact was, it was my therapist I wanted to believe in. His had been the sole voice for so long, towing me through the dark turbulence that I never expected to survive, that I could not bear to let go. I did not believe then, do not believe now, that he planted the story of Sam through hypnotic suggestion (although he certainly hadn't let me off the hook until he had ransacked every cobwebby corner of my mind in search of worse). But I was, am, certain of one thing only: whether the story of Sam was fact or a fiction, it had emanated from me.

Snapshot of myself as a child of seven or eight. She's leaning against the white siding of the school where her grandmother was teaching at the time, smiling at the camera as she's been told to do even as she squints into the sunglare. She hasn't yet been diagnosed as nearsighted. Her long brown hair is braided, just as

I wear my hair today. Her dress is plain cotton, undoubtedly home-sewn by her mother; her shoes, probably her "good" shoes for the occasion of the picture, are strapped patent leather. To my eye, she looks self-conscious. When I look again, I wonder about that self-consciousness, because this little girl is squinting out of a long-ago ranch culture that has not yet awakened from the long nightmare of World War II to apprehend the changes that the coming century will unfold.

Then I remember that although she did not know the word for it, that child has already felt the first onset of the depression that will dog her for years.

So what am I left with? Do I believe that the child in that snapshot was raped by someone named Sam? Or do I believe that, years later and under hypnosis, I invented the rape?

While I can gather certain circumstantial threads and weave them into a plausible case for the memory being genuine, I have to admit that the violence in the meadow still seems removed from me. The details—Sam, the cobbled-together vehicle, the puffing exhaust—remain more vivid for me than the details, say, of a short story I wrote ten or twelve years ago, and yet I continue to feel less a participant in that scene than an observer. I have had occasion to sit up at night, trying to comfort a friend who had been raped, and I could observe her devastation, but I could not feel it.

Or have I woven these same gathered threads into whole cloth? If so, why? Am I to suppose—and here awakens the ghost of Freud, deciding that the women who complained to him of incestuous fathers were indulging in wish-fulfillment—that the story of Sam is a metaphor for some buried childhood guilt?

Or is the story of Sam as meaningless and empty of truth as those disjointed accusations or admissions that are said to rise from the lips of patients emerging from anesthesia? Dig deep enough into any of us, and what's unburied will be a novel?

After those sessions under hypnosis, my depression lifted. And although I had lived with gradually worsening depression up until that time, for the past twelve years I have been free of it, and I have gone about my life, teaching and bringing up my younger children. Sometimes I feel sad, and sometimes my mood is lowered, but in twelve years I have never—touch wood—sunk into that black hole that is inexplicable to those who have never suffered from depression and instantly familiar to those who have. Who knows, maybe relief comes with aging.

I like to think about the child in the snapshot who squints into the blinding sunglare. I wouldn't warn her to beware the meadow grass, I'd want her to take her chances. But I would tell her, if I could, to cherish her self-consciousness. And to brace herself for a lifetime of asking questions with no answers.

But she didn't need to be told.

author's commentary

Where did you come from, where you gonna go?
Whatcha gonna do there, Cotton-eye Joe?

Only two people can answer these questions. One of them is old Cotton-eye Joe himself—and why do we think he wouldn't lie to us about what he's been up to? The other is the fiction writer, who knows everything. Not that the fiction writer can't be coy about what she knows, making the rest of us keep turning pages to find out what Joe's going to do next. But because she's created her world and put Joe in it, the fiction writer has got the say over that world as long as she can make us believe in it. If we stop believing in her world, of course, we'll stop trusting her.

The nonfiction writer, however, is stuck with the world she's been set down in. Her job is to understand her world as best she can, and it's a tough job, because there's none of fiction's lofty omniscience for her, none of fiction's blithe appropriation of, say, Cotton-eye Joe's point of view. No getting into Joe's head for the nonfiction writer. Her point of view is always limited, and she's always an unreliable narrator. We love to read her stuff, because we think we're getting close to the bone, we think we're getting the truth, but just let us catch her in a lie and we'll be highly indignant with her.

Why, then, with all these stops and bars, would anyone want to write nonfiction?

What the nonfiction writer likes is to ask the kinds of questions that used to drive her mother crazy. How come? Why? She picks off scabs, looks to see what's underneath. For all the freedom of writing fiction, the pleasures of dipping and diving from one point of view to another, of appropriation and invention, she—well, part of the time, anyway—prefers to speculate and ponder without all the scaffolding of plot getting in her line of sight. If all that speculating and pondering lead her to seeing her world from odd angles, to crossing lines and questioning rules, so much the better. She's got just one dead-set obligation, and that's to her reader, always ready with the child's question: did that really happen?

It did. As close as I can come to telling about it.

MARY CLEARMAN BLEW grew up on a small cattle ranch in Montana, the site of her great-grandfather's original 1882 homestead. She has written or edited eleven books, including *All but the Waltz: Essays on Five Generations of a Montana Family* and *Balsamroot: A Memoir.* In 2004 she received the Western Literature Association's Distinguished Achievement Award and Lifetime Membership. She teaches at the University of Idaho in Moscow, Idaho.

bernard cooper

Theresa Sanchez sat behind me in ninth grade algebra. When Mr. Hubbley faced the blackboard, I'd turn around to see what she was reading; each week a new book was wedged inside her copy of *Today's Equations*. The deception worked; from Mr. Hubbley's point of view, Theresa was engrossed in the value of *x*, but I knew otherwise. One week she perused *The Wisdom of the Orient*, and I could tell from Theresa's contemplative expression that the book contained exotic thoughts, guidelines handed down from on high. Another week it was a paperback novel whose title, *Let Me Live My Life*, appeared in bold print atop every page, and whose cover, a gauzy photograph of a woman biting a strand of pearls, head thrown back in ecstasy, confirmed my suspicion that Theresa Sanchez was mature beyond her years. She was the tallest girl in school. Her bouffant hairdo, streaked with blonde, was higher than the flaccid bouffants of other girls. Her smooth skin, plucked eyebrows, and painted fingernails suggested hours of pampering, a worldly and sensual vanity that placed her within the domain of adults. Smiling dimly, steeped in daydreams, Theresa moved through the crowded halls with a languid, self-satisfied indifference to those around her. "You are merely children," her posture seemed to say, "and I can't be bothered." The week Theresa hid *101 Ways to Cook Hamburger* behind her algebra book, I could stand it no longer and, after the bell rang, ventured a question.

"Because I'm having a dinner party," said Theresa. "Just a couple of intimate friends."

No fourteen-year-old I knew had ever given a dinner party, let alone used the word "intimate" in conversation. "Don't you have a mother?" I asked.

Theresa sighed a weary sigh, suffered my strange inquiry. "Don't be so naïve," she said. "Everyone has a mother." She waved her hand to indicate the brick school buildings outside the window. "A higher education should have taught you that." Theresa draped an angora sweater over her shoulders, scooped her books from the graffiti-covered desk, and just as she was about to walk away, she turned and asked me, "Are you a fag?"

There wasn't the slightest hint of rancor or condescension in her voice. The tone was direct, casual. Still I was stunned, giving a sidelong glance to make sure no one had heard. "No," I said. Blurted really, with too much defensiveness, too much transparent fear in my response. Octaves lower than usual, I tried a "Why?"

Theresa shrugged. "Oh, I don't know. I have lots of friends who are fags. You remind me of them." Seeing me bristle, Theresa added, "It was just a guess." I watched her erect, angora back as she sauntered out the classroom door.

She had made an incisive and timely guess. Only days before, I'd invited Grady Rogers to my house after school to go swimming. The instant Grady shot from the pool, shaking water from his orange hair, freckled shoulders shining, my attraction to members of my own sex became a matter I could no longer suppress or rationalize. Sturdy and boisterous and gap-toothed, Grady was an inveterate backslapper, a formidable arm wrestler, a wizard at basketball. Grady was a boy at home in his body.

My body was a marvel I hadn't gotten used to; my arms and legs would sometimes act of their own accord, knocking over a glass at dinner or flinching at an oncoming pitch. I was never singled out as a sissy, but I could have been just as easily as Bobby Keagan, a gentle, intelligent, and introverted boy reviled by my classmates. And although I had always been aware of a tacit rapport with Bobby, a suspicion that I might find with him a rich friendship, I stayed away. Instead, I emulated Grady in the belief that being seen with him, being like him, would somehow vanquish my self-doubt, would make me normal by association.

Apart from his athletic prowess, Grady had been gifted with all the trappings of what I imagined to be a charmed life: a fastidious, aproned mother who radiated calm, maternal concern, a ruddy, stoic father with a knack for home repairs. Even the Rogerses' small suburban house in Hollywood, with its spindly Colonial furniture and chintz curtains, was a testament to normalcy.

Grady and his family bore little resemblance to my clan of Eastern European Jews, a dark and vociferous people who ate with abandon—matzo and halva and gefilte fish; foods the goyim couldn't pronounce—who cajoled one another during endless games of canasta, making the simplest remark about the weather into a lengthy philosophical discourse on the sun and the seasons

49

bernard cooper

and the passage of time. My mother was a chain-smoker, a dervish in a frowsy housedress. She showed her love in the most peculiar and obsessive ways, like spending hours extracting every seed from a watermelon before she served it in perfectly bite-sized, geometric pieces. Preoccupied and perpetually frantic, my mother succumbed to bouts of absentmindedness so profound she'd forget what she was saying mid-sentence, smile and blush, and walk away. A divorce attorney, my father wore roomy, iridescent suits, and the intricacies, the deceits, inherent in his profession had the effect of making him forever tense and vigilant. He was "all wound up," as my mother put it. But when he relaxed, his laughter was explosive, his disposition prankish: "Walk this way," a waitress would say, leading us to our table, and my father would mimic the way she walked, arms akimbo, hips liquid, while my mother and I were wracked with laughter. Buoyant or brooding, my parents' moods were unpredictable, and in a household fraught with extravagant emotion it was odd and awful to keep my longing secret.

One day I made the mistake of asking my mother what a "fag" was. I knew exactly what Theresa had meant, but hoped against hope it was not what I thought; maybe fag was some French word, a harmless term like "naïve." My mother turned from the stove, flew at me, and grabbed me by the shoulders. "Did someone call you that?" she cried.

"Not me," I said. "Bobby Keagan."

"Oh," she said, loosening her grip. She was visibly relieved. And didn't answer. The answer was unthinkable.

For weeks after, I shook with the reverberations from that afternoon in the kitchen with my mother, pained by the memory of her shocked expression and, most of all, her silence. My longing was wrong in the eyes of my mother, whose hazel eyes were the eyes of the world, and if that longing continued unchecked, the unwieldy shape of my fate would be cast, and I'd be subjected to a lifetime of scorn.

During the remainder of the semester, I became the scientist of my own desire, plotting ways to change my yearning for boys into a yearning for girls. I had enough evidence to believe that any habit, regardless how compulsive, how deeply ingrained, could be broken once and for all: the plastic cigarette my mother purchased at the Thrifty pharmacy—one end was red to approximate an ember, the other tan like a filter tip—was designed to wean her from the real thing. To change a behavior required self-analysis, cold resolve, and the substitution of one thing for another: plastic, say, for tobacco. Could I also find a substitute for Grady? What I needed to do, I figured, was kiss a girl and learn to like it.

This conclusion was affirmed one Sunday morning when my father, seeing me wrinkle my nose at the pink slabs of lox he layered on a bagel, tried to convince me of its salty appeal. "You should try some," he said. "You don't know what you're missing."

"It's loaded with protein," added my mother, slapping a platter of sliced onions onto the dinette table. She hovered above us, cinching her housedress, eyes wet from onion fumes, a mock cigarette dangling from her lips.

My father sat there chomping with gusto, emitting a couple of hearty grunts to dramatize his satisfaction. And still I was not convinced. After a loud and labored swallow, he told me I may not be fond of lox today, but sooner or later I'd learn to like it. One's tastes, he assured me, are destined to change.

"Live," shouted my mother over the rumble of the Mixmaster. "Expand your horizons. Try new things." And the room grew fragrant with the batter of a spice cake.

The opportunity to put their advice into practice, and try out my plan to adapt to girls, came the following week when Debbie Coburn, a member of Mr. Hubbley's algebra class, invited me to a party. She cornered me in the hall, furtive as a spy, telling me her parents would be gone for the evening and slipping into my palm a wrinkled sheet of notebook paper. On it were her address and telephone number, the lavender ink in a tidy cursive. "Wear cologne," she advised, wary eyes darting back and forth. "It's a make-out party. Anything can happen."

The Santa Ana wind blew relentlessly the night of Debbie's party, careening down the slopes of the Hollywood hills, shaking the road signs and stoplights in its path. As I walked down Beachwood Avenue, trees thrashed, surrendered their leaves, and carob pods bombarded the pavement. The sky was a deep but luminous blue, the air hot, abrasive, electric. I had to squint in order to check the number of the Coburns' apartment, a three-story building with glitter imbedded in its stucco walls. Above the honeycombed balconies was a sign that read *Beachwood Terrace* in lavender script resembling Debbie's.

From down the hall, I could hear the plaintive strains of Little Anthony's "I Think I'm Going out of My Head." Debbie answered the door bedecked in an empire dress, the bodice blue and orange polka dots, the rest a sheath of black and white stripes. "Op art," proclaimed Debbie. She turned in a circle, then proudly announced that she'd rolled her hair in orange juice cans. She patted the huge unmoving curls and dragged me inside. Reflections from the swimming pool in the courtyard, its surface ruffled by wind, shuddered over the ceiling and walls. A dozen of my classmates were seated on the sofa or huddled together in corners, their whispers full of excited imminence, their bodies barely discernible in the dim light. Drapes flanking the sliding glass doors bowed out with every gust of wind, and it seemed that the room might lurch from its foundations and sail with its cargo of silhouettes into the hot October night.

Grady was the last to arrive. He tossed a six-pack of beer into Debbie's arms, barreled toward me and slapped my back. His hair was slicked-back with Vitalis, lacquered furrows left by the comb. The wind hadn't shifted a single hair. "Ya ready?" he asked, flashing the gap between his front teeth and leering into the darkened room. "You bet," I lied.

Once the beers had been passed around, Debbie provoked everyone's attention by flicking on the overhead light. "Okay," she called. "Find a partner." This was the blunt command of a hostess determined to have her guests aroused in an orderly fashion. Everyone blinked, shuffled about, and grabbed a member of the opposite sex. Sheila Garabedian landed beside me—entirely at random, though I wanted to believe she was driven by passion—her timid smile giving way to plain fear as the light went out. Nothing for a moment but the heave of the wind and the distant banter of dogs. I caught a whiff of Sheila's perfume, tangy and sweet as Hawaiian Punch. I probed her face with my own, grazing the small scallop of an ear, a velvety temple, and though Sheila's trembling made me want to stop, I persisted with my mission until I found her lips, tightly sealed as a private letter. I held my mouth over hers and gathered her shoulders closer, resigned to the possibility that, no matter how long we stood there, Sheila was too scared to kiss me back. Still, she exhaled through her nose, and I listened to the squeak of every breath as though it were a sigh of inordinate pleasure. Diving within myself, I monitored my heartbeat and respiration, trying to will stimulation into being, and all the while an image intruded, an image of Grady erupting from our pool, rivulets of water sliding down his chest. "Change," shouted Debbie, switching on the light. Sheila thanked me, pulled away, and continued her routine of gracious terror with every boy throughout the evening. It didn't matter whom I held—Margaret Sims, Betty Vernon, Elizabeth Lee—my experiment was a failure; I continued to picture Grady's wet chest, and Debbie would bellow "change" with such fervor, it could have been my own voice, my own incessant reprimand.

Our hostess commandeered the light switch for nearly half an hour. Whenever the light came on, I watched Grady pivot his head toward the newest prospect, his eyebrows arched in expectation, his neck blooming with hickeys, his hair, at last, in disarray. All that shuffling across the carpet charged everyone's arms and lips with static, and eventually, between low moans and soft oscillations, I could hear the clack of tiny sparks and see them flare here and there in the dark like meager, short-lived stars.

I saw Theresa, sultry and aloof as ever, read three more books—*North American Reptiles, Bonjour Tristesse,* and *MGM: A Pictorial History*—before she vanished early in December. Rumors of her fate abounded. Debbie Coburn swore that Theresa had been "knocked up" by an older man, a traffic cop, she thought, or a grocer. Nearly quivering with relish, Debbie told me and Grady about the home for unwed mothers in the San Fernando Valley, a compound teeming with pregnant girls who had nothing to do but touch their stomachs and contemplate their mistake. Even Bobby Keagan, who took Theresa's place behind me in algebra, had a theory regarding her disappearance colored by his own wish for escape; he imagined that Theresa, disillusioned with society, booked passage to a tropical island, there to live out the rest of her days without restrictions or ridicule. "No wonder she flunked out of school," I overheard Mr. Hubbley tell a fellow teacher one afternoon. "Her head was always in a book."

Along with Theresa went my secret, or at least the dread that she might divulge it, and I felt, for a while, exempt from suspicion. I was, however, to run across Theresa one last time. It happened during a period of torrential rain that, according to reports on the six o'clock news, washed houses from the hillsides and flooded the downtown streets. The halls of Joseph Le Conte Junior High were festooned with Christmas decorations: crepe-paper garlands, wreaths studded with plastic berries, and one requisite Star of David twirling above the attendance desk. In Arts and Crafts, our teacher, Gerald (he was the only teacher who allowed us, *required* us, to call him by his first name), handed out blocks of balsa wood and instructed us to carve them into bugs. We would paint eyes and antennae with tempera and hang them on a Christmas tree he'd made the previous night. "Voilà," he crooned, unveiling his creation from a burlap sack. Before us sat a tortured scrub, a wardrobe-worth of wire hangers that were bent like branches and soldered together. Gerald credited his inspiration to a Charles Addams cartoon he'd seen in which Morticia, grimly preparing for the holidays, hangs vampire bats on a withered pine. "All that red and green," said Gerald. "So predictable. So boring."

As I chiseled a beetle and listened to rain pummel the earth, Gerald handed me an envelope and asked me to take it to Mr. Kendrick, the drama teacher. I would have thought nothing of his request if I hadn't seen Theresa on my way down the hall. She was cleaning out her locker, blithely dropping the sum of its contents—pens and textbooks and mimeographs—into a trash can. "Have a nice life," she sang as I passed. I mustered the courage to ask her what had happened. We stood alone in the silent hall, the reflections of wreaths and garlands submerged in brown linoleum.

"I transferred to another school. They don't have grades or bells and you get to study whatever you want." Theresa was quick to sense my incredulity. "Honest," she said. "The school is progressive." She gazed into a glass cabinet that held the trophies of track meets and intramural spelling bees. "God," she sighed, "this place is so . . . barbaric." I was still trying to decide whether or not to believe her story when she asked me where I was headed. "Dear," she said, her exclamation pooling in the silence, "that's no ordinary note, if you catch my drift." The envelope was blank and white; I looked up at Theresa, baffled. "Don't be so naïve," she muttered, tossing an empty bottle of nail polish into the trash can. It struck bottom with a resolute thud. "Well," she said, closing her locker and breathing deeply, "bon voyage." Theresa swept through the double doors and in seconds her figure was obscured by rain.

As I walked toward Mr. Kendrick's room, I could feel Theresa's insinuation burrow in. I stood for a moment and watched Mr. Kendrick through the pane in the door. He paced intently in front of the class, handsome in his shirt and tie, reading from a thick book. Chalked on the blackboard behind him was THE ODYSSEY BY HOMER. I have no recollection of how Mr. Kendrick reacted to the note, whether he accepted it with pleasure or embarrassment, slipped it into his desk drawer or the pocket of his shirt. I have scavenged that day in retrospect, trying to see Mr. Kendrick's expression, wondering if he acknowledged me in any way as his liaison. All I recall is the sight of his mime through a pane of glass, a lone man mouthing an epic, his gestures ardent in empty air.

Had I delivered a declaration of love? I was haunted by the need to know. In fantasy, a kettle shot steam, the glue released its grip, and I read the letter with impunity. But how would such a letter begin? Did the common endearments apply? This was a message between two men, a message for which I had no precedent, and when I tried to envision the contents, apart from a hasty, impassioned scrawl, my imagination faltered.

Once or twice I witnessed Gerald and Mr. Kendrick walk together into the faculty lounge or say hello at the water fountain, but there was nothing especially clandestine or flirtatious in their manner. Besides, no matter how acute my scrutiny, I wasn't sure, short of a kiss, exactly what to look for—what semaphore of gesture, what encoded word; I suspected there were signs, covert signs that would give them away, just as I'd unwittingly given myself away to Theresa.

In the school library, a Webster's unabridged dictionary lay on a wooden podium, and I padded toward it with apprehension; along with clues to the bond between my teachers, I risked discovering information that might incriminate me as well. I had decided to consult the dictionary during lunch period when most of the students would be on the playground. I clutched my notebook, moving in such a way as to appear both studious and nonchalant, actually believing that, unless I took precautions, someone would see me and guess what

I was up to. The closer I came to the podium, the more obvious, I thought, was my endeavor; I felt like the model of The Visible Man in our science class, my heart's undulations, my overwrought nerves, legible through transparent skin. A couple of kids riffled through the card catalogue. The librarian, a skinny woman whose perpetual whisper and rubber-soled shoes caused her to drift through the room like a phantom, didn't seem to register my presence. Though I'd looked up dozens of words before, the pages felt strange beneath my fingers. *Homer* was the first word I saw. *Hominid. Homogenize.* I feigned interest and skirted other words before I found the word I was after. Under the heading HO.MO.SEX.U.AL was the terse definition: *adj. Pertaining to, characteristic of, or exhibiting homosexuality. –n. A homosexual person.* I read the definition again and again, hoping the words would yield more than they could. I shut the dictionary, swallowed hard, and, none the wiser, hurried away.

As for Gerald and Mr. Kendrick, I never discovered evidence to prove or dispute Theresa's claim. By the following summer, however, I had overheard from my peers a confounding amount about homosexuals: they wore green on Thursday, couldn't whistle, hypnotized boys with a piercing glance. To this lore, Grady added a surefire test to ferret them out.

"A test?" I said.

"You ask a guy to look at his fingernails, and if he looks at them like this . . . ," Grady closed his fingers into a fist and examined his nails with manly detachment, ". . . then he's okay. But if he does this . . . ," he held out his hands at arm's length, splayed his fingers, and coyly cocked his head, ". . . you'd better watch out." Once he'd completed his demonstration, Grady peeled off his shirt and plunged into our pool. I dove in after. It was early June, the sky immense, glassy, placid. My father was cooking spareribs on the barbecue, an artist with a basting brush. His apron bore the caricature of a frazzled French chef. Mother curled on a chaise lounge, plumes of smoke wafting from her nostrils. In a stupor of contentment she took another drag, closed her eyes, and arched her face toward the sun.

Grady dog-paddled through the deep end, spouting a fountain of chlorinated water. Despite shame and confusion, my longing for him hadn't diminished; it continued to thrive without air and light, like a luminous fish in the dregs of the sea. In the name of play, I swam up behind him, encircled his shoulders, astonished by his taut flesh. The two of us flailed, pretended to drown. Beneath the heavy press of water, Grady's orange hair wavered, a flame that couldn't be doused.

I've lived with a man for eleven years. Some nights, when I'm half-asleep and the room is suffused with blue light, I reach out to touch the expanse of his back, and it seems as if my fingers sink into his skin, and I feel the pleasure a diver feels the instant he enters a body of water.

I have few regrets. But one is that I hadn't said to Theresa, "Of course I'm a fag." Maybe I'd have met her friends. Or become friends with her. Imagine the meals we might have concocted: hamburger Stroganoff, Swedish meatballs in a sweet translucent sauce, steaming slabs of Salisbury steak.

School was over, but equations were insolvable, American history riddled with holes, "Ola, Paco" the extent of my Spanish. My report card was peppered with C's and D's. Arts and Crafts was the only subject at which I'd excelled, thanks to my fascination for Gerald. An ashtray in the shape of my hand, a pig fashioned from a Clorox bottle, a landscape composed of feathers and felt—I left junior high with a collection of ludicrous souvenirs, my academic future in question.

In the last week of school, a bespectacled girl sat next to me in the cafeteria. I had seen her in my classes, but we'd never spoken. She introduced herself and inquired about my grades. I was startled, then decided there was no harm in telling her of my poor standing. Jennifer pursed her lips and shook her head at my answer, and it took me a moment to realize that she was expressing a sense of injustice rather than pity. She drew on her straw, cheeks imploding. Milk gurgled in the carton. "You're bored," she concluded. "You need a challenge." Jennifer had thin lips, limp hair, and I suspected that her forwardness was a compensation for her bland appearance. Still, I was flattered by her faith in my intelligence, and encouraged her to go on. "There's lots of ways of being smart," she said. "Getting good grades is only one." Jennifer dismantled her hamburger, shunted the patty to the side of her plate. Then she aimed her gaze toward me. Thick lenses magnified her eyes. "I've watched you in class."

bernard cooper

Jennifer phoned that summer and invited me to her house for dinner. I took the bus down Hollywood Boulevard and transferred at Highland. The bus shuddered past a body shop that customized cars for television shows. Parked behind a chain-link fence were the Batmobile and a futuristic car I recognized from an episode of *The Twilight Zone*. Warm air blustered through the window of the bus, the sunset pink and green and blue. I got off in Studio City and walked up Wonderland Avenue, all the while telling myself that this was a date, a bona fide date. Jennifer was after me; her interest in my intellect hinted, no doubt, at a deeper passion. I imagined us in CinemaScope, clamped in a kiss that would make all other kisses seem pale and preliminary. That I found her in no way attractive seemed like a minor point. I savored the scent of my Aqua Velva and knocked on the door.

No one answered. I knocked again. Finally the door swung open, the man behind it incredulous, blinking. "No need to knock," he said. "We don't stand on ceremony here." I followed him into a living room strewn with books and records. A cat clawed the sofa, kapok spilling from one of its cushions. An aquarium glowed in the corner. Pipe smoke marbled the air.

Jennifer emerged from an archway and said, "Bernard, you've met George?" I shook the man's hand, and for one wild second, thought he might have been her husband.

"He knocked," said George.

"We never lock the door."

Throughout high school and well into college, I continued to harbor the dread of being discovered, of finding myself the subject of scorn, but my worry lessened, almost without my willing it to lessen. I still shook with the reverberations from that afternoon in the kitchen with my mother, pained by the memory of her shocked expression, and most of all her silence, but something slowly overtook me: I began to enjoy my status as an outsider, to foster my difference as ardently as I had once resisted it; this uniqueness, after all, allowed me the perspective of a writer, taught me to rely on my private reserves of imagination, gave me a fierce and protective regard for my own sensibility, the tenacity and temperament to create an alternative world with words.

During those years, I confided to friends my desire for men, and many admitted similar feelings. Eventually, I met teachers and students who were gay, whose joy and confidence were exemplary.

If you are gay or lesbian, I can promise with a fair amount of certainty that the struggle for self-acceptance will enrich you. The hurt you accumulate along the way becomes material for art, heightens your political and social awareness, offers you the basis of community with others who have transcended deceit. The point is that you accumulate, not lose, gain, not forfeit. Especially in the face of AIDS, especially in this decade of rampant homophobia, you'll discover how insistent, how enduring, how valuable a thing desire is.

author's commentary

Dick Cavett once asked the drag queen Holly Woodlawn, "Holly, just tell me one thing: when you wake up in the morning, are you a man or a woman?"

"Who cares," answered Miss Woodlawn, "as long as you're beautiful."

Her retort seems to me particularly apt when it comes to defining this area of literary endeavor we call "creative nonfiction." What matters first and foremost is that a piece of writing disarm us with its beauty; definitions and categories be damned.

But here we are, wanting to know what this form is, or might be. I tend to think of creative nonfiction in the broadest possible terms: a text that can accommodate the objectivity of reportage, the characterizations and taut dialogue of fiction, and the distilled imagery and imaginative leaps of poetry. A mongrel among purebreds, creative nonfiction borrows freely from all genres and recombines them in ways that resist easy categorization. Because it blurs the boundaries between genres, many people, editors and marketing departments in particular, become a little confused and agitated when it appears on their desks. Certainly this presents obstacles for the writer of creative nonfiction. But more and more adventuresome readers and publishers are willing to believe that such an ambiguous creature actually exists, and that it deserves the same exposure as a novel or a collection of poems. It seems to me, in fact, that the form's elusiveness is its primary virtue. Creative nonfiction is by nature quixotic, malleable, likely to change identity from page to page, or at least be categorized differently from reader to reader, some of whom will argue that Annie Dillard's tribute to the tenacity of a weasel, say, is a prose poem, while others will consider it a short story, and still others, an essay.

Whatever one calls this form, it is immediate and alive precisely because it invents itself as it goes along.

Creative nonfiction is a close relative to that old and venerable form, the essay. Perhaps the term "essay" is most evocative as a verb: "To essay, to attempt, the test or trial of the nature of a thing." However we define it here today, I hope our definition of creative nonfiction can stay as liquid and unpredictable as the form itself.

Just to complicate matters, I often think of my work as memoir, though it reads, people tell me, as though it were fiction. Many people seem to believe that there is a strict demarcation between fiction and memoir, and further, that what is exposed in a memoir, as opposed to a work of fiction, is the writer him– or herself, standing naked before the reader, bathed in the light of indisputable truth. In fact, the writer of the memoir raises the same smoke screen as the writer of fiction—the smoke screen of language. Anyone who works with language will tell you that words are infinitely variable, rough approximations at their best; to change a single word is to change the very landscape of recollection, and since there are thousands of words in any given memoir, it seems unlikely that the memoir is pure and reliable, while the novel and the short story are, by contrast, fabrications. Both fiction and nonfiction are forms that require great stamina and imagination, though the writer's intent—to create a made-up universe, or to honor the universe in which he finds himself—may vary.

The memoir is not an untainted reflection of fact, because facts are arguable, and memory is fallible. But what appeals to me as an autobiographical writer is memory's weakness as well as its power, its limitations as well as its reach. In other words, I'm drawn to the pathos of recall, a species of self-reflection that's riddled with gaps and exaggerations and wishfulness. I enjoy introducing into my memoirs, at a strategic moment, some reference to the unreliability of memory. I like to stop the narrative and say, "I can't be sure, but this is how I think it might have been." I find it bracing to throw the whole act of reminiscence into question; a memoir may not only reveal what is known, but may also ask what is knowable.

In writing memoirs, I make every effort to present myself and others in the most frank and tempered way possible, careful to neither aggrandize nor blame. Writing has never been for me a way of settling grudges or a substitute for psychotherapy. I have known few celebrities and have led a rather insular life; I have nothing extraordinary to report except that, when viewed with the kind of concentration writing demands, life is an amazement worthy of words. I also write because our lives must end, and memoirs give me the sense—a false sense, I realize—that people and places can be fixed in time. And yet no matter how clear I am about my reasons for choosing this form again and again, I know that each memoir is provisional, only one version of the life lived, an expression whose ideal is elusive.

I make no apologies for the fictions that are woven through my work. These fictions bring me closer to, rather than farther away from, the truth. In one memoir, for example, I show my father doffing his hat at the burial of a chicken—the setup is too complicated to explain here, but he actually did attend such a funeral. I wasn't there to see the hat-doffing firsthand, but I've extrapolated this detail from a lifetime of intimacy with the man, and I can assure you that he would have doffed his hat, or would have wanted to if he hadn't. Now, correct me if I'm wrong, but this gesture, which conveys both my father's reverence and the absurd protocol of the ceremony, cannot possibly be more of a strain on the reader's credulity than a chicken's funeral, for which I have documented proof.

An interviewer recently told me that he was disappointed by memoirs because, in book after book, he was meeting a construct and not the real person. "You want to be really disappointed," I told him, "just think how many times this happens when you meet someone face-to-face." He was operating from the assumption that each of us consists of a single, unchanging, comprehensible self. Or that, outside the realm of print, we come to each other with open hearts and clear motives. While I often wish this were true, I have grave doubts, and one of the many feats of a good memoir is that it makes the person behind the prose seem, for several pages, candid, consistent, and complete.

This singularity of character comes at great cost to the writer of memoirs, who must drink large quantities of coffee and spend a small fortune in hysterical phone calls to sympathetic friends in order to face his autobiography-in-progress, making that dismal mess into a commodity distinguished by its control and restraint.

I become squeamish when reviewers praise me for my honesty. Honesty alone is not a virtue, a point made all too clear by the dozens of painfully honest and thoroughly unreadable manuscripts that have come under my scrutiny. So, if honesty alone doesn't ensure a compelling piece of prose, what does? Paradoxically, it is artifice, the rigors of arranging and rearranging words until the words are as close to right as they will ever be. After the hard work is done, the personal nature of the subject matter becomes somewhat technical for the memoirist, but entirely palpable for the reader. This is the kind of translation—from the personal to the universal—that makes the difference between one's journal, fit for private consumption, and one's memoir, fit for a readership of discerning strangers.

Unfortunately, I became so exhausted during the course of writing *Truth Serum,* my collection of memoirs, that there was no time to prepare for the incomparable discomfort of having my personal life discussed on the radio by moderators who had never read my book, or of being given a letter grade in *Entertainment Weekly,* which made me feel as if I will never escape the dreaded report card. Even worse than those indignities, however, is my irresistible urge to tell you, at the risk of sounding egomaniacal, that I got an "A." This meant more to me—I was never a model student—than is easy to admit, and I wish my parents had lived not to read my work, which would only have confused and probably embarrassed them, but to see that I got a good grade in a glossy magazine, which they would have considered definitive proof of my worth as a person and theirs as parents.

Anyway, this question of truth versus imagination, or nonfiction versus fiction, will never be settled. Nor perhaps should it be. First and foremost I hope that my work, always a mixture of imagination and fact, will wake up beautiful.

BERNARD COOPER has published two collections of memoirs, *Maps to Anywhere* and *Truth Serum,* as well as a novel, *A Year of Rhymes.* His work has appeared in *Story, Ploughshares, Harper's, The Paris Review,* and *The New York Times Magazine,* and in anthologies such as *The Best American Essays* and *The Oxford Book of Literature on Aging.* His recent publications include a collection of short stories, *Guess Again.* He is the author of *The Bill from My Father: A Memoir* (February 2006), which is being made into a Warner Brothers film by director Dean Parisot.

How to Date a Browngirl, Blackgirl, Whitegirl, or Halfie

junot díaz

Wait for your brother and your mother to leave the apartment. You've already told them that you're feeling too sick to go to Union City to visit that tía who likes to squeeze your nuts. (He's gotten big, she'll say.) And even though your moms knows you ain't sick you stuck to your story until finally she said, Go ahead and stay, malcriado.

Clear the government cheese from the refrigerator. If the girl's from the Terrace stack the boxes behind the milk. If she's from the Park or Society Hill hide the cheese in the cabinet above the oven, way up where she'll never see. Leave yourself a reminder to get it out before morning or your moms will kick your ass. Take down any embarrassing photos of your family in the campo, especially the one with the half-naked kids dragging a goat on a rope leash. The kids are your cousins and by now they're old enough to understand why you're doing what you're doing. Hide the pictures of yourself with an Afro. Make sure the bathroom is presentable. Put the basket with all the crapped-on toilet paper under the sink. Spray the bucket with Lysol, then close the cabinet.

Shower, comb, dress. Sit on the couch and watch TV. If she's an outsider her father will be bringing her, maybe her mother. Neither of them want her seeing any boys from the Terrace—people get stabbed in the Terrace—but she's strong-headed and this time will get her way. If she's a whitegirl you know you'll at least get a hand job.

The directions were in your best handwriting, so her parents won't think you're an idiot. Get up from the couch and check the parking lot. Nothing. If the girl's local, don't sweat it. She'll flow over when she's good and ready. Sometimes she'll run into her other friends and a whole crowd will show up at your apartment and even though that means you ain't getting shit it will be fun anyway and you'll wish these people would come over more often. Sometimes the girl won't flow over at all and the next day in school she'll say sorry, smile, and you'll be stupid enough to believe her and ask her out again.

Wait and after an hour go out to your corner. The neighborhood is full of traffic. Give one of your boys a shout and when he says, Are you still waiting on that bitch? say, Hell yeah.

Get back inside. Call her house and when her father picks up ask if she's there. He'll ask, Who is this? Hang up. He sounds like a principal or a police chief, the sort of dude with a big neck who never has to watch his back. Sit and wait. By the time your stomach's ready to give out on you, a Honda or maybe a Jeep pulls in and out she comes.

Hey, you'll say.

Look, she'll say. My mom wants to meet you. She's got herself all worried about nothing.

Don't panic. Say, Hey, no problem. Run a hand through your hair like the whiteboys do even though the only thing that runs easily through your hair is Africa. She will look good. The white ones are the ones you want the most, aren't they, but usually the out-of-towners are black, blackgirls who grew up with ballet and Girl Scouts, who have three cars in their driveways. If she's a halfie don't be surprised that her mother is white. Say, Hi. Her moms will say hi and you'll see that you don't scare her, not really. She will say that she needs easier directions to get out and even though she has the best directions in her lap give her new ones. Make her happy.

You have choices. If the girl's from around the way, take her to El Cibao for dinner. Order everything in your busted-up Spanish. Let her correct you if she's Latina and amaze her if she's black. If she's not from around the way, Wendy's will do. As you walk to the restaurant talk about school. A local girl won't need stories about the neighborhood but the other ones might. Supply the story about the loco who'd been storing canisters of tear gas in his basement for years, how one day the canisters cracked and the whole neighborhood got a dose of the military-strength stuff. Don't tell her that your moms knew right away what it was, that she recognized its smell from the year the United States invaded your island.

Hope that you don't run into your nemesis, Howie, the Puerto Rican kid with the two killer mutts. He walks them all over the neighborhood and every now and then the mutts corner themselves a cat and tear it to shreds, Howie laughing as the cat flips up in the air, its neck twisted around like an owl, red meat showing through the soft fur. If his dogs haven't cornered a cat, he will walk behind you and ask, Hey, Yunior, is that your new fuckbuddy?

Let him talk. Howie weighs about two hundred pounds and could eat you if

junot díaz

65

he wanted. At the field he will turn away. He has new sneakers, and doesn't want them muddy. If the girl's an outsider she will hiss now and say, What a fucking asshole. A homegirl would have been yelling back at him the whole time, unless she was shy. Either way don't feel bad that you didn't do anything. Never lose a fight on a first date or that will be the end of it.

Dinner will be tense. You are not good at talking to people you don't know. A halfie will tell you that her parents met in the Movement, will say, Back then people thought it a radical thing to do. It will sound like something her parents made her memorize. Your brother once heard that one and said, Man, that sounds like a whole lot of Uncle Tomming to me. Don't repeat this.

Put down your hamburger and say, It must have been hard.

She will appreciate your interest. She will tell you more. Black people, she will say, treat me real bad. That's why I don't like them. You'll wonder how she feels about Dominicans. Don't ask. Let her speak on it and when you're both finished eating walk back into the neighborhood. The skies will be magnificent. Pollutants have made Jersey sunsets one of the wonders of the world. Point it out. Touch her shoulder and say, That's nice, right?

Get serious. Watch TV but stay alert. Sip some of the Bermúdez your father left in the cabinet, which nobody touches. A local girl may have hips and a thick ass but she won't be quick about letting you touch. She has to live in the same neighborhood you do, has to deal with you being all up in her business. She might just chill with you and then go home. She might kiss you and then go, or she might, if she's reckless, give it up, but that's rare. Kissing will suffice. A whitegirl might just give it up right then. Don't stop her. She'll take her gum out of her mouth, stick it to the plastic sofa covers and then will move close to you. You have nice eyes, she might say.

Tell her that you love her hair, that you love her skin, because, in truth, you love them more than you love your own.

She'll say, I like Spanish guys, and even though you've never been to Spain, say, I like you. You'll sound smooth.

You'll be with her until about eight-thirty and then she will want to wash up. In the bathroom she will hum a song from the radio and her waist will keep the beat against the lip of the sink. Imagine her old lady coming to get her, what she would say if she knew her daughter had just lain under you and blown your name, pronounced with her eighth-grade Spanish, into your ear. While she's in the bathroom call one of your boys and say, Lo hice, loco. Or just sit back on the couch and smile.

But it usually won't work this way. Be prepared. She will not want to kiss you. Just cool it, she'll say. The halfie might lean back, breaking away from you. She will cross her arms, say, I hate my tits. Stroke her hair but she will pull away. I don't like anybody touching my hair, she will say. She will act like somebody you don't know. In school she is known for her attention-grabbing laugh, as high and far-ranging as a gull, but here she will worry you. You will not know what to say.

You're the only kind of guy who asks me out, she will say. Your neighbors will start their hyena calls, now that the alcohol is in them. You and the blackboys.

Say nothing. Let her button her shirt, let her comb her hair, the sound of it stretching like a sheet of fire between you. When her father pulls in and beeps, let her go without too much of a goodbye. She won't want it. During the next hour the phone will ring. You will be tempted to pick it up. Don't. Watch the shows you want to watch, without a family around to debate you. Don't go downstairs. Don't fall asleep. It won't help. Put the government cheese back in its place before your moms kills you.

author's commentary

It's strange and painful to grow up in a society, culture, world where children are taught early which skin colors are the most desirable and which are not. The adults in my family were more than eager to pound it into us kids' heads the toxic racial hierarchies that they were raised on in the Dominican Republic, where dark-skinned people were considered neither attractive nor normal and light-skinned people were like gods. What a sickness: brown people and black people telling their children that people lighter than them were best. Early memories: being advised by an uncle to pursue only white-girls—They're the best, he insisted in front of his own brown wife; my mother using the word prieta as a synonym for ugly and blanca as a synonym for

67

beautiful, even though none of her children were blanco. The confusion that these sorts of daily imbedded racisms provoked in me and in so many of my friends, the self-loathing they seeded. Being a young person of color in the United States, at least in my decades, the 1970s and the '80s, often meant wrestling with issues of self-hatred. This was the one thing that linked us all—from my American-born Chinese friend to my Egyptian buddy. And yet it wasn't anything that people talked about. It was a law, in a way, but not a law that got mentioned. It was a silence, and if I am anything I am an artist who is drawn to silences.

But I was also interested in portraying that period in my boyhood when the accumulated wisdom of the older boys was something that I aspired to, no matter how ridiculous and nonsensical their insights were. Most of their lore focused on girls: the getting, fucking, and relative virtues of the different kind of girls in our town. When I was nine, ten, eleven, I took any advice I could get, what with adolescence just around the corner and me with no fucking idea of what came next. As an immigrant I was especially vulnerable to this kind of hand-me-down knowledge; I didn't know jack about the country I was living in and any maps that would ease my way, even if they were fabricated and falsified ones, were better than nothing.

JUNOT DÍAZ, author of the celebrated short story collection *Drown,* was born in Santo Domingo, Dominican Republic. He is a graduate of Rutgers University and received his Master of Fine Arts degree from Cornell University. His fiction has appeared in *Story, The New Yorker, The Paris Review, Best American Short Stories 1996* and *1999,* and *African Verse.* He lives in Cambridge, Massachusetts, and has recently published his first novel, *The Brief Wondrous Life of Oscar Wao.*

Excerpt from Notes from a Writer's Book of Cures and Spells

marcia douglas

Work into the night my love—
letters small and tight—
until the moon, eating her own flesh,
disappears.

The time has come now to pay respect to the muse, for it is she who has guided you here thus far. Honor the history of your craft and make her doll with special care, tracing her back one chosen word at a time.

invitation

First you start with her belly—a large mango seed that you wash with rainwater, then leave on the zinc roof to dry in the sun. After three days, lean your ladder against the wall and climb back up to take a look. The seed will be shrunken and bleached white. Hold it carefully in your palm; feel it warm as a fresh egg.

Use your penknife to make a thin slit through the seed's side; then soak it overnight in a half cup of white rum. Next morning, check on it again before leaving it to dry on the roof once more. After four days, you will see that the slit has widened, the inside a faint yellow.

Sit at the kitchen table and stuff the belly well with ground pimento, thyme, salt, pepper, and a little rosemary; then write the word "speak" on a piece of tobacco paper, folding it tight and sliding it inside. Tie the stuffed belly with a strip of muslin, winding it securely.

The head is to be made from a guinep seed. After it is washed and sun-dried, write her name—Sister, Sister, Sister—around and around in tiny letters, then wear it tied tight right over your navel. After seven days, take it off and attach it to the mango belly.

The arms and legs are next—twigs broken from a tamarind switch. Spanish moss will do for her hair and two seashells for her breasts. A bag of glass beads makes perfect embellishment. Attach them one by one—red and green and blue; then adorn with gold thread as you see fit. Paint a generous mouth and two eyes wide open; a single cowrie should hang from her hair.

pouring libation

Feed Sister yellow cornmeal and white rum. Place fresh bougainvillea at her feet along with a bowl of uncooked rice filled with coins. When you are ready, tie a red ribbon around a ballpoint pen. Put it in your bag along with a loaf of bread, a bottle of soda, a packet of powdered milk, a kerosene lamp, two red candles, and a small hand mirror. Go outside and keep on walking until you come to a place where the road splits like your legs pushing out a child. Choose the path with the most gravel. To the left there will be a julie mango tree with a snake carved into its bark. When you see this, switch your bag to the other shoulder and keep on going. You will need to hurry if you are to make it to the river before sundown. The last thing you need is for your shadow to beat you there, snatching away the words waiting at the water bottom.

As soon as you arrive, take the bread from the bag; break it into small pieces and cast it in an arc upon the water. Open the bottle of soda and pour it slowly; sprinkle the milk powder and watch it disappear downstream. This is the time to light the red candles and the kerosene lamp. When at last you reach for the pen, the ink will ooze like shed blood. Do not lift your hand from the page. Do not stop to scratch your scalp, slap the mosquito at your ankle, or brush the fly from your chin. Most of all, do not worry about the crocodile eyeing you from the other side of the river. Cut your eye, spit over your shoulder, and keep on writing. You must write until there is no more ink left in your pen.

signs and wonders

Later, when the moon appears, the dogs upstream will begin barking. You will know when Sister is ready, her chest softly rattling—took-took, took-took—like so many seeds. From the corner of your eye, catch a glimpse of her sitting on a warm rock to the side, her face in her palm. Know that she has traveled from a long way—two hundred years through cane fields, swamp, grass-lice, wind, rain, and mango blossom. See how twigs fall from the nutmeg tree each time she blinks to adjust her eyes to river light.

She has come to observe your hand busy as a small bird, reminding her of a night long ago, when she leaned against a moonshine windowsill, scratching on wood and dry leaf with a pen stolen from Massa and marked with his initials. How she hungered for words then, devouring them wherever they could be found—the bottoms of cracked plates, the inside soles of shoes, the rims of old biscuit tins. She worked into the night, tiny letters like soldier ants, racing across bark.

A quick glance at Sister, and see how she cranes her neck, closes her eyes, listening to the rhythm of your pen. Someone is probably throwing stones into the river, trying to distract you, but do not look up or you will break the spell, ink turning to scab before it reaches the page. Concentrate instead on the two flickering candles with long red tears, for it is your busy hand that keeps Sister breathing, and whatever you do, you must not lose her. Write write write her name over and over, bringing her back to the next morning, her fingers stained night blue and hidden in shallow pockets against her thighs. When Mistress called, she quickly took the egg basket and scurried away so she could wash with water from the chicken trough. She washed and washed, but the blue remained. Two brown eggs fell onto the floor. A door banged shut; footsteps approached from across the yard.

As you write the word "yard," fireflies circle the kerosene lamp, and you notice a man's foot on the rock beside you. Resist the temptation to run away. There is no escape now; Sister has taken you all the way back—two hundred years through the smell of molasses. Hold your head still as the man sharpens his machete. Pretend to be interested in crushed corn on the ground. Leaves rustle underfoot, and you hear Sister scream, her voice high-pitched and broken in the evening sky.

This is the scene in which blood trickles everywhere, words lodged in your throat like fresh bone. As Sister's amputated fingers are hurled through the air, stuff your scarf in your mouth to stop your lips from trembling. Grab the fingers quick before the dogs arrive. Bloody nails dig into your skin now, and you want out of this story, as far away as you can possibly hide. You almost dash your pen to the ground, but then for one brief moment, Sister's eyes meet yours.

Remember a woman who got stuck in a story, wandered around and around, and never came back? They found her shoes by the edge of the river with a note inside which read, *The word made flesh* . . . Better to have stayed at home—hung the clothes on the line, stirred the cornmeal porridge, swept under the bed. But you cannot change your mind anymore; you are too far gone. A small crow cries in the lime tree behind you.

closing the space

This is the time for the hand mirror in your shoulder bag. Reach for it with your left hand and lean it against the rock in front of you. The mirror sees trouble before you do and will always remember the way back home. Sister still screams a trail of red, and you must hurry before she disappears. Chase the trail all the way through the bush; howl if you must, your voice joining hers; follow the course of the river as she runs downstream.

You will see Sister pause at the river's mouth; note how she beckons you with her bottomless eyes. Late as it is, the moon has almost eaten all its flesh; the crocodile sleeps at the water's edge. In the square of the hand mirror, glance back down the path from which you came. Way at the end of it, you will see your little yellow kitchen, the table set with clear glass plates. A lizard stretches on a straw mat by the stove. Sugar ants cluster around crumbs on the window-sill. As Massa's hungry dogs race toward Sister, spell out her name; press into the page as you urge her on, your pen almost empty.

You have heard stories of slaves in flight, flying back to Africa, but this is not that story. You have heard stories of women walking out into the ocean, drowning themselves, but this is not that story.

In this story, you must follow Sister's heels until the river falls into the waiting sea. In wee morning light, the Caribbean is thick as dark ink. You wade into the water, and it licks your flesh with a warm blue tongue. Massa's three dogs arrive only inches behind you, hesitating at the water's edge. Sister turns around and grabs at your collar, pulls you down flat against the ocean floor. You hold on to each other, plaits afloat in blue fluid. When you open your eyes, you see the dog's paws paddling above. Your lungs are swollen, and you cannot hold your breath much longer, soon you must rise up for air. You turn to look at Sister and notice her face: The sockets of her eyes are generations deep; the pupils like searchlights burrow into yours. As your head fills with yellow light, you recognize each other as next of kin. She pulls a string from her navel—two hundred years long—coils it into a ball, presses it in your hand. You want to reach her, to make some gesture—

But you are out of air. Somewhere a whip cracks, and you rise from the water, arms extended. As your blood pumps faster, the dogs hurl themselves at Sister's flesh. Do not try to save her—there is no more time and not enough ink for indecision. Keep one eye on the mirror and turn now, go. Run back down the gravel path, past the julie mango tree, and back to the place where the road splits like your legs throwing away a child. Dry your tears on your sleeve and keep on going. Do not look back; this scene cannot be revised.

As you enter the yard, the little ball unravels behind you, expanding in the wind like a long red cloth. Fold it carefully before you enter the house; then write your name in the middle of your hand. Trace the lines of your palm, crisscrossed and dusty. Call yourself out loud—hear how your voice has changed.

author's commentary

The protagonist in *Notes from a Writer's Book of Cures and Spells,* set in Jamaica, is a storyteller, Flamingo Tongue, whose life becomes intertwined with her characters. The text of the book is organized as a writer's notebook and includes Flamingo's sketches, writing charms, and story jottings, as well as an appendix of dreams and other material. The extract here in *The Art of Friction* is taken from one of her many interactions with "Sister," the muse who lures her into the heart of the story.

I believe writing is akin to spell casting. The writer and characters cast spells on each other in a reciprocal fashion, and in turn, on the reader/listener. In the language of fiction manuals we use the term "craft"; and in *Notes,* my character, Flamingo, attunes herself to the "craftiness" of what it means to tell a story. In the world of this story, then, "craft" brings to mind the trickster, Anancy, as well as the obeah/spirit world of the Caribbean. As the text unfolds, Flamingo activates charms by communicating with a story-witch and making soul dolls—one for each character. Color plates of Flamingo's soul dolls also appear in the appendix of the novel.

In writing this meta-fiction, I made Flamingo's soul dolls on her behalf. I followed her prescription and made the "Sister" doll from seeds, pods, twigs, shells, and other found materials gathered from trips to Jamaica. In addition to Sister, I made six other dolls—Dahlia, Alva, Millie Donovan, Made in China, Mrs. Ying, and Madda Shilling. As I made each doll, I contemplated her/his role in the story. This was a very useful and fulfilling experience, with the narrative and the doll-making becoming interconnected and inseparable one from the other.

Because of the meta-fictional nature of this novel, some readers question, "Where does fiction begin and truth end?" I see myself as very separate from Flamingo. As I wrote this text and made the dolls, I stood somewhere in Flamingo's shadow, but at a necessary distance. This distance enabled the story; the process being part experience and memory, but mostly imagination. In the space between these two elements—memory and the imagination—alchemy can take place, and it is this alchemy that most enchants me as a writer. The relationship between the writer and her characters involves a mutual exchange. The writer finds the words and the character feeds the imagination. As the process comes full circle, the final spell is cast when a reader/listener engages with the text. In writing this piece I was very conscious of my storytelling and what it means to be a woman-of-words in Caribbean story space.

MARCIA DOUGLAS was born in England and grew up in Kingston, Jamaica. She is the author of a collection of poetry, *Electricity Comes to Cocoa Bottom* (1999), as well as the novels *Madam Fate* (1999) and *Notes from a Writer's Book of Cures and Spells* (2005). Douglas teaches creative writing at the University of Colorado, Boulder.

A Primer for the Punctuation of Heart Disease

jonathan safran foer

☐ The "silence mark" signifies an absence of language, and there is at least one on every page of the story of my family life. Most often used in the conversations I have with my grandmother about her life in Europe during the war, and in conversations with my father about our family's history of heart disease—we have forty-one heart attacks between us, and counting—the silence mark is a staple of familial punctuation. Note the use of silence in the following brief exchange, when my father called me at college, the morning of his most recent angioplasty:

"Listen," he said, and then surrendered to a long pause, as if the pause were what I was supposed to listen to. "I'm sure everything's gonna be fine, but I just wanted to let you know—"

"I already know," I said.

"☐"

"☐"

"☐"

"☐"

"Okay," he said.

"I'll talk to you tonight," I said, and I could hear, in the receiver, my own heartbeat.

He said, "Yup."

■ The "willed silence mark" signifies an intentional silence, the conversational equivalent of building a wall over which you can't climb, through which you can't see, against which you break the bones of your hands and wrists. I often inflict willed silences upon my mother when she asks about my relationships with girls. Perhaps this is because I never have *relationships* with girls—only *relations*. It depresses me to think that I've never had sex with anyone who really loved me. Sometimes I wonder if having sex with a girl who doesn't love me is like felling a tree, alone, in a forest: no one hears about it; it didn't happen.

?? The "insistent question mark" denotes one family member's refusal to yield to a willed silence, as in this conversation with my mother:

"Are you dating at all?"
"□"
"But you're seeing people, I'm sure. Right?"
"□"
"I don't get it. Are you ashamed of the girl? Are you ashamed of me?"
"■"
"**??**"

¡ As it visually suggests, the "unxclamation point" is the opposite of an exclamation point; it indicates a whisper.

The best example of this usage occurred when I was a boy. My grandmother was driving me to a piano lesson, and the Volvo's wipers only moved the rain around. She turned down the volume of the second side of the seventh tape of an audio version of *Shoah,* put her hand on my cheek, and said, "I hope that you never love anyone as much as I love you¡"

Why was she whispering? We were the only ones who could hear.

¡¡ Theoretically, the "extraunxclamation points" would be used to denote twice an unxclamation point, but in practice any whisper that quiet would not be heard. I take comfort in believing that at least some of the silences in my life were really extraunxclamations.

!! The "extraexclamation points" are simply twice an exclamation point. I've never had a heated argument with any member of my family. We've never yelled at each other, or disagreed with any passion. In fact, I can't even remember a difference of opinion. There are those who would say that this is unhealthy. But, since it is the case, there exists only one instance of extraexclamation points in our family history, and they were uttered by a stranger who was vying with my father for a parking space in front of the National Zoo.

"Give it up, fucker!!" he hollered at my father, in front of my mother, my brothers, and me.

"Well, I'm sorry," my father said, pushing the bridge of his glasses up his nose, "but I think it's rather obvious that we arrived at this space first. You see, we were approaching from—"

"Give . . . it . . . up . . . fucker!!"

"Well, it's just that I think I'm in the right on this particu—"

"GIVE IT UP, FUCKER!!"

"Give it up, Dad¡" I said, suffering a minor coronary event as my fingers clenched his seat's headrest.

"Je–sus!" the man yelled, pounding his fist against the outside of his car door. "Giveitupfucker!!"

Ultimately, my father gave it up, and we found a spot several blocks away. Before we got out, he pushed in the cigarette lighter, and we waited, in silence, as it got hot. When it popped out, he pushed it back in. "It's never, ever worth it," he said, turning back to us, his hand against his heart.

~ Placed at the end of a sentence, the "pedal point" signifies a thought that dissolves into a suggestive silence. The pedal point is distinguished from the ellipsis and the dash in that the thought it follows is neither incomplete nor interrupted but an outstretched hand. My younger brother uses these a lot with me, probably because he, of all the members of my family, is the one most capable of telling me what he needs to tell me without having to say it. Or, rather, he's the one whose words I'm most convinced I don't need to hear. Very often he will say, "Jonathan~" and I will say, "I know."

A few weeks ago, he was having problems with his heart. A visit to his university's health center to check out some chest pains became a trip to the emergency room became a week in the intensive-care unit. As it turns out, he's been having one long heart attack for the last six years. "It's nowhere near as bad as it sounds," the doctor told my parents, "but it's definitely something we want to take care of."

I called my brother that night and told him that he shouldn't worry. He said, "I know. But that doesn't mean there's nothing to worry about~"

77

jonathan safran foer

"I know~" I said.

"I know~" he said.

"I~"

"I~"

"□"

Does my little brother have relationships with girls? I don't know.

↓ Another commonly employed familial punctuation mark, the "low point," is used either in place—or for accentuation at the end—of such phrases as "This is terrible," "This is irremediable," "It couldn't possibly be worse."

"It's good to have somebody, Jonathan. It's necessary."

"□"

"It pains me to think of you alone."

"■ ↓"

"?? ↓"

Interestingly, low points always come in pairs in my family. That is, the acknowledgment of whatever is terrible and irremediable becomes itself something terrible and irremediable—and often worse than the original referent. For example, my sadness makes my mother sadder than the cause of my sadness does. Of course, her sadness then makes me sad. Thus is created a "low point chain": ↓ ↓ ↓ ↓ ↓ ... ∞.

❋ The "snowflake" is used at the end of a unique familial phrase—that is, any sequence of words that has never, in the history of our family life, been assembled as such. For example, "I didn't die in the Holocaust, but all of my siblings did, so where does that leave me? ❋" Or, "My heart is no good, and I'm afraid of dying, and I'm also afraid of saying I love you. ❋"

☺ The "corroboration mark" is more or less what it looks like. But it would be a mistake to think that it simply stands in place of "I agree," or even "Yes." Witness the subtle usage in this dialogue between my mother and my father:

"Could you add orange juice to the grocery list, but remember to get the kind with reduced acid. Also some cottage cheese. And that bacon-substitute stuff. And a few Yahrzeit candles."

"☺"

"The car needs gas. I need tampons."

"☺"

"Is Jonathan dating anyone? I'm not prying, but I'm very interested."

"☺"

My father has suffered twenty-two heart attacks—more than the rest of us combined. Once, in a moment of frankness after his nineteenth, he told me that his marriage to my mother had been successful because he had become a yes-man early on.

"We've only had one fight," he said. "It was in our first week of marriage. I realized that it's never, ever worth it."

My father and I were pulling weeds one afternoon a few weeks ago. He was disobeying his cardiologist's order not to pull weeds. The problem, the doctor says, is not the physical exertion but the emotional stress that weeding inflicts on my father. He has dreams of weeds sprouting from his body, of having to pull them, at the roots, from his chest. He has also been told not to watch Orioles games and not to think about the current Administration.

As we weeded, my father made a joke about how my older brother, who, barring a fatal heart attack, was to get married in a few weeks, had already become a yes-man. Hearing this felt like having an elephant sit on my chest—my brother, whom I loved more than I loved myself, was surrendering.

"Your grandfather was a yes-man," my father added, on his knees, his fingers pushing into the earth, "and your children will be yes-men."

I've been thinking about that conversation ever since, and I've come to understand—with a straining heart—that I, too, am becoming a yes-man, and that, like my father's and my brother's, my surrender has little to do with the people I say yes to, or with the existence of questions at all. It has to do with a fear of dying, with rehearsal and preparation.

jonathan safran foer

✂🕸 The "severed web" is a Barely Tolerable Substitute, whose meaning approximates "I love you," and which can be used in place of "I love you." Other Barely Tolerable Substitutes include, but are not limited to:

→|←, which approximates "I love you."
🝆 □, which approximates "I love you."
🝐, which approximates "I love you."
✖🝒, which approximates "I love you."

I don't know how many Barely Tolerable Substitutes there are, but often it feels as if they were everywhere, as if everything that is spoken and done—every "Yup," "Okay," and "I already know," every weed pulled from the lawn, every sexual act—were just Barely Tolerable.

∶∶ Unlike the colon, which is used to mark a major division in a sentence, and to indicate that what follows is an elaboration, summation, implication, etc., of what precedes, the "reversible colon" is used when what appears on either side elaborates, summates, implicates, etc., what's on the other side. In other words, the two halves of the sentence explain each other, as in the cases of "Mother∶∶ Me" and "Father∶∶Death." Here are some examples of reversible sentences:

My eyes water when I speak about my family∶∶I don't like to speak about my family.

I've never felt loved by anyone outside of my family∶∶my persistent depression.

1938 to 1945∶∶□.

Sex∶∶yes.

My grandmother's sadness∶∶my mother's sadness∶∶my sadness∶∶the sadness that will come after me.

To be Jewish:: to be Jewish.

Heart disease:: yes.

← Familial communication always has to do with failures to communicate. It is common that in the course of a conversation one of the participants will not hear something that the other has said. It is also quite common that one of the participants will not understand what the other has said. Somewhat less common is one participant's saying something whose words the other understands completely but whose meaning is not understood at all. This can happen with very simple sentences, like "I hope that you never love anyone as much as I love you¡"

But, in our best, least depressing moments, we *try* to understand what we have failed to understand. A "backup" is used: we start again at the beginning, we replay what was missed and make an effort to hear what was meant instead of what was said:

"It pains me to think of you alone."
"← It pains me to think of me without any grandchildren to love."

{} A related set of marks, the "should-have brackets," signify words that were not spoken but should have been, as in this dialogue with my father:

"Are you hearing static?"
"{I'm crying into the phone.}"
"Jonathan?"
"□"
"Jonathan~"
"■"
"??"
"I:: not myself~"

"{A child's sadness is a parent's sadness.}"

"{A parent's sadness is a child's sadness.}"

"←"

"I'm probably just tired¡"

"{I never told you this, because I thought it might hurt you, but in my dreams it was *you*. Not me. *You* were pulling the weeds from my chest.}"

"{I want to love and be loved.}"

"☺"

"☺"

"↓"

"↓"

"🌡"

"☺"

"□↔□↔□"

"↓"

"↓"

"⏭⏹⏮"

"■ + ■ → ■"

"☺"

"👂□"

"▷◁"

"◉□❖●◆○○□◆⊙●"

"■"

"{I love you.}"

"{I love you, too. So much.}"

Of course, my sense of the should-have is unlikely to be the same as my brothers', or my mother's, or my father's. Sometimes—when I'm in the car, or having sex, or talking to one of them on the phone—I imagine their should-have versions. I sew them together into a new life, leaving out everything that actually happened and was said.

It was said—although no one seems to know by whom, originally—that an ant is not an entomologist. That is, just because you are something, that doesn't mean that you are an expert about that thing, or that you could explain the doings of that thing, or would necessarily choose to be that thing. The kinds of questions being raised in this book, about fiction and creative nonfiction, are, frankly, questions I don't ask myself. Or not when writing. Too often, self-questioning wants to become self-consciousness during the creative process. And self-consciousness is the enemy of creativity. Creativity depends on ignoring boundaries, not transgressing them. Better to be an ant, at least until you've finished a draft.

I've never had any desire to create something new, or experimental, or even unique. I've never tried to work within any particular form or to challenge a form. And when I squint my eyes a certain way, I can honestly say that I've never had any *intentions* with my writing. What I mean is, I've never known what it was that I wanted to create in advance of creating it. I've never wanted to know. Otherwise the very best that I could do would be to meet my expectations. Joseph Brodsky once said, "The rhyme is smarter than the poet." That strikes me as true.

If I sat down assuming I would write fiction, and ended up with something that someone else would call creative nonfiction, fine. If I ended up with poetry, that would be fine, too. If I ended up with a painting, or a song, or a play . . . So long as it was necessary.

JONATHAN SAFRAN FOER is the author of two best-selling novels, *Everything Is Illuminated* and *Extremely Loud and Incredibly Close,* and the editor of an anthology, *A Convergence of Birds.* His books have been translated into twenty-nine languages and he is the winner of numerous literary prizes from around the world. As winner of the American Place Theater's Literature to Life Award 2006, his most recent novel, *Extremely Loud and Incredibly Close,* is regularly performed for students by the APT.

STEFAN KIESBYE

"In German art, a battle of death and life is raging," Eric von Vessen quotes Paul Schultze-Naumburg, who was director of the Weimar Art Academy in the 1930s and coined the maxim "Art must be created from blood and soil." Von Vessen has a high forehead, fine, sand-colored hair and thin mustache. He is good-looking in a ruggedly intellectual way. He'd be able to blend in on a construction site as well as at a conference on European architecture, both of which he does regularly.

Born in 1948, von Vessen, after a career as architect with Eber and Carp in South Florida, where he developed shopping plazas and residential areas, found himself "longing for a challenge." He'd made a fortune in his profession, his wife Elise inherited her father's pharmacy empire, and his life at age fifty could not have been more comfortable. "It was deadening," he exclaims, "absolutely deadening."

He confesses that the approaching new millennium made him review his work of twenty-five years. He concluded that everything he'd built had been built "for today, and therefore was already crumbling. It was as if I had planned and built ruins. Dozens of the malls I designed have been torn down, the developments have turned into slums." Von Vessen had to build for the future if he wanted to be remembered. He dreamed of an architecture that was large, well crafted, and everlasting, imagined monuments of pride.

Von Vessen, who had acquainted himself with the work of Hitler's favorite architect, Albert Speer, during college, found that Speer had answers for his questions.

"I understood," he says and laughs, "that Speer was maybe the last architect who had the imagination and the power to transform an entire country. What he didn't have," von Vessen adds wistfully, "was time."

In 1999, the architect sold his stakes in Eber and Carp and bought the estate of John Erring, "a vast piece of nothingness," in southeast Nevada. "It was ideal," von Vessen notes. Speer, if the Nazis had stayed in power, would have had to tear down large parts of Berlin to create what he and Hitler envisioned for the

German capital. "Tear down the old, erect the new. For us, it was much easier. We were able to start from scratch."

Just in time to celebrate the new millennium, von Vessen and his crew of 640 started work on Germania, the city Hitler and Speer could not finish. "Oh yes," the architect says, "we had plenty of champagne ready for the occasion."

During research for what von Vessen simply calls "his life," he had a lucky strike of monumental proportions. "Speer built a model of Germania, 1:50, back in the 1930s. There were photos, of course, but the model was thought to have been lost during air raids on Berlin in '45." One day back in the spring of '99, von Vessen received a call from New England. "This guy, Albert Leary, he had heard of my plans for building Germania through the press. We had tried to keep a low profile, but a project of that scale . . . He had an old barn, he said on the phone, but refused to tell me what he kept in there. He just said I'd be a fool if I wouldn't make the trip." Von Vessen, after receiving a second call, decided to give it a shot. In May of that same year, he arrived in Entport, New Hampshire.

"So we go to his barn, and this guy is behaving like an insane magician. We have to pull away tons of straw and wood, and I'm starting to curse my curiosity when we finally pull out this gigantic wooden crate." Von Vessen stretches his arms like an angler to indicate how big his find was. "We have to work half an hour to open the front of the crate: more straw—I was going crazy." But he stayed and after another hour, "there, in the middle of this red New England barn, stood the Great Hall, Albert Speer's model of Germania's centerpiece."

Leary's father, a major in the U.S. Army, had shipped his souvenir to America after '45, in a transaction that, von Vessen claims, "took guts and a good deal of bribery."

The architect bought Speer's Kuppelhalle, and today, weeks after his own Great Hall has been opened to the public, it occupies a special place in Germania's Reichskanzlei. "The model helped me through all the tough times, it was a source of inspiration, it kept up my faith."

Some of the hard times arrived when outraged citizens organized a protest tour and arrived in Nevada with banners demanding "Down with the Nazis" and "Stop Fascism."

"They smeared buildings and monuments, left their garbage everywhere,

stefan kiesbye

and threatened to hurt workers. The police wouldn't do a thing," von Vessen remembers, and after the first wave of angry opponents, he brought in security. "I didn't imagine Germania with watchmen and fences. It was a city I wanted to give to my people, to all citizens of this country. But policing Germania was the only way to protect my vision."

His vision has been called "neofascist," a "Triumph of the Ill Will," and a "monument to Hitler and his genocidal politics." But von Vessen won't have any of that. He claims that condemning Speer's architecture is an act that confuses politics and aesthetics. "His ideas are judged by Hitler's killings." This view, von Vessen claims, doesn't do justice to the architecture realized in 1930s Germany. "We look at Speer's buildings and think, Ooh, how shocking, these buildings breathe Nazism, breathe murder and death, when really, all over Europe, you see the same style of neoclassicism, and think nothing of it. The evil people associate with Germania is a false interpretation. Hitler also built the autobahn, and people use highways without thinking, Oh my God, this asphalt is absolutely terrifying."

Yet so far, he hasn't convinced the growing lobby of people who want Germania to be shut down. The State of Nevada has tried to stop work on Hitlertown, as Germania is widely known in the region. After an unfavorable court decision, von Vessen had to let construction rest for several weeks, but the architect won the appeal. And although his case still awaits hearing in front of the Supreme Court, in the meantime, "Germania is growing, definitely."

The new Great Hall seats 234,000, is 250 meters wide, and 290 high. Stone was imported from all over the Americas, Italy, and Germany. "We ran into problems early on," von Vessen admits. "More than 200,000 people breathing and perspiring under a dome—it seemed impossible to avoid fog rendering the interior invisible." But the installation of an intricate ventilation system—each of the green plush seats is vented and can be cooled or heated—was a giant step in the right direction. "It shrank seating capacity, but something had to give." In the end, the problem was solved by breaking with Speer's original plans. "We made the dome retractable," von Vessen says, and adds with a smirk, "Who knows? We may be awarded an NFL expansion team one day."

Yet, as of today, Germania's population is a meager 5,823, half of them construction workers and security guards. The rest are small entrepreneurs who supply the town with food and other daily necessities. When Hitler made plans to build his new Reichshauptstadt, Berlin was a thriving metropolis. Life would have been altered and redirected by vast reconstruction projects—the Spree River was to be rerouted to accommodate the ambitious North-South axis—but four million people were ready to make Germania their own.

Who will walk and drive along the 38.5 kilometer–long Paradestrasse, the North-South axis Hitler was dreaming of? Who will promenade under the 117 meter–high, 170 meter–wide, and 119 meter–deep Triumphbogen? Paris's Arc de Triomphe could be placed within von Vessen's monument. As of yet, only workers and security guards in their black-and-blue uniforms are regulars on Germania's streets.

"We take our cues from Vegas," Elise von Vessen says in front of the Great Hall. She is ten years younger than her husband, tanned and in good shape. She's wearing a light Armani suit and likes to show new visitors around. She's also in charge of a national advertising campaign that tries to bring new businesses and hotel chains to Germania. "You build it, they come. It's not as easy as in the movies, but we will achieve our goals. It's a matter of imagination and daring." In 2001, more than fifty thousand Americans and tourists from overseas flocked to Germania. Elise von Vessen plans to quadruple the numbers each year. "The city is growing, and we will keep the public interested in our wonderful buildings," she promises. "People are already coming. Now we have to convince them to stay."

Her husband of twenty years can only shake his head at questions about his city's future. One day in his office at the Reichskanzlei, comfortably dressed in a blue sweat suit—he is an avid jogger and ran with both Jimmy Carter and Bill Clinton—he tries to answer them nevertheless. "However much I hated doing malls, the knowledge I gained comes in handy. You don't build where the infrastructure is too weak to support you. The time of our forefathers who built settlements in the desert and hoped the railroad might lay tracks through their town are over." Work on a highway connecting Germania with Interstate 80 has been underway since the previous year and is close to completion. An airport reminiscent of Berlin Tempelhof will open soon.

stefan kiesbye

Also planned for the immediate future is the Soldatenhalle, a gargantuan building that, in Hitler's plans, was supposed to house a Hall of Honor with sarcophagi holding the remains of high-ranking military officers. Now it will house a casino with more than six hundred first-class rooms. The Reichskanzlei too will invite visitors to gamble. The extravagant marble mosaics and tapestries were once said to document the fascists' drive toward power. Now the offices Hitler imagined will be turned into five-star restaurants and about three hundred high-end luxury suites.

Without investors, even a rich man such as von Vessen would not have been able to erect "a single wall of the Kuppelhalle." But support has been steady and is growing nation- and worldwide. "Our sources won't dry up anytime soon." As proof, developments, town houses, and several signature high-rises are going up in Germania. "Our workers: they need modern housing, they need stores. Trailers will be outlawed soon around here. We have created 2,500 jobs; long-term, more will be created each year." Certain sections of Germania, starting with the area close to the Triumphbogen, will see luxury mansions. "It will be as desirable as Beverly Hills, Paris, and Venice taken together. We have a unique opportunity here, and we won't let it slip away."

Others seem to share von Vessen's optimism. "You see," Ernest B., a construction worker putting the finishing touches on a row of pseudo-Gründerzeit apartment houses, says, "we're developing the West all over again." Isn't he concerned about the public's often hostile reaction to Germania? Don't the security guards scare off tourists? "No," he says. "When the people come, the guards will be gone. This is just the kind of project that thrives in this country. Yeah, you might have some rough stretches, but the sky's the limit for your imagination."

Many of the newly built apartments are still empty. Does that worry him? "They're real nice. Wait till the casino and the girls come. We have jobs here. I mean, there'll be jobs for the next fifty, sixty years. And it doesn't matter where you find a job, not even what job it is. It's important you have one." He points to the slogan on his dirty-white T-shirt, "Germania—I've seen the future." "We're in the right place at the right time."

A state official who speaks on the condition of anonymity explains, "In Idaho or Montana, this guy would have fallen on his face, but this is Nevada. Once the court gives him the green light, there'll be nothing to stop him. Casinos and prostitution—Hitlertown is well equipped for the challenge. This is a place to die for. It will be a hip place to live, party, and spend lots of money."

But von Vessen wants more than a fun place. "This project is bigger than myself, my money, influence. It's bigger than anyone can imagine right now. Yes, the city has to grow, take its time, but however long that will take, the Great Hall will be here when it's needed. Hitler was the last visionary leader, a leader who was willing to form a country after his ideas." Von Vessen keeps a photo of the Führer in his desk. "Totalitarian, yes, cruel, yes again, but visionary nonetheless. Take Napoleon or Caesar. They were despots, yet were—and still are—revered. We still go to Europe to look at the remains of what they created. With Germania, I give people the chance to experience what Hitler intended them to see. His vision was once cut short, but is now here to stay."

author's commentary

In the 1980s I moved to live in West Berlin, out of reach of West Germany and its soulless *Wirtschaftswunder* and walled off from the East and its particular brand of socialism. It was an island, a big, peaceful city, ruled by the Allies and subsidized by the West. Rents were controlled, and salaries bolstered by Berlin bonuses. I was paid extra to live in the city.

I was well educated about World War II and the Holocaust, but on a walk in front of the Reichstag, I discovered something new to me. The city had set up billboards and maps, documenting the history of the Third Reich, and on one of them, it showed a model of Germania, the capitol building Hitler and his favorite architect Albert Speer had planned to build after razing much of contemporary Berlin.

Yes, Nero had tried to burn Rome, but to destroy an already thriving city to rebuild and rename it? Just because Hitler wasn't fond of Berlin and wanted something flashier for his capitol? It was nuts, yet I was intrigued by the scale of the project. You had to be crazy, you had to have a vision, and you needed nearly unlimited resources to even think about pulling it off.

Then I forgot about it.

89

stefan kiesbye

In 2003, I found that what I liked reading best were the "On and Off the Avenue" paragraphs I found every week in *The New Yorker*. They were short and a safe haven from the wordy, overwritten, and figurative-language-crazy stories and articles I came across everywhere. Instead, stories, in these paragraphs, were only hinted at. I got snippets of people and places, and with my little knowledge of New York, I had to conjure up all the pictures myself. The New York in my head was nothing like the real place. It was better.

In response to "On and Off the Avenue," I wrote thirteen pieces about places and people in the United States I'd like to visit or meet. For one of the first stories, I remembered how Berlin had narrowly escaped obliteration, and imagined that if Germania should ever be erected, it had to happen as a theme park in America.

In terms of style I stuck to the unadorned prose of journalism, because what good is a bizarre fact of life if it is clad in funky garments? To add any beautiful language, or to turn the tale into a "well-written story," would have taken the sting out of Hitlertown. Only if I underplayed the monstrosity and outrage of building Germania in the Nevada desert could I leave room for the reader's recognition that somebody will already have thought about this project, and that its realization is improbable and yet not entirely unlikely.

The fiction, as I see it, is not the invention of a place like Hitlertown, but the journalistic language insisting on its authenticity and factuality. And I hope that pieces like this also open our eyes again to magazine and newspaper articles and their fabrication. For me, fantastic events hold little magic, since in the magic realm, just as in dreams and cartoons, anything can happen. Yet I have never trusted the "real" world, have never felt comfortable or safe in it, and undermining what we commonly assume is true fills me with deep pleasure.

One of the unnerving aspects of Nazi Germany is that no ruler after Hitler has had such sweeping visions and the means to implement them. In that regard he is a descendant of Caesar and Napoleon. To be sure, the world is better off without him, and yet, if you look at contemporary entertainment (and my own story), he is still all over the place. He is a popular reference point, a menace we now have domesticated and turned into a cartoon to render the horrors enjoyable in literature and the movies. From *Indiana Jones* to *Hellboy,* from Philip Roth's *The Plot against America* to the *Miami Vice* movie starring Jamie Foxx and Colin Farrell—the Nazis and their modern offspring still provide our most feared and most beloved enemies. Hitler was the last of a breed of iconic dictators (with Stalin never being able to capture the world's imagination), ready to turn reality into what he thought reality ought to be. Whatever he could imagine he needed others to see with their own eyes.

In fiction we can approach society's taboos and the current version of what we think we have agreed upon as reality. Discussions about gay and lesbian marriage, the use of marijuana, the Iraq War are battlefields of the status quo, of what we allow ourselves to say. In every election candidates do not say what they think but what they think people want them to think. Reality is the fiction of the many, but if we want to discuss currently unspeakable matters, we have to fabricate our own version of what we see.

The centerpiece of Germania, that terrifying successor to Berlin, was the Große Halle, an auditorium with seats for 200,000 people. Their breath would have shrouded the inner space in fog, and yet, who has ever dreamt that big again?

STEFAN KIESBYE, author of *Next Door Lived a Girl,* a novella, received an MFA in creative writing from the University of Michigan. Some of his work can currently be read in the magazines *Hobart* and *Pindeldyboz,* and in *Stumbling and Raging: More Politically Inspired Fiction,* an anthology edited by Stephen Elliott. Kiesbye lives in Ann Arbor with his wife Sanaz and teaches at Eastern Michigan University.

1980

Pac-Man became the first computer game hero. He was originally supposed to be Puck-Man (he was, after all, shaped like a hockey puck), but with the threat that rampaging youth might scratch out the loop of the P on machines in arcades, Pac-Man was born, a name with literally no meaning.

Median household income: $17,710.00
Median cost of a house: $76,400.00
These things hardly mattered or even meant anything to anyone who was just moving out of his or her parents' house and had found an apartment for $200/month, which could be afforded on a $100 a week part-time minimum wage paycheck while finishing a fifth and sixth year of college.

Ted Bundy was sentenced to death by electrocution.

Brooke Shields purred in her Calvin Klein advertisement: *You know what comes between me and my Calvins? Nothing!* Shields also showed off what she had to offer as an actress in *The Blue Lagoon.* Anyone who went on a first date with the person he or she eventually married will remember this film, especially if either of them, having lost one of their brand-new bought-with-birthday-money soft contact lenses in the middle of the first viewing, for some reason still wanted to see how the movie ended and had to go see it twice.

Ronald Reagan visited the White House to get his job briefing from President Carter. Carter would subsequently disclose that the president-elect asked hardly any questions and did not take notes.

John Lennon was shot, ostensibly for being a phony, by a fan carrying *The Catcher in the Rye.* Doctors at the emergency room that received Lennon's dead or dying body later said they could not have recognized him.

In fact there were few people less phony. As an emblematic death, it was the end of rebellion. Some people, though, were in the throes of being engaged, pawning high school rings to buy silver wedding bands.

1981

The hostages held in Iran for over a year were released on the day of Ronald Reagan's presidential inauguration. In his inaugural speech, Reagan took credit for the release.

The public heard the first news report about a gay man's mysterious death from an immune-deficiency disease. Later, when the media continued reports of the pandemic, the disease was defined as one that affected "homosexual men, intravenous drug users, and Haitian men." The inclusion of Haitian men in this early description was eventually dropped without explanation.

The army suggested, *Be All You Can Be.*

The Reagan administration tried to count ketchup as a vegetable in subsidized school lunches.

The minimum wage was raised to $3.35. At 40 hours a week, for 52 weeks a year, this would net $6,968, no taxes. The poverty threshold for 1981, for a single person, was $4,620. Two thousand three hundred forty-eight dollars of breathing room for the year. Some people, however, went to college, and could now make $10,000 a year working behind a desk at a hospital, or as a salesman (-person) for a cement company, or as a first-year elementary schoolteacher, or even earn a little more than that as a grocery checker.

Reagan Budget Director David Stockman said in an interview for *Atlantic Monthly,* "None of us really understands what's going on with all these numbers." He then conceded that trickle-down economics "was always a Trojan horse to bring down the top [tax] rate." And then, regarding the tax bill, "Do you realize the greed that came to the forefront? The hogs were really feeding."

Striking air traffic controllers were fired by President Reagan. Unfortunately Barry Manilow wasn't available to fill in (see 1986).

Britain's Prince Charles married Princess Diana on live TV, and Americans began an(other) immersion in Royal-watching. Some other people got married this same year. Some of them did so without the Diana-style wedding dress and hundred-yards-of-lace train. A few of them opted for a minister's office on a Thursday night, the bride wearing a brown corduroy skirt, the groom in white jeans (his best pants).

"Honey, I forgot to duck," Ronald Reagan supposedly said to Nancy after he was shot by John Hinckley Jr. It was immediately assumed that John Hinckley was crazy.

1982

Bob Jones University, which did not allow admission of nonwhite students, was granted a tax-exempt status by the Reagan administration. A few months later, Reagan told Chicago high school students that the plan was not designed to assist segregated schools, because "I didn't know there were any. Maybe I should have, but I didn't."

The poverty rate rose to 15 percent and the national unemployment rate reached 10.8 percent. There was a new plan, under consideration by the Reagan administration, to tax unemployment benefits. According to a spokesman, it would "make unemployment less attractive."

President Reagan did not like the media constantly reporting about economic distress. "Is it news that some fellow out in South Succotash someplace has just been laid off, that he should be interviewed nationwide?"

He would have been pleased to hear that after six years of college, some people considered themselves fortunate, almost blessed, to be allowed to teach college composition for $250 per month per class; or rewarded to have started at box boy as an undergraduate and in six short years become night manager.

An ad from Mattel for children's computers said, *Now you can get a smarter kid than Mom did.* Why did the advertisement use *get* and not *have?* Did college composition teachers discuss the awkwardness of this sentence? And why was Mattel advertising computers for children when some people, even those who taught college composition, were still using electronic typewriters with "correctible" lift-off letters?

Responding to the buzz regarding Nancy Reagan's appetite for fancy gowns, a White House spokesman said that the First Lady's only intention was to help the national fashion industry. Some people, especially those who rode bikes to work—without making a connection or considering it a protest—stopped wearing skirts entirely (even that brown corduroy wedding skirt).

Bottles of Tylenol were laced with cyanide in Chicago-area stores and pharmacies. Seven people with headaches died of poisoning.

The Equal Rights Amendment also died.

Four thousand one hundred fifty followers of the Rev. Sun Myung Moon (2,075 of them women) were married in a mass ceremony in Madison Square Garden. Later in 1982, Rev. Moon was found guilty of (among other things) conspiracy to obstruct justice.

"You know," Ronald Reagan reportedly said to the Lebanese foreign minister, "your nose looks just like Danny Thomas's."

1983

The navy thought maybe it should eliminate expenses such as $780 screw-drivers, $640 toilet seats, and $9,606 Allen wrenches.

HIV was identified. By this time Haitian men were no longer blamed for carry-ing the disease. Fashion prognosticators predicted ultrathin would soon not be considered stylish, since those suffering with AIDS were ravaged by weight loss. Plumpness, however, did not find its way into contemporary style. Anyone who was still a virgin in 1980 when she met her future husband, then got married in 1981, was probably not ever going to experience uninhibited sexual experimen-tation or promiscuity.

Just Say No (also) became the (only) official antidrug slogan.

The same year Karen Carpenter died of anorexia at the age of 32 (which would not do anything to help chubbiness come into fashion), a new pop star named Madonna released her first album. Her voice was compared to Minnie Mouse on helium. Some people, however, weren't buying new albums at the same rate they had when they lived with their parents. So they might own several Car-penters, but no Madonna. One of the Beach Boys also died this year, but no one remembers where she was when she heard Dennis Wilson drowned. This might have meant something, but nobody wondered what.

A White House spokesman said "preposterous" to conjecture about an inva-sion of Grenada. The following day, because the media were not permitted to cover the mission, the press received, from the White House PR office, photos of Reagan in his pajamas being briefed on the invasion of Grenada.

"I think some people are going to soup kitchens voluntarily," said Ed Meese (who, it turned out, was the same guy who came up with the plan to tax unemployment benefits). "I know we've had considerable information

that people go to soup kitchens because the food is free and that
that's easier than paying for it . . . I think that they have money."

The minimum hourly wage was still $3.35.

Ed Meese (whatever his official position, he seemed to do and say a lot)
gave a Christmas speech at the National Press Club: "Ebenezer Scrooge
suffered from bad press in his time. If you really look at the facts, he
didn't exploit Bob Cratchit. Bob Cratchit was paid 10 shillings a week, which
was a very good wage at the time. . . . Bob, in fact, had good cause to be happy
with his situation. His wife didn't have to work. . . . He was able to afford the
traditional Christmas dinner of roast goose and plum pudding. . . .
So let's be fair to Scrooge. He had his faults, but he wasn't unfair to anyone."

1984

Ronald Reagan, preparing for a speech, was asked to test the
microphone. He said, "My fellow Americans, I've signed legislation
that will outlaw Russia forever. We begin bombing in five minutes."

Penthouse produced its first issue with a man on the cover (George Burns).
Inside, the nude centerfold was an underage Traci Lords. In most countries, including the United States, it is (still) illegal to own or view this issue. The same
edition includes photos of the first Black Miss America, Vanessa Williams, a
few years younger, and nude. Although it was not illegal to look at her photos,
Miss America was asked to resign.

Advertisement for Softsoap: *Ever wonder what you might pick up in the shower?*
Advertisement for Sure: *Raise Your Arm if You're Sure.*
Advertisement for Wendy's: *Where's the Beef?*
(Still an) advertisement for the army: *Be all you can be.*

Despite complaining that it cost too much to administer, Reagan signed the CIA Information Act of 1984, an amendment to the 1966 Freedom of Information Act. At the time the cost of administering the act was less than the Pentagon spent each year on marching bands.

Replacement umpires worked the playoff baseball games when umpires went on strike. Once again, Barry Manilow wasn't available (see 1986).

In a presidential election debate, Reagan accounted for much of the defense budget going toward "food and wardrobe" (see 1985). The Great Communicator went blank in the middle of another answer, then said, "I'm all confused now," before giving his closing statement. Afterward Nancy beseeched Reagan's aides: "What have you done to Ronnie?" Reagan later claimed that if he'd worn as much makeup as Mondale, he would have looked better in the debate.

The Census Bureau reported that 35.3 million Americans were living in poverty and that this was 15.2 percent of the population, an 18-year high. In a televised interview, Reagan said, "You can't help those who simply will not be helped. One problem that we've had, even in the best of times, is people who are sleeping on the grates, the homeless who are homeless, you might say, by choice."

Median household income: $22,415, up 20 percent since 1980; median cost of a house: $97,600, up 27 percent since 1980. Minimum wage: still $3.35/hour; still $6,968 for 40 hours of work, 52 weeks a year. Some people say this was the best year of their lives. Especially people who were right at the median, or even a little below. Especially if things like that didn't matter. Especially since they'd just left home in 1980 and doing their own laundry and grocery shopping—even laundry and grocery shopping for two—was still fun.

1985

Many of the gala celebrations planned for Reagan's reinauguration were postponed because the official inauguration day fell on Super Bowl Sunday.

After 99 years, Coca-Cola marketed "New Coke"; three months later, after consumer objection, it reinstated Coca-Cola Classic. Some wondered whether the whole snafu was a planned promotional gimmick.

While most of the American public will only remember the Great Communicator demanding, "Mr. Gorbachev, take down this wall," President Reagan also said, prior to his visit to West Germany, that he would not be visiting any site of a former concentration camp because it would inflict too much shame on a country where "very few alive remember even the war." (Whereas most American veterans were in their 60s and quite alive.) But the White House pronounced that Reagan would lay a wreath at the Bitburg military cemetery, an integrated home to the tombs of American and Nazi soldiers (although there are no Americans' graves there). President Reagan defended his West Germany itinerary: "I know all the bad things that happened in that war. I was in uniform for four years myself." (His uniform, more aptly called *wardrobe,* was in the training films he starred in.)

The number of Barbie dolls sold surpassed the American population. Some people had contributed more Barbie dolls than they would children (as in 2 dolls to 0 children). This worked, because that median income figure was for two people, not three (or four, or five . . .). Even though that wasn't some people's reason for not procreating.

A congresswoman, discussing Ronald Reagan's response to the balanced-budget bill, said, "We tried to tell him what was in the bill but he doesn't understand. Everyone, including Republicans, was just shaking their heads."

A *San Francisco Chronicle* reporter filed suit, under the new Information Act, to obtain FBI files that would prove then–California Gov. Ronald Reagan spent years trying to launch an illicit "psychological warfare campaign" against "subversive" students and faculty. The *Chronicle*'s questions were referred to Ed Meese (this guy again?), Reagan's chief of staff while he was governor (then *too?*). Meese (repeating the party line) said he did not remember planning any such activities. While it would take 17 years for the *Chronicle* to win the challenge and get documents that in fact proved these things true, in 1985 the FBI only released documents that appeared to have altered Reagan's part as a mole for the FBI in the McCarthy era. Some people, if they'd watched the news more often than ESPN or reruns of *Kung-Fu,* might have wondered if their own activities in the 1970s, including visiting a "known commune" (which has the same root word as communism), might have given them their own FBI file. But maybe some people knew, without knowing, that it was better to only know now as much as you did then, when you visited the known commune not knowing anything except you were there to get some grass.

1986

In thorny contract negotiations with musicians, management of the San Diego Symphony canceled the season and locked out the musicians. But even before negotiations officially broke down, management (already knowing there would be no symphony season)—to help pay for the newly refurbished former vaudevillian concert hall—booked shows by East Coast ballet companies, East Coast orchestras, and Barry Manilow.

The first postal killing happened in Oklahoma, netting 14 postal workers.

Ed Meese (who now, apparently, had a different job) suggested that employers should begin covertly watching their workers in "locker rooms, parking lots, shipping and mail room areas, and even the nearby taverns" to apprehend them with drugs. (*Just Say No* may not have been working. This was plan B.)

On November 25, as the Iran-Contra scandal simmered, Ed Meese said, "The president knew nothing about it." On November 26, on national television, Meese said, "The president knows what's going on." A month later Meese suggested maybe Reagan did give his approval to the deal, while he was under sedation after surgery. (What was Meese's job again?)

California Highway Patrol Officer Craig Peyer—who, it turned out, had a history of stopping young women driving alone and talking to them for lengthy periods—pulled college student Cara Knott off the freeway and directed her to drive down a dark, unused off-ramp. Their encounter ended when Peyer strangled Knott and threw her body off a bridge. The day after Knott's disappearance, local TV news chose Officer Peyer to do a safety-on-the-road segment. Shortly after this case, the California Department of Transportation became the first (and only such agency) to install emergency call boxes—one every mile on every one of the state's freeways. Less than ten years later, the boom of cellular phones made the call boxes seem relics from another era, or monuments to Knott.

An advertisement for Nike said, *Improve your husband's sex life.* It would have been politically correct (not) to propose that Cara Knott would still be alive if Mrs. Peyer had worn her Nikes to bed.

The space shuttle *Challenger* exploded, live on national television. Decades later, a new generation will be defined as those who weren't alive when Kennedy was shot, but who knew exactly where they were when the *Challenger* blew up. This simplistic division ignores those who not only recall clearly when they heard the Kennedy news (recess canceled in first grade), *and* when they heard about John Lennon (the afternoon of their last final exam of the fall semester of their senior year of college), but now also remember when the *Challenger* exploded (while they were doing sit-ups on the living room floor with the TV on before going back to the Laundromat to pick up the white load so there'd be clean underwear for work that evening).

1987

"I hope I'm finally going to hear some of the things I'm still waiting to learn," President Reagan said as the Iran-Contra hearings began. In his January Tower Commission interview about the affair, Reagan conceded that he authorized the arms sale to Iran. In February, Reagan told the Tower Commission that now he remembered that he did *not* sanction the arms sale. While narrating his (re)recollection from a memorandum, Reagan also read aloud his stage instruction (which some remember to say "be earnest," but they may be confusing it with the time George Bush Sr. read aloud his stage instruction, "message: I care"). President Reagan, in a *Washington Times* interview, reminisced wistfully about the time when Joseph McCarthy and the House Un-American Activities Committee exposed subversives.

The acronym AIDS—first used in 1982 when more than 1,500 Americans were diagnosed with the disease—was not uttered by Ronald Reagan in public until 1987, by which time 60,000 cases had been diagnosed, and half of those people had died. (Perhaps he was hoping it was still a mysterious disease among Haitian men, and maybe medical research money could go to beefing up immigration laws.) During a rally to protest the administration's (lack of) AIDS policies, Washington police wore large yellow rubber gloves when they arrested 64 demonstrators.

Gary Hart withdrew from the presidential race when a sexual misdemeanor was exposed. One might propose that his candidacy died to save the future President Clinton.

Playtex became the first to use live lingerie models in TV ads for the Cross Your Heart Bra. One might say this tested the waters for pantyshield companies who would in the future use live actresses to rave about a product that's "not for your period, just those other little leaks."

At the Iran-Contra hearings, no one, not even the president, ever definitively found out what he knew or when he knew it.

Prozac was approved by the FDA. Some people needed it right away. Even anyone who had used audacity, cunning, and acumen to successfully fake a psychological exam and earn a 4F draft deferment in 1969—that same someone might come home from an hour on the grocery workers' picket line and cry, and be curled up in a fetal ball by the time anyone else came home, and not be able to afford Prozac without health insurance.

1988

The Bureau of Labor Statistics said that more than 6 million persons who worked or looked for work at least half of the year had family incomes below the official poverty level in 1987.

> President Reagan on Michael Dukakis's campaign for the
> presidency: "You know, if I listened to him long enough, I would
> be convinced that we're in an economic downturn, and that
> people are homeless, and people are going without food and medical atten-
> tion, and that we've got to do something about the unemployed."

A (new) Nike advertisement said, *Just Do It.*
Visa said, *It's Everywhere You Want to Be.*
The army continued to say, *Be All You Can Be.*

A General Motors advertisement said, *This is not your father's Oldsmobile.* This campaign was credited with helping hasten the eventual demise of Oldsmobile, as the message confirmed for baby boomers the notion that Oldsmobile had been a make preferred by their fathers.

One and a half million acres of Yellowstone National Forest burned. For the fortunate who actually had that archetypical 1950s and early '60s baby boomer upbringing where the family station wagon, festooned with tourist decals, was certain to pull into Yellowstone at least once, this might have signaled the final death of childhood. Just to confirm that biological clocks had been completely distorted, Old Faithful began to change its schedule.

For anyone driving an Oldsmobile, the fires in Yellowstone, therefore, might have been beyond devastating. Oldsmobiles aside, other factors contributing to early midlife crises might have included the incursion of the first college-educated Gen-Xers into the job market the previous year (calculating birth year 1965, plus 22 for the quickest course to finishing college, discounting child-geniuses). College composition teachers had already noticed the attitude change in their students, and the number of business majors who wore Bush campaign pins. Then the morning of the election, when the pedestrian overpass spanning the freeway beside the university was adorned with Dukakis posters, some people actually thought "maybe all is not lost."

In his last television interview as president, when asked to comment on his presidency overlapping with a sizable upsurge in the number of homeless people, Ronald Reagan wondered if many of these were homeless by "their own choice." He extended this analysis to people without jobs. For the second time he clarified his point by referencing the number of newspaper classified job listings (for computer programmers, nurses, and many of the varieties of engineers—electrical, aerospace, mechanical, and architectural, but not so many environmental).

1989

A new East German government prepared a law to lift the travel restrictions on East German citizens. On November 9, a government spokesman was asked at a press conference when the new East German travel law would come into force. His answer seemed flustered: "Well, as far as I can see, . . . straightaway, immediately." Within hours, tens of thousands of people had gathered at the wall, on both sides. When the crowd demanded the entry be opened, the guards stood back, and the wall was disengaged, peacefully. It's possible the East German plan to allow "private trips abroad" never intended the complete and total opening and then destruction of the wall. Did Ronald Reagan, almost one year out of office, try to take credit? (Yes.)

Prodemocracy demonstrators in Tiananmen Square were

fired on by Chinese soldiers. Between 400 and 800 people were killed. (Reagan did not take the blame.)

Although he denied betting on baseball games, Pete Rose was banned for life from Major League Baseball. Why does it seem that Tiananmen Square and the Berlin Wall faded from the news quicker than Rose's fall from fame?

Ted Bundy was executed in Florida's electric chair. This event did not muster much outcry. There is still more debate over whether Rose should be allowed back into baseball than the efficacy of the death penalty, although, admittedly, Rose is a slightly better example for debating baseball's betting rules than Ted Bundy is for a discussion of capital punishment. However, while Bundy simply solidified for the Right their belief in society's moral right to kill undesirables, the execution only caused shades of gray for the Left, some of whom were distracted further by the realization that even mating with someone of the same political persuasion didn't guarantee a sublime unison, and some kinds of disillusionment could not be fixed, even with Prozac.

Since 1980, the median income went up $11,196, or 63 percent. The median cost of a house went up $72,400, or 94 percent. The overall cost of living rose 48 percent, while the minimum wage was still $3.35/hour. If you went to college, but didn't major in business or engineering, medicine or law, you could probably hover right near the median 2-person household income of $28,906, provided you sustained the 2 people in the household.

Some people got married this year; actually 2,403,268. A nearly as impressive number, 1,157,000, were divorced.

Although later the 1980s would be called—usually by patronizing college students who'd grown up in soft middle-class homes—an era of superficiality and decadence, some people never got to be yuppies or conspicuous consumers or marital swingers or weekend cokeheads. Maybe they already were all they were going to be.

cris mazza

The Word According To

If everything I wrote weren't *true* to me, I probably shouldn't be writing. But *truth* and *nonfiction* are not the same species, any more than *truth* is the opposite of *fiction*. *Fiction* and *nonfiction*, especially in the context of literature, are, fundamentally, not distinctions of veracity but are literary methods of arranging material. The word *material* itself is purposely vague here, since it could mean *time*, it could denote focus or camera angle, it could pertain to the amount of *drama* (as Aristotle defined it), could indicate *information*, even "*facts*." *Fiction* could contain information that is 100 percent factually true, and still be fiction. *Nonfiction* (in my opinion) could lie by omission, could be unreliable due to the nature of memory or angles of perceptions, and would still be *nonfiction*. And both would still be "truth" as their authors define it.

One difference between *fiction* and *creative nonfiction* (I make this distinction to remove the genres of history, political analysis, nutrition, etc.) that I can't put aside is that in *creative nonfiction*, I am, as reader, never expected to (and in my case can't) forget there is an admitted, unhidden, often unabashed writer who sat at a keyboard (or pad of paper) and created the piece of writing that I am now reading. The author, the piece's speaker—in indicating it is *nonfiction*, that "I am telling you about something I know or that happened to me"—is also admitting that he or she is writing the piece, afterward, from some position of retrospect. (For this reason, I've always been bemused at the use of present tense in creative nonfiction and memoir.) Sometimes in fiction the author creates a narrator who is speaking from the position of "author," and that aspect (the rendering of experience into language) becomes part of what the fiction is about. But this is not an inescapable quality of fiction, and most often, even in fiction written in the first-person POV, the reader does not, is not expected to, and shouldn't be aware of or perceive the *author* sitting at a desk writing the piece. This "admission" (that "I am this piece's author") can be liberating in nonfiction. There's no pretense this way, no feigning; in fact, the point of view of the piece (the undeniable presence of the piece's author) becomes its basic "truth" (and that "truth" can then extend into "truth" as the author perceives it). This doesn't tie nonfiction any more closely to "just the facts." Perhaps *this* is the tension between the two genres: which one is more true? And it becomes a *friction* between them because the answer is *neither*. They continue to fight for the distinction.

As primarily a fiction writer, who has written one memoir, my innate stance is how fiction's "truth" is something I create through manipulation. This would on its surface seem a contradiction, but it is, I believe, manipulation—more than "imagination," more than "pathos"—that contains the charisma of fiction.

One could argue that my story "Trickle-Down Timeline" doesn't have a character, and is therefore not fiction (and some editors have, in fact, called it an essay). One could also argue there is indeed a character, or two of them—named, in variations, *someone* and *anyone*—and that this is, in fact, what makes it fiction, despite the use of "real" events from history and the chronology ignoring cause-and-effect relationships. My reason for defining it as fiction is that it is manipulation of material, technique, and form, and even though admitting this *might* be admitting that any political statement the piece may be making is the result of skewed information, I would argue that's how every "truth" is arrived at: the material that impacts us the hardest forms our "truth." So my manipulation is intended to enhance a desired impact, but is still a piece of fiction because it's the manipulation that counts, the arrangement, the selection (and elimination), the choice of verbs, adjectives, and adverbs, the zoom in and pan back. Plus those characters—doesn't their life "change" through adversity, isn't that "drama"?

I could've, however, called it an alternative essay and argued that side of it.

CRIS MAZZA is the author of a dozen books of fiction, including the critically acclaimed *Is It Sexual Harassment Yet?* and the PEN Nelson Algren Award–winning *How to Leave a Country*. She also has written a memoir, *Indigenous: Growing Up Californian*. Her most recent novel, *Waterbaby,* came out in 2007. A native of Southern California, Mazza grew up in San Diego County. Currently she lives fifty miles west of Chicago. She is a professor in the Program for Writers at the University of Illinois at Chicago.

Seven Stories about Being Me

wendy mcclure

the story of the curly hand

It seems that when my hands are not in use at least one is almost always curled up into a soft fist, with the thumb out and the fingers bent over the palm. I went twenty-seven years without noticing this until the guy I was dating pointed it out to me. "Look at your hand!" he'd say. "You're doing it again."

"I think you do it when you are very relaxed," he said. I don't know if that's true.

Later, another boyfriend said, "I think you do that because you're retarded."

the story of the grape slurpee when i was seven

It was bought for me at the 7-11. It came in a big tall cup with a picture of Velma from *Scooby-Doo* on it. For about a year afterward I regarded Velma from *Scooby-Doo* with some trepidation simply because of what happened later on that night with the grape Slurpee and me. And trust me, you don't want to know what happened with the grape Slurpee and me.

the story of the lane bryant jeans

"Hey," he'd said. "Show me the jeans you wore when you were *really* fat." This sort of thing really fascinated him for some reason.

I'd already gotten rid of the very biggest stuff, though. In my closet, I had only one last pair of jeans that I hoped I'd never have to wear again. They were from Lane Bryant, in a bootcut style that had been terribly misinterpreted by the plus-size fashion industry. They pooched out at the hips; they flared out too much below the knee; the prefaded denim was too stiff. They tried hard, so fucking hard, those jeans, but they were stupid and clowny, and they were all clumsy with wide pylon legs; they were blocky and massive like concrete supports built to hold up your ass like it was the I-94.

He held them up and looked at the prefrayed cuffs. "Hmm," he said. "These are almost cool," he said. "No they're not," I replied. Then he took off his own jeans and put them on. I was laughing. He buttoned them up. The jeans fit his waist and then hung down everywhere else, just a little, and *just so,* he seemed to be thinking. He was checking himself out in the mirror.

"You are *not* going out in my Lane Bryant jeans."

"Why not?" he said. "I like them. Don't they look good?"

"They . . . uh . . ." I looked at him. They actually did look sort of okay. "I don't think I can answer that," I said. "Because I know they're my Lane Bryant fat girl jeans."

"But they look pretty good, right?"

"I guess," I said. "I guess it doesn't matter that they're Lane Bryant jeans."

We went out to a bar. We met up with my friend Leigh.

"Know where I got my jeans?" he asked Leigh.

"Um . . . where?"

"Lane Bryant," he said proudly, emphasizing each syllable while I rolled my eyes. "Mm-hmm. Lane Bryant."

"I have no response to that," Leigh said.

I talked to his roommate a few days later. "Yeah, so he came home," she said, "and he was all, 'Do you like my jeans? They're *Venezia.*' He fucking loves them."

"Is he always this way?" I asked her.

It's true they looked better on him. And he was wearing them when we broke up. I noticed and everything. I didn't much like that he kept them. But what the hell was I going to do, ask for them back?

the story of the lumps in my leg

There are two of them in my right thigh and nobody can see them but I can feel them. They seem to be about the size of marbles. My doctor says they're probably "fatty tumors" and that they're usually harmless. I sure as hell hope so.

But what a nice phrase, *fatty tumor.* I like the compound creepiness of it. Kind of like *Nazi pustule* or *apocalypse wart* or just plain *shit fuck death!* In my leg.

the story of neapolitan

What does it mean that I have hardly any stories about eating? I don't know.

My favorite ice cream for a long time was Neapolitan. I have always liked how it has that certain orderly three-flavor rigor; most definitely a fascist kind of beauty. When I was in junior high I would sit down at the kitchen table with an open carton and explore various Neapolitan propositions: was the divide between chocolate and strawberry an arbitrary line, or was it a plane? Was it perfectly parallel to the vanilla/strawberry divide? I'd find out with my spoon.

We usually bought the brands in boxes that opened at the short end—the ones that had the flap that said, "Please Fold This Side In First"—and I liked entertaining the idea that I might close the box again sometime. I would sit down with the box and steal and steal and steal. It was stealing because each bite had nothing to do with the next one or the last.

the story of the broken uterus

The gynecologist hadn't come in yet and there was nothing to read and the only thing even remotely of interest in the exam room was a life-size plastic model of the female reproductive system. That I was willing to shuffle across the room wrapped in a paper sheet to get it should give you an idea of how very fucking bored I was.

There was a ridged seam that ran down the middle of the uterus and clearly it did not serve an anatomical function. I don't know why I decided to try and *open* the thing, because it's not like I had a deep need to see a cross-section of the ovaries; I guess I thought the whole deal could just swing open like a *Star Wars* playset. And it did, sort of.

But then I could tell it wasn't really supposed to be opened. Uh-oh.

the story of blue

I was in fifth grade and on a school bus on a field trip. I had the wheelie seat and I kept thumping my feet against the metal hump.

We were going to the history museum but we couldn't get on the expressway yet because of traffic, so the school bus had to go through *Chicago,* the killer part of Chicago. We went through the killer neighborhood and the killer park and everything. But when you looked out, all you could see was that it was snowing. We weren't in school and we were going someplace else, and it was snowing enough to make everything all right. And then a killer pothole broke the back axle of the bus.

There was some bouncing and bumping, and more bumping, and then shrieking and banging. I wasn't quite in my seat at the time, and suddenly I was *really* not in my seat. Everything looked like when the movie film would clatter against the projector and you'd have to turn the thing off.

Off, and then I was slumped in my seat and everyone was around me, and I could hear my teacher's voice saying *Don't throw up Wendy don't throw up* and I was thinking something along the lines of *Well, in just a moment I think I am going to really disappoint you, Mrs. Smitherman.*

But then I didn't. I didn't throw up, but something else was going on: something was droning in my ears, a sort of *uhhhhhhh* sound. It took a moment to realize it was coming out of me, out of my mouth, from the bottom of my stomach up through my chest, and it hurt to get it out, at least until I figured out that what I had to do was breathe, and then I did, and that hurt too, but not as much.

I had been slammed against the edge of the seat in front of me hard enough to knock the wind out of me. *You turned blue,* someone told me. I had heard of that happening to people when they couldn't breathe, but I couldn't imagine what that would look like. Now it had happened and I still didn't know. All the commotion had knocked me over to the wrong side of knowing.

In order to get back I would have to tell everyone who hadn't seen what happened. So I told people *I was blue* for months and months. In fact, I told the story to anyone who would listen.

This was a piece I put up on my Web site, poundy.com, in March 2004, as part of a semiregular journal about my weight and body image issues that I had been publishing online for the previous few years.

I think I can put this piece into a couple of different contexts. The first one is oddly technical: around this time, applications like Blogger and Moveable Type were starting to become more common for online writers, but I was still employing the older practice of building all my Web pages nearly from scratch and uploading them one file at a time. It took at least twenty more steps to put a journal entry online this way, compared with the simple "click this button to publish" method associated with blogging and online writing these days. This difference hardly seemed relevant at the time, but looking back I think it influenced what I wrote. I would write longer journal entries, more "important" ones (or so I'd think), in order to make the royal-pain-in-the-ass process of upgrading my Web site worthwhile. They were more like essays than the quick jotted-off blog bits, more inwardly focused and introspective. At the same time, though, I was becoming increasingly aware that I had an audience—that people were reading my life as a story told in installments.

Which brings me to a second, more personal context: my occasional discomfort with having an online diary. Sometimes it felt too immediate to write on a day-to-day basis; I had the unsettling sense that I was obligated to a "plot" of some kind. Or else, if I didn't post an entry for several days (for whatever reason), I wondered how readers would interpret the silence. So I guess I wrote this piece sort of offhandedly, as a way to step back from the intense commitment of the journal while at the same time satisfying the basic tenets of it—to tell the truth *and* tell a story. I may have also been responding to the way online writing was becoming increasingly short-form (as in blog entries) and yet consisting so much of personal accounts. Rather than try to narrate events in my life as they happened and tell a larger story that I couldn't always see or understand (and to believe otherwise, I think, is to make your life a living fiction), I imagined my life and my body breaking apart into little stories, pieces of a whole to be assembled later.

WENDY MCCLURE is the author of *I'm Not the New Me,* a memoir, and *The Amazing Mackerel Pudding Plan,* a collection of annotated diet recipe cards from the 1970s. She lives in Chicago, where she works as an editor and a writer. In November 2000, she started the Web site *Pound* (www.poundy.com) to write about body image, weight issues, and diet culture because she thought there was a lot more to say about this kind of stuff. She also writes the pop culture column for *Bust* magazine.

Tagore to the Max   PETER MICHELSON

peter.michelson

In October of 1912 Ezra Pound wrote from London to Harriet Monroe, founding editor of *Poetry* in Chicago, that he had "the scoop of the year" for the magazine—"six poems at least" of Rabindranath Tagore's *Gitanjali*. "And nobody else," he continued with immense satisfaction, "will have *any*. . . . This means that we [by which he meant the magazine for which he had just become foreign correspondent] have got to be taken seriously and *at once*." *Poetry,* then but two monthly issues old, and Tagore, in his fifty-first year, were alike at the threshold of historically significant careers in the English-speaking world. Tagore's own translation of *Gitanjali,* from which Pound had secured the first six poems, would be published in England and the United States within the next year, introduced by William Butler Yeats. In the next year, too, he would also publish *The Gardener* and win the Nobel Prize.

But in the fall of 1912 Tagore was largely unknown to the reading public in the West. His poems were featured in *Poetry*'s third issue in December and were promptly "welcomed" in a *Chicago Tribune* editorial. Shortly thereafter Tagore's son wrote requesting some copies of the poems' first English appearance for his father. Young Tagore was studying chemistry at the University of Illinois, and his father was visiting him there. A surprised and delighted Harriet Monroe immediately invited the poet to Chicago.

A month or so before this correspondence a slight thirty-three-year-old furrier and poet appeared at the *Poetry* office, which was already becoming a gathering place for poets. His quiet manner had a compelling intensity, and as the frequency of his visits increased Harriet Monroe found herself consulting his opinion of the poetry manuscripts flooding in. His own poetry had, as she would later write, a "slow working delicate talent," and she found his judgment of new poets suggestive and helpful. Gradually he spent more and more time at the magazine office and less and less time tending his small furrier shop. Harriet Monroe worried about him, as did his wife, of whom Harriet Monroe was especially fond. She could see that poetry was becoming a necessity of life for him and that the tension between it and his work and family responsibilities was beginning to strain his mind. At the same time his peculiar imagist poems and verse plays were earning him a small but distinctive reputation among poets. Likewise his reviews and essays in *Poetry,* which astutely charted the terrain of possibilities in what was being called the new poetry—now known as modernism—Ezra Pound, H.D., William Carlos Williams, Mina Loy, Wallace Stevens, and others.

In reviewing Pound's *Lustra* he perceived in poems like "The Return" the "infinite possibilities of the fantastic-real" as an access to "what we cannot but call the mystery of life." It was a characteristic quality of his own poems and one that drew him to the natural mysticism of Tagore's *Gitanjali* and *The Gardener.* But by late 1919 the fantastic had all but completely lured him from the real world. His wife took their two sons to her parents' home across the continent in Seattle, secured work there, and sent for him.

Harriet Monroe took him to the train. "He was as gentle as ever," she wrote later, "when I confided him to a sympathetic porter, but soon after his arrival in Seattle a mental hospital had to be his refuge." It was so until he died there in 1953, nearly but not quite forgotten. A decade later William Pratt published an anthology entitled *The Imagist Poem.* From it, in company with Pound, H.D., Williams, Stevens, and other onetime confreres, he made his final and long-delayed communication with the world. It was called "Midnight," and it celebrated a brooding surge of spring blossoming, and in a rush, transformed that fantastic-real hour. His name was Max. The younger of the two infant sons his wife, Sara, took west from Chicago was my father.

In January of 1913, when Rabindranath Tagore came to Chicago at Harriet Monroe's invitation, however, Max had not yet taken leave of the real world. Or at any rate he had taken no more leave of it than had Rabindranath Tagore. How much leave that was Max did not know. He knew only that he had been enthralled a month earlier when he read the first six poems of *Gitanjali*—in manuscript, then again in galley proofs, and finally in *Poetry*'s pages. "Oh, grant me my prayer," Tagore had written, "that I may never lose the bliss of the touch of the one in the play of the many." Max had breathed spontaneous affirmation. "I was not aware of the moment when I first crossed the threshold of this life," Tagore had written. "What was the power that made me open out into this vast mystery like a bud in the forest at midnight?" *Yes,* Max breathed again. He knew the surge of being that burst upon the aegis of that mysterious and timeless hour. Three years later he would initially publish an homage to Tagore's image. He would call it "Midnight," the poem that would be his posthumous farewell to the world, an evocation of life crossing the threshold.

Max met Tagore at the *Poetry* office on Cass Street in Chicago. The small office had but one piece of hospitable furniture, an aging wicker armchair. Tagore's entrance was stately. To Harriet Monroe he seemed a tall patriarchal figure in his gray Bengali robe accentuated by a flowing gray beard. In a revealing observation she noted particularly that "His features were regular and Aryan, his skin scarcely darker than a Spaniard's." The poet's attentive eyes scanned the office and the face of each person to whom Harriet Monroe introduced him—her associate editor Alice Corbin Henderson, Mrs. William Vaughn Moody, at whose home the poet would be staying, two young poets, and Max. It was a modest reception, but the poet would later read his poems publicly and be received more sumptuously. Tagore's observant survey of the room was reciprocated by the brooding intensity of Max's dark eyes. With characteristic dignity and poise the poet seated himself in the waiting armchair. To Max, Tagore transformed the creaking wicker to oiled teak or gleaming ebony, some rich oriental wood of which ageless thrones are made. Instinctively Max lowered himself to a lotuslike posture on the floor before the chair, as if—though he had no distinct awareness of it—to avoid an elevation above the poet's line of sight. Tagore immediately recognized the gesture that Max himself did not. But Max at that moment did recall Pound's comment on Tagore in a letter Harriet Monroe had shown him, that he'd just "come from dinner with the *really* great man who is only vaguely aware of the seething literary wire-pulling that swishes beneath his Olympus." Even as Max had the thought Tagore's benign smile intimated intuitive communion between them.

Max was not at all surprised. As soon as he had read the *Gitanjali* hymns he felt affinity with Tagore's spiritualism. If Max had been born a Jew, he had even more been born a pantheist. Had not the sprites of the trees, the birds, the seasonal atmospheres, the very light and dark always spoken to him, not spoken exactly but reverberated as if by voice? And had he not been fearful, even to paranoia, of acknowledging their voices? But here in the large-souled celebration of Tagore's poems was confirmation—that the playful, often teasing voices of the many were a chorus harmonizing with the spirit of the One, that to hear them and record the hearing in his poems was not madness, as he had feared, but an evocation of nature's mystery manifold and one. He would feel this even more later in 1913 when *The Gardener* was published, where he felt the dialogue of nature's multiplicity with the transcendent One went beyond even that of *Gitanjali*. But at that moment the conclusion of Tagore's sixth *gitanjali* came to mind, for he had committed them nearly verbatim to memory.

Max was not a man for idle conversation, much less flattery or even politeness. He was far too intense, especially where poetry was concerned. And poetry was almost his only concern. He spoke, when he spoke at all, directly from the heart. Just then his heart was filled with Tagore's poems. "But there, where spreads the infinite sky for the soul to take her flight," he murmured in a voice barely audible, yet just enough so that Tagore could make out the words, "reigns the stainless white radiance. There is neither day nor night, nor form nor color, and never never a word." The last phrase lingered in the subdued timbre of Max's voice. He looked with the full candor of innocence into Tagore's eyes, as if offering the poet the homage of his own verses. Again, Tagore understood the gesture that Max himself did not. "Yes," the poet said simply, nodding his great gray head slowly and returning Max's level gaze. For that moment the two were alone in a timeless space. The elder poet was filled with compassion for the *yatra* he sensed in the younger poet's soul. Max was filled with the silent interstices resonant in the poet's words, a silence that hovered eloquently. "Thank you," Max said at last. He lowered his eyes, head bowing almost imperceptibly. "Thank you," he said again, whispering. The clenched hands resting on his knees unfolded slowly, like a blossom opening at midnight.

The poet sat back in the armchair. His leonine head turning now to include others, silent themselves in the moment's singularity, restored time to its flow.

Tagore, as Harriet Monroe would later describe this visit, would go on to delight and instruct his hosts on a variety of subjects, especially with his "satirical-humorous observations of western civilization" with its odd, and to him surprising, "separation of religion from life." They particularly enjoyed his chanting his verses in the original Bengali, which Tagore's high tenor rendered beautifully. Pound had written to Harriet Monroe that Tagore "has sung Bengal into a nation," and here by serendipity they were hearing the beauty of history at first hand. But Tagore also had a politics, and he protested the British colonization of India bitterly. "India has been conquered more than once," he said, "but when the conquest was over life would go on much as before. But this conquest is different, it is like a great steel hammer, crushing persistently the spirit of the people." Of course he said this in spirited English. But then as Walt Whitman—a man and poet in Tagore's own mold—would say: "Do I contradict myself? Very well, then, I contradict myself."

Tagore's Nobel Prize made him a world icon of poetry and spiritual sensibility. There are those who say that he honored the prize more than it honored him. Be that as it may, it was the prize that drew international attention to his work and made him a world figure. If he is not read much in the West today, his iconography continues nonetheless. As for Max, it was poetry that drew his attention, for to his mind there was no prize commensurate with Tagore's achievement. In retrospect, one of Tagore's achievements was to give Max his poetic life. Yeats once told Pound that Tagore was "greater than any of us—I read these things and wonder why one should go on trying to write."

Max, though, read those things, and they inflamed his voice and vision. In the next seven years he produced a steadily growing body of poetry, prose, and plays that drew the admiration of his more famous contemporaries. And in his work those manifold voices of nature—of the trees, the creatures, of the very air itself—those voices of being's mystery and not its madness, those voices that had received the benediction of Tagore, imparted to him their mysteries. He gave them language, language and sensuously impassioned mystical images. But then, before his slow working delicate talent had fully found itself, the voices went bad. They resented any time he took from the muse. And the muse, cruel in the purity of her attentions, had no interest in feeding, clothing, or sheltering his family. Max shared her resentment. But he and his family nonetheless had their needs. In this crucible, the lyrical voices deserted him. Others took their place. They told him there were plots against him. They told him to wait outside the post office and assassinate the president. They told him and anyone else who was listening that Max was going mad.

After a full and productive life Tagore died at the beginning of the world war that would lead to the shelving of the British hammer battering the spirit of India. Whether Tagore anticipated that I don't know. When independence came Tagore's was an honored cultural legacy for the new nation. Max died in obscurity twelve years later, though there is a sense in which he died when he entered the mental hospital in 1920. Tagore revisited Chicago several times, but he and Max never met again. They had said, after all, what they had to say to one another. Max, too, would pursue "the stainless white radiance." On Tagore's way he had sung, "When . . . I looked upon the light . . . the inscrutable without name and form had taken me in its arms in the form of my own mother." On that same trek Max, too, had come upon the inscrutable. And it took him, too, in its arms. But the comforting maternal form had been replaced, as Tagore might have said sadly, by the demonic arms of the rakshasas.

It is quite possible that Max, a childhood Lithuanian immigrant to America, knew those indigenous Indian antagonists better than Tagore was ever obliged to do. He had in any event long since buried his memory of the poet. Indeed, any recollection whatsoever of poetry would induce a violent paranoiac reaction in that otherwise gentle man. As, even more sad to say, would the sight of his wife, Sara. So much so that by the end of his first decade of internment she had to leave him to exorcise his demons as best he could. By the time of his death it seems certain that he no longer remembered Sara, who had died in the interval, or his sons, let alone suspected a grandson would one day relate his brief and, as it happened, fatal encounter with the great spirit of Rabindranath Tagore.

author's commentary

Writers exist in the face of uncertain achievement. Or, as William Faulkner once put it, the measure of a work is the magnitude of its failure. There is a sense in which the English essay (which I prefer to "creative nonfiction") as a form developed in response to this problem. Francis Bacon's essays in the seventeenth century set a sturdy, yeomanlike example—short serviceable expositions of greater and lesser topics that permitted the writer more intellectual latitude than such tomes as his *Novum Organum*. It was left to the Romantic essayists—especially William Hazlitt, Charles Lamb, and Leigh Hunt—to open the form to personal exploration and intellectual flirtation, to a greater range of aesthetic success and failure. In their hands the essay took on the challenge of artifice and spontaneity and began to be an art form as well as an expository tool. From there it began its inevitable trajectory toward the intersection of fact and fiction.

As a kind of corollary to Werner Karl Heisenberg's indeterminacy principle, it is now a commonplace that all narrative—scientific, historical, legal, etc.—is necessarily fictive to a greater or lesser extent. I write essays because they are in a great tradition, are fictive to a greater or lesser extent, and they allow, even invite, a narrative caprice that generates a useful dialectic with reality.

At the time I wrote "Tagore to the Max" there was a conjunction of two unlikely events. First, I had just completed a labor of many years, collecting the extant works of Max into an edition, for which I had written a biographical essay about him. Because there was little data available about Max's life, what there was stimulated a good deal of speculation. Second, at that point an editor from Calcutta asked me to write a piece about Rabindranath Tagore's poetic presence in contemporary America. Because Tagore's presence in this country is fainter than it once was, and I had little to say about him, I was about to decline the invitation. But I recalled Harriet Monroe's account of both poets in her autobiography, and I thought that perhaps I could synchronize their stories and answer some of my lingering questions about Max and understand more about the mystical lyricism of both poets.

By what I hope is an astute mixture of fact and fiction I was able to work out a story line. My narrative then had some components that intrigued me. Not so much that a young poet meets an older poet at the apex of his career, but that the younger poet strives to engage the older poet's imaginative milieu, which proves productive poetically but destructive personally, that the two come from antithetical cultures, where the wages of poetry, to say nothing of mysticism, are quite different, and finally that so transcendent a moment carried the seeds of pathos if not tragedy. I will not diminish the reader's pleasure nor insult his or her perceptivity by indicating just where fiction enhances fact or vice versa. To be honest, I'm not sure I know anymore. But I will say that if this encounter did not happen altogether as reported, it all *could* have happened. Moreover, in the process of writing this piece I learned a good deal about Tagore and about Max and about the valency of poetry. I hope the reader will be able to say the same.

PETER MICHELSON, a sometime director of the University of Colorado's Creative Writing Program, has published personal essays, literary essays, fictions, and poetry in a variety of journals. He is the author of six books, including *Speaking the Unspeakable* and *When the Revolution Really*, and editor of *The Extant Poetry and Prose of Max Michelson, Imagist*.

What struck me most—in the initial moments of surprise, before I realized that all of it made sense—was that my father had not gone to any great lengths to hide anything. The letter, the notepad, the Boston Symphony Orchestra program, and the photograph were simply lying in the bottom drawer of his old rolltop desk. Simply lying there! And I wondered, did he mean for me to find them? He must have known my mother would not ever look through his desk, even after his death. He must have known I would have to, after hers.

The sepia envelope, brittle and thin, was stamped with a 1946 New York City postmark and addressed to William Foster, 741 Western Avenue, Holliston. I had never known my father lived there. Inside lay a single folded sheet of paper.

This twilight state without you is agony. I think of you, of that new concerto, and I am like some precious Stradivari, plucked and left to quiver.

Such language! And relating to my father of all people. There was no signature, no return address, just these smoldering words, written in spiky, elegant handwriting I didn't recognize, sent to him long before he met my mother.

At first, the leather notepad seemed to offer no clues. It had a smoky, charred smell, like outdoor cushions my mother once bought at a fire sale. They made my father so nauseated he asked her to throw them out. The cover's gold, circular stamp read *United Shoe Machinery Corporation, Boston, Mass., 1945.* Inside were pages of my father's infamous lists:

granite 9573UJ
Dr. Coty's Mist
eucalyptol
liq. pit.

Cryptic, but that was my father. "Just answer the question you're asked," he used to counsel. "Then zip it up."

Equally peculiar was the BSO program, announcing the first performance of Samuel Barber's cello concerto, in April 1946. This concerto was my father's favorite piece. It inspired my playing from childhood. Yet in all the years of listening to it, of watching me try to master it, he never once mentioned he'd been to its premiere.

Why?

And the strangest thing, too weird, was this week's performance schedule: we were playing the piece in Symphony Hall, for only the second time since that premiere so long ago.

Coincidence? Or life happening for a reason?

I gazed down at the snapshot, a laughing couple standing in front of a hedge. I thought about how I would never know who these people were, or why my father saved their picture, then I looked more closely. The man *was* my father, lean and blond—so young!—his arm around a woman as tall as he was who was caught in the motion of turning her head toward him, laughing.

The motion had caused the woman's face to blur. I fished around in the boxes I'd packed for my father's magnifying glass and held it over the picture with the distinct sense that he'd done this, too: strained in vain to get a sharper look. I could make out the separate strands of the woman's platinum Forties-style waves, the weave of her dress, splattered with large flowers, but I could not clearly see her face.

I wondered what had become of her. I had never seen my staid, dignified father look like this—infatuated, almost giddy. On a second pass through the notepad, I found her name—my name, but not my name—on the next-to-last page:

Edith Worth
333 E. 54th St.
PLaza 5-1095

Then: *Edith, Edith, Edith*—these last three wildly scattered around the page. And folded and tucked into the back pocket of the notepad, a marriage certificate.

Edith Mary Worth and William Henry Foster, May 22, 1946

It was like a symphony's finale making sense of disparate parts. I knew there had always been a void in my father's history, a time, after the war, when he had never been quite clear about what he'd done or where he'd lived. But both my parents had been private people, evasive about intimate matters, like many of their generation. I knew the facts: they had married in 1963 when my father was forty-nine and my mother thirty-seven. I didn't know much else.

Francine would know, I thought. She had been more than a housekeeper the last twenty years, she'd been my mother's best friend. But she was out getting more boxes, so I waited, a half-hour passing swiftly while memories shifted and re-formed: the times I'd surprised my father at his desk, the motion of his hand shutting the drawer, the way he'd look down at that hand, and then, finally, at me. Those old images sandwiched together like glass slides: my father alternately slack-jawed/distracted/happy. The happy times he'd turn to me and say, "Edith is my joy!" and pluck me off the floor and onto his lap to recite "The Children's Hour," the poem I loved best because my unlovely, old-fashioned name was in it in a way that made it pretty and new:

From my study I see in the lamplight
Descending the broad hall stair,
Grave Alice, and laughing Allegra,
and Edith with golden hair.

Edith with golden hair. I had golden hair. Was it possible that Edith was my mother? Even though their marriage took place more than twenty years before I was born? The dates made it unlikely, but it would account for the distance—never acknowledged, and certainly amiable enough—that had always existed between my mother and me.

The last time she and I had talked was a Thursday, almost a year ago. I'd been feeling guilty about the fact that I hadn't seen her for a while and stopped in between a morning rehearsal and the evening's performance. I found her in the study, the glass doors of the bookcase hanging open, my father's law books in disarray.

"Edie!" she said, waving me in. "I've decided to turn this room into an aviary."

Her manner was so firm and decisive that I could only look at her stupidly. She was more assertive since my father died. She even looked healthier. She'd joined a birding group and her arms were heavily freckled from being out in the sun, her face tan under a white cotton headband.

I wasn't very nice. "You can't get rid of Dad's stuff," I said, snatching the back of my old chair, where I had spent so many evenings practicing my cello while my father went over cases.

"Don't try to talk me out of it," she said. "I've decided. In fact, I've already put in a call to Francine."

"For what?"

"For help. I'm just waiting for her to call me back. She'll be glad to see me do this, finally. It's my house, after all."

"Francine has no business telling you what to do with Dad's stuff."

"It's my business, Edie." Her voice was firm and annoyingly pleasant. "Perhaps you should focus on fixing your own life instead of trying to run mine."

She rarely criticized so bluntly. Even though I knew she thought my marriage ended because of my devotion to work, which she considered excessive, the most she'd ever said—and that under her breath—was that I should have stepped aside once in a while and let the spotlight shine on my husband.

"Tim's lack of success has nothing to do with me," I said flatly. "He'll never be successful because there's too much 'me' in his playing."

She had no idea what I was talking about. I reached for the rolltop impatiently. "At least let me choose what I want of Dad's," I said. But she laid a hand on my arm.

"No, no, dear. I want to put that in storage, as is."

She was wearing this new assertiveness with pride, like a merit badge. "Fine!" I said. I threw off her hand. Then I caught our reflections in the hall mirror and saw our faces—hers stricken, mine hard and satisfied—like a stranger might. I came close to mustering up an apology and later, of course, wished that I had, but an apology just wasn't as satisfying as leaving in that huff.

Hours later, the personnel manager met me at the stage door and told me that my mother had suffered a stroke. Her healthy appearance had been just that: appearance.

The creak and swing of the back screen door announced Francine's return. I found her in the dining room, planted in front of the hutch, ready to bubble-wrap the Christmas plates.

She jerked her head toward the study. "Finished?"

"I filled a lot of trash bags."

"Stick them outside. My guys—they pick them up." Francine was raised in remote Quebec. Words dropped from her mouth like bricks.

I didn't waste time. "Did you know my father had a first wife?"

There was the slightest hesitation in her packing, I was sure of it, but she shook her head and said, "First wife?" as if the idea was nuts.

But if she knew the truth, then she would also know why I was not told. Loyal to my mother, she would reveal nothing.

"Because," I said, thinking fast, "right before my mother had the stroke that day? She did a lot of talking."

She looked at me sharply and I scrambled to keep her interest. "Maybe it was some kind of premonition, but she did a lot of talking."

"What did she say?"

"Something about—a wife."

Her eyes narrowed. "Huh?"

"She wasn't ready to talk about it, she said."

"So why didn't you ask later?"

"She couldn't speak in the condition she was in." Which was true. "I hoped she would recover." There hadn't been much chance of that, but I'd hovered, hoping that behind those roving eyes, something saw and appreciated that I was there and sorry.

I could see that although Francine didn't quite believe me, there was something more. But she said, "I don't know about any wife" with some finality, and for the next minute, there was just the sound of scissors cutting bubble wrap, the rip of tape across plastic teeth.

There had always been this barrier between us, and I didn't know how to penetrate it. "Take those," I said impulsively, gesturing to the holly-trimmed plates she'd always admired.

She backed away as if I'd said something scandalous. "I will not!"

"*Why?*"

"These are for Jane's grandchildren."

I almost laughed at how that remark completely bypassed me. "Grandchildren? I've had exactly two dates in the past two years, both with self-involved prima donnas that made Tim look humble."

"There's plenty nice guys out there, you're just too caught up in how they look or are they artists. Anyways—" She looked toward the dining room, where my mother had lain in the rented hospital bed those last months, head turned toward the deck railing, watching finches and swallows fly among the feeders Francine had lined along the deck. "I wouldn't want Jane to think I was after her things."

"She wouldn't think that—" I caught sight of something on the top shelf. "My mother's poems," I said, reaching for the old Stouffer's candy box, recognizing it at once. Years before, my mother had written poems about birds, about winter in New England, and sent them to *Yankee Magazine.* The editor's name had been, maybe still was, Jean Burden, and the name had seemed appropriate. My mother's hopefulness, the way she checked the mail each day, her continued disappointment, became a burden that I took upon my twelve-year-old shoulders. I'd sensed that something important was riding on those poems.

"She went through a poetry phase," I said. "She kept them a secret from my father. Wanted to surprise him when one was published. 'Just hand him the magazine,' she said. Finally, she stopped writing them."

"I didn't know about these." Francine seemed almost affronted.

"Well it was before you came."

"Still."

"After all that rejection, she was probably embarrassed."

"Aren't they any good?"

I scanned them. "No." There was no natural cadence, no form to the poems. But they were felt. One of the titles was "From My Center." So much was making sense now. Remembering how badly she had wanted to present my father with a poem. The way she had glamorized her name as "Jayne" for a while. She must have known, or at least felt, that something was missing.

I remembered, too, how sacred personal privacy in our home was. Who started that? Her? Him? There were no locks, no keys; there was only trust. "The strongest lock," my father called it.

"She should have showed them to me."

"What's your interest in poems, Francine?" Over the years I'd sometimes wondered—then quickly shoved the thought away—about the nature of unmarried Francine's affection for my mother. Her cleaning company employed a hundred people who cleaned stadiums and apartment buildings. There was never any need for Francine to personally scrub our floors.

"I just would have appreciated them is all."

"I'm sure you would," I said. I meant to sound sincere, but must have come off sarcastic, because she snatched up the carton, brushed past me, and dumped it into the hall.

"Oh, from the time I first came here, I saw how it was. You and him always going off to them concerts, leaving her out."

It was no good pointing out that my mother never liked the symphony.

"Maybe she changed her mind," Francine said.

"All she had to do was say so."

Francine's square, stubborn face took on the distinct look of a bulldog once she got going on a subject. "And then, when he sold the practice, she thought they'd buy a little Cape Cod place, but no. He buys you *that*." She gestured down the hall to where my Gagliano's case leaned against the wall. "Giant fiddle costing more than a house. Crazy."

I could almost imagine my mother there, silently siding against me. She'd been the type of person who never came right out and told you something was bothering her. No, you were supposed to read her mind.

Of course, it hadn't been she who had encouraged my music. It was my father, when I was barely old enough to hold an instrument, who played Rach-

the art of friction

maninoff and Sibelius with the volume turned up so I could leap around the living room. It was my father who drove me to my cello lessons year after year, who encouraged me to audition for Juilliard when I was feeling too intimidated to try, who understood that it was Tim's professional jealousy that ultimately poisoned my marriage.

"If my mother had a problem with my cello, she should have said something."

Francine gestured across the hall to the deck. "What are you going to do with them bird feeders?"

My mother had been like this—changing conversational gears like a bad driver. Her conversations with Francine had made for odd music, cacophonic, annoying to listen to. Birds, they'd be talking about one minute, then a certain kind of furniture polish, then grandchildren—or rather, Jane's lack of them.

"Pack them," I said. "The Realtor said the auction people will take them. She thinks they're some kind of folk art."

"Huh. That one's got her head you-know-where." Over the weeks of packing, Francine and I had ripped up the wall-to-wall in the living room, as the real estate agent advised ("Hardwood floors are what people want"); we had pulled down drapes ("Buyers today want light-filled spaces"). Francine was fed up.

"I'm sure she knows what she's doing."

"Since when's a bird feeder a work of art? Your mother would have a laugh over that one."

"My mother wasn't perfect, you know," I said, remembering, for some reason, how I once gave my mother a bird for her birthday, a parakeet from Woolworth's. She'd stiffened, and the sight of that bird with aqua-dyed feathers seemed to me suddenly and obviously grotesque. I cried that I'd chosen such a gift and tried to fake why I bought it. "We'll let it go," I said, "and watch it live in one of your birdhouses." But my mother said it would die if we let it outside, and for the next nine months, until it did die, the bird lived in a white wire cage in our living room, and I could never pass it without a messy mix of shame and pity.

I'd never known my mother well enough to know what she liked. I'd always guessed wrong.

"What's perfect?" Francine said.

maryanne o'hara

I lugged the trash bags out to the curb, glad for the excuse to get away from Francine. I would have to figure things out on my own. Maybe my father and this Edith tried for years to have a child. She finally got pregnant, only to die in childbirth. No, the dates just didn't fit. All I knew was that my father eventually married his secretary, Jane, who had often recounted the story of how they got together: *I used to make a tuna macaroni dish he loved. I'd bring him some for lunch. Every Tuesday. One day, he said he wanted to see what it was like to eat tuna macaroni on a Monday night.*

How disappointed I was in that story, when I was old enough to understand it. I remembered quizzing him. Why did you marry so late? Why did you bother? How did it feel to be so old having a kid?

He was sitting at his desk, and there was something about its order, about his precise way of pausing to think before answering, that lent assurance to his words. "I wanted you," he said. "I wanted a child. Age just didn't factor in."

Age factored in later. He was eighty-four, I was thirty-three the day he died—a luminous April morning with sailboats skimming the Charles River, which I could see from my chair by his hospital bed. My mother was running some errands; I was watching him fall in and out of sleep. I couldn't get a childhood memory out of my mind—the day I'd grasped so fearfully just how old he was. We were in Vermont, in a cabin we'd rented for years, during a late-afternoon storm. I was standing against the tattered screen door, intoxicated by the breeze on my face, watching the lightning flash blue over the mountains, when my father appeared beside me. "*The pain of finite hearts that yearn,*" he said in his quoting voice. He pressed his palms against the screen. "Mr. Robert Browning." The backs of his hands were spotted, ridged with bulging blue veins. He was old, I realized then, as old as my friend Laura's grandfather, who'd died in May.

From his bed, he murmured something, and I leaned across the bed-rail. His eyes were on me, watery blue and rimmed red.

"Don't give up," he said.

I shook my head, confused. Give up music?

He shook his head with all the impatience he could muster. "Love."

At that point, I was only recently separated from Tim and this kind of talk made me weary. "Oh, Dad, really," I said. I no longer believed in romantic love, at least not in a lasting sense. I'd married a fellow cellist expecting shared vision, that sort of thing, but Tim kept a mental relationship scorecard—who gave what and when—and criticized my every performance, even though I was the one with the BSO seat.

He closed his eyes. The lids were nearly translucent. "We use the word *love* as if it has a concrete, agreed-upon definition. But it is barely defined, I think."

He dozed off, and I watched his ribs rise and fall under his johnny. I steeled myself—there were so few breaths left.

Then he spoke my name. "Edith." He said it in an odd way, as if my name was just a word, a dreamy half-murmur of a statement.

"Daddy?"

His eyes flickered open. He waved a weak hand toward the sailboats. "I thought I could not sail beyond the border of love." His gaze turned inward. "Here is Kundera quoting his Rubens: *First you must understand this apparent contradiction: beyond the border of love there is love.*"

The silence in the room became rhythmic. A red second hand ticked its way around the clock.

"What are you saying, Daddy?"

His eyes remained fixed on the window and I wasn't sure whether to press for an explanation.

"Oh, too much," came the eventual answer.

After Francine went home, I stayed up late, looking, with no luck, for more information. The next morning, onstage at Symphony Hall, I was buzzing with lack of sleep. Even though I was eager to do the Barber, I wanted to get through the rehearsal so I could get to Holliston and investigate town records. A canvas curtain, meant to simulate the acoustics of the full hall we would have for the evening's open rehearsal, hung in front of the stage. The curtain cut the orchestra off from the rows of hard leather seats—unchanged since that premiere in 1946—that I wanted to peer at, just to try to get a handle on the fact that my father actually sat there while Raya Garbousova played the piece for the first time.

I studied the program notes. The premiere was performed on April 6. Edith's letter was postmarked April 19, and sent from New York. It was a month before their marriage. She'd heard the new concerto and had felt herself, alone and apart from him, to be like *some precious Stradivari, plucked and left to quiver.*

I've always believed that a truly great performance, if recorded somehow, is art at its purest: transcending its fleeting presence to become endlessly present. Like a painting. Like poetry. The recording might not even have to be an actual reproduction of the music, but some witness to it that conveys the soaring spirit of the original—like Edith's testament as witness to that first performance.

There was no guest soloist—Ilya, our principal cellist, was doing it. When Arkil, the guest conductor, raised his baton, the rest of us plunged into the first movement: a startling, jagged, unrelentingly forward-moving orchestral progression that subsides as the solo cello snakes its way in. Immediately, with dismay, I heard that Ilya was not quite good enough to perform this piece. Few people are. Masterfully played, the early solo is like a skater twisting and turning but all the while gliding smoothly forward. Ilya's skates were dragging, and I decided that I would draw slower, then sink quicker, into the strings when my chance came to play this—as it would, as it must. Because the coincidence of performing this piece, now, was like my father encouraging me one more time.

In the afternoon, I made my way out to Holliston. In the town hall, the young clerk, a pregnant girl who was filing when I came in, perked up when I told her what I was looking for. "I love stuff like this," she said. We searched deeds, then moved to fire logs and newspaper microfiche and finally to the 1947 birth and death ledgers.

Edith was not my mother. The truth was simpler, and sadder, than that. A short piece in the *Holliston Gazette* clarified:

We note the tragic passing of Mrs. William Foster (formerly Edith Worth), on Sunday, the 27th of April. Mrs. Foster, a violinist with the Greater Boston Ladies' String Quartet, reentered her burning house at 741 Western Avenue for reasons unknown and there perished. Services will be held at the First Congregational Church in Mount Hope, New York, on Wednesday at nine o'clock in the morning. Cause of the fire is under investigation.

So she *had* been a musician. I wondered—with a cringe, I must admit—about my father's motives for encouraging me in music. For naming me Edith. He definitely guided me, but the euphoria came from inside, of course it had. Every teacher said it: I was born to play, my vibrato came naturally.

"And here's the cert," the clerk said, leaning over a black ledger filled with handwritten birth and death records.

NAME: *Foster, Edith M.* CAUSE OF DEATH: *flame burns.*

"What a horrible way to put it," I said, lingering over the cold fact of my name on a death ledger.

The clerk laughed. She was sweetly unaffected. "They were very straightforward then." She was young and about to have a child and other people's pain was an abstraction. "There's a man listed in one of these books as 'self-strangulation by necktie.'"

Shush, I wanted to say. I was thinking of the notepad, and how paper and leather, shut in a drawer for more than half a century, could still retain the smell of fire.

"The poor woman," the clerk said. "A relative?"

"Sort of." And wasn't she, in a way? If she had not died, I would never have been born.

I asked for a copy of the ledger. According to it, she was twenty-five years, five months, and three days old when she died. She was buried in her birthplace: Mount Hope, New York.

Outside, I started the car but sat for a while, gripping the wheel, trying to put it all together. The few facts triggered more questions, but there was no one else to ask. I was the last of my parents' line, truly an only child. There was an older cousin in Montreal, a woman I didn't know. A memory stirred—this cousin, Carole, visiting when I was a child. Jealous of my doll bed, my dresses. Whispering mean things to me, threatening to snap my bow. *Your dad was in a loony bin.* Me not believing anything Carole said, telling her to shut up.

He started his practice in 1960. Where was he after 1947?

Your dad was in a loony bin.

Back at the house, I found Francine on the deck, wrapping bird feeders in newspaper. I held out the ledger copy, but her wrapping hands didn't even pause.

"What exactly did she tell you that day?" she finally asked.

"She didn't say anything."

"So how did you find out?"

"I found stuff, in my father's desk."

"Huh." She eyed me closely. "So what *did* she talk about that day?"

It occurred to me that Francine was after something specific. "Other things," I said, deliberately vague.

For a long while she didn't say a thing. There was only the distant sound of some neighbor's weed whacker. When she finally spoke, it was with resolve and rancor. "She was afraid you wouldn't understand, that you'd lose respect for her."

"I wouldn't," I said, a reflex. But I thought of my mother's face in the mirror that day I lashed out at her newfound assertiveness. The cedar railing was warm under my hand; I gripped it tight. The scent of field-flowers, the catbirds calling, these were things I associated with my mother.

"I wouldn't," I said again. "Lose respect."

People are supposed to respond to touch, to the sound of their own names. I touched Francine's arm and said, "I wouldn't, Francine," but she shook me off.

"I've only got bare facts," she said stubbornly.

She told me what she knew; I filled in the rest.

A simple kitchen fire, grease probably, and both of them in the living room, reading the newspaper, perhaps. It was a Sunday afternoon. My father always liked reading on a Sunday. A Sunday afternoon in April, so the day was probably chilly, with a bit of a breeze.

It hadn't been too bad at the start, Francine said. After they realized it was spreading too fast for them to extinguish, they simply ran out the front door and down the porch steps. People gathered. Someone called the fire brigade.

For a while, perhaps, no one spoke. Fires have a way of mesmerizing people. I pictured the laughing Edith of the snapshot, pictured her leaning against a tree, watching the flames while neighbors crowded around. The fire bell clanged, louder and louder; all eyes turned to watch the truck arrive. Nobody noticed Edith running back inside.

Francine said she must have noticed that my father was nowhere in sight. With all the confusion and noise, she must have panicked, blindly and completely, jumping on the assumption that he had returned to the burning house.

Behind the house, well back from the blaze, my father was standing with a few of the men, considering the damage. They were probably talking insurance policies and reconstruction costs when he heard his name, heard Edith screaming his name. He ran for the porch, but the heat threw him back. There were hands pulling at him, pulling him from the black, pressing wet rags to his face, pressing him to the grass, his ears filling with the crack and pop of timber burning, with the shattering of glass as the windows exploded from their casings.

"And your father had a nervous breakdown after that," Francine said. "He was in some sanitarium for a while and then he got out and there was about a decade of working in different law firms, then settling here in Wellesley, starting the practice. Then your mother went to work for him."

A sanitarium. I let that truth sink in. He must have been consumed by guilt, by grief, to end up in such a place.

"And that's it," she said, firmly. "That's all I know."

But what did anyone know?

Maybe I'd gotten it wrong. Maybe he wasn't reading. Maybe that quiet Sunday habit came later. Maybe Edith was playing her violin, maybe they were engrossed in listening to a new recording. Maybe they were so engrossed in each other they forgot dinner was on the stove and never heard the first hiss and crackle.

Imagining this, imagining a young couple madly in love, I wondered how my mother could possibly have allowed me to be named Edith.

Maybe when I was born she did not yet know. Or knew about the wife but not her name, or knew her name but not the nature of the death.

Or maybe she had her own peculiar understanding.

She was thirty-seven when they married, a woman well into spinsterhood by the day's standards. She was probably grateful to have found a husband, grateful for a baby.

Whatever the reason, I wished she had felt she could tell me.

Francine picked up a lighthouse-shaped feeder and set to wrapping it. "You got a show tonight?"

"An open rehearsal."

She busied herself with paper and masking tape, but her movements were rough. She kept clearing her throat. Finally, she squared her shoulders and looked me in the face. "That day she did all that talking . . ." She shifted her weight from foot to foot; she cleared her throat again.

I looked at her.

"That day she went sick, she left a message on my machine. She wanted to talk to me. About the house. Big changes."

Right. She had wanted help creating her aviary.

She fussed with a piece of newspaper, inching closer, her face darkening to red. She lifted her chin, but her eyes darted back down to the deck floor. "Do you know," she asked, "what she wanted to ask me?"

It was the look on her face that got me. It was that same humble, hopeless mix I'd seen on my mother's face when she went for the mail during those po-etry-submitting days. I saw that hope and thought: what is the harm in giving her what she wants? What is the harm?

"She wanted to know," I said slowly, "if you wanted to move in here with her." When her eyes jerked up and held mine, I knew I'd gotten it right. I felt a surge of that overwhelming generosity of spirit that can course through you when you least expect it. It was as if I were finally giving my mother the right gift. "Keep each other company," I said.

I pretended not to notice how hard Francine tried not to look emotional. I gave her time. I wrapped the log-cabin feeder and blocked any squeamish feel-ings from my head. When her packing movements returned to their normal briskness, I said, "So tell me what you know."

She grunted. She peeled a sheet of paper from the stack. "I did."

"No. What you know about how my mother felt," I said.

"How do you think she felt, you being named after that woman?"

"It must have taken some pretty impressive understanding on her part."

She laughed quietly. "Sorry to disillusion you."

"That wasn't how it was?"

"Your mother said no but your father filed your name that way anyway."

The dismay on my face must have stirred Francine's sympathy. "Sometimes you're such a pup," she said, in a tone that sounded almost affectionate. "Do you have any idea what the not-so-very-old days were like? He was *the man*. And once the deed was done, it was done. And she figured, 'Well, I'll call her Edie. Well, if it makes him happy.'"

"Did she feel awful, knowing he'd been so devoted to someone else?"

"No."

"No?"

"That first wife, she was still new. The marriage hadn't had time to slide into habit. It was still in that strappy high-heel stage. Hadn't become the worn old shoe. Your mother knew that."

"I don't understand why they never told me."

"Don't you?" There was a look of good-natured disdain on Francine's face. "We grew up in a time when people kept their business to themselves. Not like now, with every*one* telling every*body* every*thing*."

"But I'm not everybody. I'm their daughter."

She threw up her shoulders. "It was a different time. It really was. And anyway, what's the point in people knowing everything?"

"It's the way people are. We want to know." I was thinking out loud. "We want to know and be known."

"Your father couldn't talk about her," Francine said. "And your mother certainly didn't *want* to." She put down the bird feeder she was wrapping; she looked off beyond the yard. "But she was okay with it. She said she liked the idea of having a man who wouldn't be out looking for something else."

Had my mother looked for something else, something she found in Francine? I studied Francine's solemn, settled face, its look of a person long disappointed by love, and decided, no.

"I remember your mother saying 'What was left was all I ever wanted.'"

I nodded. "Right."

But I didn't believe it. I remembered the poems. I remembered the "Jayne." I remembered the photograph and that look on my father's face. There's a difference between not wanting something and resigning yourself to never getting it. Nobody doesn't want ecstasy.

Then I saw the time. I had an hour to get back to Boston and onstage. Of course the traffic down Route 9 was jammed and I was late arriving. I quickly rosined my bow then slipped in the stage door to take my place behind the violins, bumping chairs and apologizing as I went. My fingers were quick and practiced plucking and tuning the strings, and finally my spine relaxed, my shoulders became fluid, in that way of perfect moments when everything comes together and each stroke, each note, is just right.

I breathed deep and looked out at the gilded simplicity of Symphony Hall. It was full. Open rehearsals tend to sell out. They're inexpensive, and conductors don't do much stopping of the music once it starts, but more than that, people seem to like being part of art-in-process.

Far out in the center section, on the aisle, was an old man I could almost imagine was my father. He was tucked under the first balcony, already closing his eyes, and something about his mild, gentle manner told me why my father never said anything about that first, beloved wife. He didn't want me to question who I was, or why I was loved, didn't want to cause pain to my mother. He might have meant to tell me, but sometimes we never find a way to say the hard things.

So he left behind evidence. Maybe there's something in all of us that wants our secrets found out, because our secrets define who we really are. I thought of how he'd mused on the word love, how he'd called it ill-defined. Maybe it doesn't matter what we call it, I thought. Maybe what we really crave is this: to be longed for by someone who recognizes, and wants, exactly who we are.

It was then that I noticed the man by the left exit doors, hands on his hips, watching me. He was slight, nondescript, the kind of person I might describe by saying he had brown hair. But he couldn't keep his eyes off me, off my bow, my darting fingers.

I couldn't know that after the rehearsal, this man would be waiting for me on the sidewalk by the stage door, that he would be embarrassed and awkward and I would think he was not my type at all but would remember Francine criticizing my choice of men, would remember my father talking about finding love beyond borders. And before I knew it this man would have drawn me into my favorite debate—about whether music could truly be recorded and thus preserved. I would argue my side and he would argue the other, and when I told him he had contradicted himself he would say, "That's all right. For every truth there is an equal and opposite truth."

I would consider this apparent contradiction. I would say, "I think that might be true, if a truth is something apart from a fact."

But I didn't know any of this when the stage door opened and the applause began, the conductor striding through, bowing, climbing the podium. The clapping quickly died down, rustling subsided. We all got into position, bows poised, fingers raised.

Then Arkil raised his arms and there was no time to dwell on anything else.

author's commentary

I wrote "Beyond the Border of Love" because I was fascinated by some facts in my own family that had no stories attached to them. After my grandmother died, I found a small leather notebook hidden in a desk drawer. Its pages were crumbling and smelled pungent and smoky. I paged through it, realizing it must have belonged to my grandfather when he was a young man in law school. Notes inside were cryptic but seemed to corroborate stories that had circulated through the family for two generations: that my grandfather had been married to another woman long before he met my grandmother, that the first wife had died in a horrific fire, and that when he married again and had a child (my mother), the baby somehow got named after the dead wife.

My mother was well into her teens, visiting distant relatives, when she first heard whispers about the "first Florence." She tried to ask her father about it, but he was good at staring straight ahead and refusing to answer a question. Her mother pretended she'd never heard of anything so ridiculous as a first wife. Then she stared straight ahead, too.

maryanne o'hara

I was struck by their secrecy, and by the fact of the notebook, sealed away for decades and still smelling of fire. How, I wondered, could any woman agree to name a new baby after a tragically dead first wife? The "facts," gleaned from the notebook, provided no insights. To figure out an answer, I began writing. What I came up with, "Beyond the Border of Love," is purely fictional, but it is also full of truth. Indeed, the story's characters try to define truth:

"For every truth there is an equal and opposite truth," one character says. The main character considers this *"apparent contradiction."*

"I think that might be true," she says, *"if a truth is something apart from a fact."*

Truth embraces apparent contradictions and blurs genre distinctions; it ultimately stands on its own.

MARYANNE O'HARA is the associate fiction editor of *Ploughshares*. *The North American Review* published "Beyond the Border of Love" in 2002 and nominated it for a Pushcart Prize.

1. *Because the beginning of the beginning is an unloaded camera, a shiny new sports car in your driveway, a small-handed wave that may or may not be the wave from that little blond girl who may or may not be your sister three hundred yards off the coast in the glistering surf, four hundred yards, and gaining distance:*

> He hears someone at the
> *No.*
> I think I hear someone at the
> *No.*
> You think you hear someone at your
> *The engine of possibility turning over, vapors igniting.*
> You answer your front door and
> *And what?*
> *Which door do you open along the hotel corridor of them?*
> You answer your front door and a little boy dressed like a little man
> dressed like a bright red, white, and blue superhero, no, the svelte, rav-
> ishing medieval princess, no, the thumb-nosed hunchback from last
> season's television hit, yes, that's it, extends his pillowcase at you and de-
> mands candy in a not-wholly-congenial polyp-throated voice.

2. *Because the beginning after the beginning of the beginning becomes time on fire, becomes the shiny sports car backing out and pulling forward and the neighborhood's arborescent landscape coalescing around it, the tie-up, the tuning fork, the thematics of the sweaty arm slipping around your waist on the rubber mat:*

> The light
> *When are we?*
> The light has already opaled by 4:30.
> *Good.*
> *Where?*

A poison tinge from the Turnpike peps the air around you.
And more?

Up and down the block scale-model pro-wrestlers, mutants, valentine-headed space aliens,

> *A lovely turn of phrase.*
> *Valentine-headed.*

and a lone Apache warrior hustles between split levels with leaf-cluttered yards bunched with plastic scarecrows and hay bundles and pumpkin arrangements.

Fleets of alert mothers cruise the vicinity in resplendent off-road utility vehicles that will never leave pavement. Pathfinders. Grand Cherokees. Blazers. Having retrieved their children, they will drive directly to the local mall where artificially cheerful policemen will X-ray their hauls for signatures of malice.

3. *Because the beginning after the beginning after the beginning (though nowhere near the middle) provides yesterday, provides the waving girl's name (Sarah . . . no, Shauna, no, Shiloh, no, Sarah), provides the density of a past tense and thereby the complication of the present:*

Tonight marks your last in what legally ceases to be your house in fewer than fourteen hours.

Everything around you except a lamp, some rumpled bedding, and a sleeping bag in the living room on the Oriental rug is boxed or draped with sheets.

Even the sound here has changed, carrying the impression of standing alone in an empty airplane hangar at dawn.

4. *Because less is more, because less is sometimes more, because what is unsaid is sometimes more important than what is said, because the hot wet feel of the arm around your waist, the blond girl (Sarah) waving and receding, two bodies engaged in the conservation of matter:*

The little boy in front of you impatiently clears his polypoid throat.

Snaggy Scree chocolate-and-bubble-gum bar in hand, you look down at him and think about complimenting his costume. It's one of the best you've seen since the spectacles commenced this afternoon just past 3:00. The clothes themselves aren't much, of course: plaid wool sports coat, buttoned white shirt, loose gray wool pants tied with a length of rope, blazingly white technosneakers.

But the mound that rises over his left shoulder, almost ripping through that sports coat, is deeply awesome, as is the way he has built up the skin over his sunken right eye into a cartilaginous lump.

The cleft lip and brown-fringed teeth are the work of a master.

Your glance drifts over his shaved squarish head.

Across the street, a mother flashes her Ford Explorer's headlights in a complicated code to attract the attention of a chubby, squat Darth Vader and an oversized dung beetle busy comparing stashes on the curb down the sidewalk from a house with a ceramic deer and two fawns in its front yard.

Waving, Darth Vader waddles forward.

5. Because of the intuitive pleasure before the perfection of counterpoint and harmony, the beginning after the beginning after the beginning is the details of the girl's, of Sarah's, hand, the cusps of dirt beneath her chewed fingernails, the small red inexplicable rash . . . no, birthmark, no, bruise behind her left ear:

Tomorrow morning the movers will arrive.

By noon you'll be somewhere near Scranton on Route 80, shooting west, because in a sense you can't think of anything else to do.

You grew up fifteen minutes from here in River Edge. You attended high school in Oradell and college in New Brunswick and married in Hackensack and worked for almost sixteen years at a technology park in Teaneck. Now you're going to leave this house, leave the East, leave your wife, who has, if the truth be known, already left you, although you are unable to articulate why in sentences that would make sense to another person.

How does that make you feel?

Standing there holding the Snaggy Scree, Superduper Jaggy Large Size, you imagine your heart is the black box flight recorder from a 747 and you wonder if it will ever reveal any significant information upon inspection.

Glare from the Ford's headlights washes across the left half of the little boy's face in front of you as the 4 × 4 swings around heavily in the street, halts, and Darth Vader clambers aboard.

The passenger door fumps shut.

The little boy in front of you, you see in the garish splash, isn't

6. *Because the only successful stories, so-called fictions, so-called creative non-fictions, are the ones about two bodies engaged in the conservation of matter, because the camera starts clicking . . . because the way the mother splashes into the surf, screaming, because the way her husband (the father) joins her in the amphetamine of potential loss, this is called the beginning of the middle, the interrupted reading:*

The little boy in front of you, you see in the garish splash, isn't really a little boy at all.

He isn't dressed *like* a hunchback.

He's wearing a lilac five-o'clock shadow and his hands are callused hammers and a great kyphos protrudes like a vestigial second head directly behind his left ear.

7. *Because, in the beginning of the middle, speech is scene, and scene is what Sarah's parents scream as they splash through the surf toward their receding child, while the young tanned man named Wallace with the baggy black swim trunks who has come to this Jersey beach with his girlfriend Toni to spend the afternoon sunning and listening to the radio on a neon-yellow towel raises his video camera and begins tracking them, saying into his mike, "Hey, babe, check this out, I think that little girl is in trouble":*

"Get away from here," you say. "Beat it."

You swing the door shut but the hunchback dwarf kicks out his foot and obstructs the door's arc. He's impressively strong for his dimensions. The door bounces open. His pillowcase bulges with hodgepodge booty like a potato sack.

"Screw you," he says. "Hand over the Snaggy Scree."

In the cozy amber foyer light, you notice each of his knuckles has a greenish-blue letter tattooed on it. The left hand spells out M–O–R–E, the right H–A–T–E.

"Get off my porch," you say, attempting to sound noteworthy. "Scram."

"Gimme the goddamn candy bar," says the hunchback dwarf.

You estimate his violence capacity.

"What are you, kidding? Is that what you are? Look at you."

"Gimme the candy bar."

"You think I'm giving a counterfeit kid a Superduper Jaggy Large Size Snaggy Scree? You're out of your mind. You know what I'm giving you? I'm giving you exactly dick, is what I'm giving you."

One of his eyes doesn't close all the way when he blinks.

"I'm asking you nicely, you putz," he says. "Gimme the candy bar."

"I'm giving you dick, exactly, is what I'm giving you."

"You want I should show you crazy? Because I'll show you crazy."

"I want you should get off my property, is what I want."

"Cuz you just go ahead and tell me that's what you want. Go on. Just say the word. I'll show you fucking *deranged.*"

A swarm of television sets with children's legs skitters onto your sidewalk, takes one look at the confrontation escalating before them, pauses, reconsiders, and skitters off into the maturing dusk.

"I'm giving you precisely dick, is what I'm giving you, precisely," you say. "Where the hell you get off, impersonating a kid like that?"

"I'm not going nowhere till I get my goddamn candy bar. Which I'm not repeating twice. Gimme the Snaggy Scree."

"Go away."

"Cuz you just say the word and it'll be my pleasure to tear you a new asshole. Look at me. I'm pleading here." He reviews me. "What?"

"What what?" you say, suspicious.

"The big lunk is like scared of a little guy like me?"

"Of you?"

He squints. Or blinks. It's impossible to tell.

"You saying I'm nothing to be scared of?" he asks, incredulous. "Is *that* what you're saying?"

"I'm saying I'll call the police, is what I'm saying, if you don't leave my premises here by the count of three."

"Son of a *chickenshit*. I'll show you crazy."

The dwarf drops his pillowcase. Candy clatters across cement. He crouches and lifts his hammer fists.

His thumb-nose grinches.

8. *Because the middle of the middle is the first time Sarah's head dips beneath the waves, the first wobble and clunk that announces your blown tire:*

The dwarf reaches into his back pocket and when his hammer fist appears again there's nothing . . . no, a switchblade, no, a slick midnight-blue snub-nosed revolver stuck in it.

It reminds you of the kind detectives used in early television police dramas from your childhood.

Only you can't tell whether it's an authentic slick midnight-blue snub-nosed revolver or a toy that looks like a slick midnight-blue snub-nosed revolver.

"What did I just say?" he says.

You realize in the few minutes you've been talking the dusk has pixeled into evening.

In another few pulses this instant will have become the past.

"What did I fucking just ask you as fucking politely as one guy can fucking ask another?" asks the dwarf.

A smile seeps into your features.

"What?" he says, astonished.

You smile some more.

"*What?* You think this is some kind of a joke? You think this is fuh—"

You reach out and slam the heavy door in his face. This time he doesn't have

the art of friction

a chance to even think about raising his foot to stop it. After the fact, you don't remember starting to move your arm.

9. Because the end of the middle which looks forward toward the beginning of the beginning of the end is the second time Sarah's head blinks out of existence, sun-sparkle on slate-blue waves off the Pacific coast, the Pacific coast or the Atlantic coast, sometimes such particulars not being especially important, sometimes the space between fiction and its mirror self being the use of an adjective, the color of seawater, the way the light coalesces on a Sunday or a Monday, what you can remember, what you can't, the sweaty arm slipping up quick as a heartbeat behind your neck, the feeling in the pit of your stomach that you can no longer control your careening vehicle as it tugs into lanes of traffic speeding around you, let us call the little girl your sister, let us say she is drowning.

Immediately diminutive clumping commences on the other side. The hunchback dwarf is furious. He's ballistic. He's trying to kick down your door. He's trying to chip through it with his switchblade, no, with the gun butt of his real gun that may not be real at all. It is impossible to tell. He's trying to ram through with his shoulder and his curses and his elbows.

Next, as suddenly as it erupts, everything goes gongingly still.

The revolver, it occurs to you, can't be loaded, even if it is authentic. If it were loaded, it would have gone off. You swim through several additional thoughts, tabulating, then bend forward and consult the peephole.

Through the fisheye lens you see the dwarf cringed in pain. He's cuddling his left foot in both palms as if it were a newborn baby. He's hopping up and down. The gun, real or fake, rests on the cement among a circus of splattered jawbreakers, candy corn, sticks of chewing gum, rolls of Life Savers, Reese's peanut butter cups, specialty jelly-bean boxes, and a single wobbling apple that revolves unsteadily to the very edge of the stoop, hesitates, and plunks off.

You watch the hunchback dwarf bounce less and less.

He lowers his foot gently to the concrete, stands erect as his tangled spine will allow, considers the evening sky. He places his hammer hands on his lower back and cracks it. Then he kneels like a ninety-year-old man claiming a nickel from the middle of the street and begins sweeping together his loot.

When he has mined the colorful mess into his pillowcase, he reaches for his revolver, slips it back into place, rises incrementally, and begins to lurch down the steps and up the sidewalk, left leg slower than right, with as much dignity as he can scrimp together.

10. *Because the beginning of the end is always sadness, call it memoir, call it magic, call it anything you want, because it remains the tiredness in the model's eyes, the unyielding feeling that you could have always done more—for the driving conditions, say, for your secondary characters, for your sister Sarah going under off the coast of New Jersey or Venice Beach or Venezuela:*

Watching his homuncular form diminish, you feel instantly bad. The black box that is your heart melts into regret.

You should open the door and invite him in.

You should apologize.

Look at him.

Look at him there.

It simply wasn't that big a deal. All said and done, what would it have taken you to play dumb? You should offer him a drink right now or maybe just open the door and hand over a Snaggy Scree and call it quits, except

11. *Because the middle of the end is called The Switch in wrestling, because one fighter obtains arm leverage to change from a defensive to an offensive position, because you know what will happen to Sarah in just a few more paragraphs, you think you know, you know the way your shiny sports car will enter the skid:*

Except as he prepares to gimp into the street, everything penetrates a darker dispensation.

Like this:

Five boys, all fifteen or sixteen, emerge from behind a massive evergreen bush and surround him. They're dressed only as themselves. They are wearing black wool ski caps and hyperbolically baggy jeans that hide their sneakers and white T-shirts three times too large even though it's the last day of October and the atmosphere is chilling.

They say something. They push him. He pushes back. A struggle flares. One teen yanks the overfed pillowcase from the hunchback dwarf's grip and holds it just out of his reach. He leaps for it, once, then backs up and brings his gun into view.

A passing Geo Tracker slows down.

Then a Toyota RAV.

Another teen drops to all fours behind him. A third shoves the hunchback dwarf over into a pile of leaves banked on the curb. The little guy receives four or five eggs in the chest and on the shoulders.

Next thing, the boys are gone.

The boys are gone and the hunchback dwarf is lying there alone, in the leaves, egg yolks on his chest and shoulders.

12. *Because in the end either you win the match or you don't, these are your options, and your options are words, ways of telling, not things in the world but inventions for making syntax work, either the sweaty arm slips from your waist or it doesn't, either the model rises and leaves or remains seated, because there are almost never any ties, because your shiny new sports car will either slow to a shuddering stop on the shoulder's gravel because you remembered the emergency brake at the last second, and you will sit there behind the wheel, shaken, respiring, or you will over-compensate during the first instants of your blown-tire skid and veer into oncoming traffic, or maybe veer perpendicularly into traffic that used to be flowing the same direction as you, because Toni already has breast cancer but she doesn't know it, because Wallace is sleeping with Toni's best friend whose name you have not imagined, because that best friend is a boy, or Wallace is not and will not, because Sarah's father (whose name you know, because he is your father, but this doesn't matter) will go on to become mayor of his town, because Sarah's mother (Sandra) will go on to become a successful elementary schoolteacher, though she will learn within five years that she is unable to conceive again, because neither parent will ever forget this day, the one with the sun-sparkle on slate-blue waves, because this*

is the day they lost their daughter, the day Sarah went under for the third time, or almost lost their daughter, the day her father, your father, reached her as she exhaled her last breath, or died trying to reach her, caught in the same riptide, no, that isn't what happened, although Sarah suffered brain damage, having inhaled water, having stopped breathing, or maybe suffered emotional scarring, or none of the above, because she never knew anything was out of the ordinary, because she wondered why her parents were running along the beach, what they were shouting about, why grownups always act so weird, others gathering with them in a herd, including that stupid-looking fat guy in the baggy black trunks with the video camera, because she was simply playing, having a little fun at their expense, because Wallace caught it all on video, her last struggle, her lack of last struggle, although none of these options ever helped Toni, because however you choose to tell her story, whichever door you choose to open for her, Toni will always reach down one sunny warm summer morning in the shower stall and her fingers will brush across that lump, the one larger and harder than she ever thought such a lump could be, and, in any version you tell, Toni will then close her eyes, close her eyes and palpate that lump over and over again, in simple wonder at the sudden fact of it, then do no more than comfortably tilt her head back into the cool chlorinated spray, hoping to enjoy this brief moment, because that is all she can do, knowing that this is for better or worse the movement of every narrative arc, the end of every end:

And that's it.

That's all, the show over, the comfortable universe reconstituted, the hunchback dwarf rising and attempting to brush himself off, then disappear into the swarms of other teratoids hustling up and down the suburban block in northern New Jersey where you grew up, where you spent your whole life until this instant.

Which is the last thing you see as you retire from the peephole. You turn and stroll through the house that is no longer your house, clicking off lights, touching things that won't be here to touch tomorrow.

You lie down among the rumpled bedding and the sleeping bag on your Oriental living-room rug.

The doorbell rings.

The doorbell rings again.

You don't answer.

You don't even contemplate answering.

You simply lie there in the blackout, remembering the dwarf's technosneak-ers flying out from under him, the arresting white flashes in the high beams, and you initiate your wait, biding your time until every trick-or-treater resigns and, eventually, withdraws.

author's commentary

Writing is editing. To set pencil to paper, fingers to keyboard, is to com-mence choosing, including this and leaving that out, consciously and un-consciously (mis)remembering, condensing, amplifying, rearranging, in-venting. The act of composition is the art of narration.

Someone once distinguished between Boring Narration, on the one hand, and Boring Narration, on the other. The first sort refers to works that are unselfconscious, predictable, compensatory, the second to those that ex-cavate, perturb, trouble, termite along. Much memoir and other iterations of so-called "creative nonfiction" fall within the first class, believing that the genre is something other than it is—namely, truthful, accurate, insightful, and self-aware.

Yet "creative nonfiction," a form of narcissistic historical writing, finds its being, as do all forms of historical writing, as a subcategory of fiction—a special subcategory, of course, but a subcategory nonetheless. Although there are remarkable exceptions (Shelley Jackson, W. G. Sebald, Lyn Hejin-ian), "creative nonfiction" usually demands for itself a privileged status with regard to evidence, personhood, past; tends to behave as if oblivious of the theoretical implications and complications extant in its own genetic construction—how, for example, as Hayden White hypothesized in his examination of nineteenth-century historiography, the version of yesterday one chooses depends as much on moral and aesthetic values as it does on such notions as "fact" and "truth."

That's why the memoirist often reminds me of the television journalist leaning into blustery rain on a gray beach, hair whipping, jacket a giant mad blue bat flapping around him, Hurricane Katrina bearing down behind, shouting at the top of his lungs into his microphone: *Boy, it sure is windy out here!*

In my novel *Girl Imagined by Chance* (FC2, 2002), as in much of my current work, I am interested in the notion of our culture being one less of production than of reproduction—both in the biological sense of rampant breeding (much to the detriment of our planet), and in the Baudrillardian sense of simulation (in our commodified, spectacular, technological society, the notion of "reality" has come to feel downright quaint). It is a short step from there to *Girl's* core narrative about a couple that in an unguarded moment invents a make-believe child to appease their friends and family, and the novel's core metaphor: photography—an art emblematic of faith in reproduction and mimesis.

I am also interested in the idea of *critifiction,* a term coined several decades ago by Raymond Federman to designate a mode of prose that hovers between fiction and fact, one profoundly concerned with the very nature of "authenticity." The consequence has been the slow emergence in my writing of an aesthetics of uncertainty. Behind it, I suspect, floats Ludwig Wittgenstein's ghost. What I've always loved about that philosopher's imagination is how it became increasingly obsessed with trying to articulate what one might be able to know about the world with anything like conviction. The more obsessed Wittgenstein became, the more honest he became. The more honest he became, the less sure he became about *anything.* Something analogous is the case with respect to photography or any sort of depiction that takes the dubious position of unselfconscious certainty with respect to its power to re-present, and to re-presentation's children, "truth" and "fact":

the more you study and think about an example, if you are being honest with yourself, the less sure you will always be about it.

By engaging in such a project, I hope to continue contemplating the ways in which we might commence undoing readings/writings of the simplistic photography we call "creative nonfiction," for such narrative naïveté is the stuff conservative artists and our current political leaders cherish repeating until it begins to sound like something approaching the "truth" about the human condition and the "facts" on which our government bases its policies.

LANCE OLSEN is author of nineteen books of and about innovative fiction, including, most recently, *Anxious Pleasures* (Shoemaker & Hoard, 2007), *Nietzsche's Kisses* (FC2, 2006), and *10:01* (Chiasmus, 2005). He teaches innovative fiction and fiction-writing at the University of Utah, and lives with his wife, assemblage-artist Andi Olsen, somatically in Salt Lake City, and digitally at www.lanceolsen.com.

agency recruitment procedures

Recruitment for the intelligence agency in Combaria takes place as follows:

An ad is placed in a newspaper read by a large number of people educated in the sciences; these people, very often, know little about politics. The ad asks for intelligent, honest, industrious young people who wish to embark on an exciting, exotic career. It invites these people to hear a lecture given by an agent and to sign up for interviews afterward. The agency makes clear that, while it will teach recruits to lie and cheat as agents of the government, it does not seek applicants who already do so. Thus, a large number of those who have always wanted to deceive but have never had legal means to do so become interested. The agency offers opportunities to deceive large segments of the population at once.

Wanting to see more of how this organization worked, I heard the lecture and put my name on the long list of people to be interviewed. In the lobby where I and the many other applicants waited, I overheard a conversation between two who seemed to have seen the recruiter already. I asked them how long they had waited in the lobby, because I had been waiting for an interview for almost an hour. I told them I was honest and thought myself a good candidate. The two looked at each other, then one spoke:

"I am with the agency. And, yes, we do want honest men. But we also want men capable of telling a lie, and those capable of this know a lie when they see one. The agency is not interviewing here today like they said they would be. You believed us. Therefore, we are not interested in you."

Then the other spoke:

"Those who did not come here are those the agency wants. They didn't believe the ad, and probably don't even believe the agency exists. And the reason they will end up working for us is that they are right: it does not exist."

"But how can you say that the agency does not exist?" I said. "You yourselves are agents."

"Yes," said the first again. "That is what we told you."

militaristic government

We've come to expect the rationales given by governments in defense of their various projects to be lies. This is especially true of militaristic governments, which do not wish to overtly disclose their policies. A militaristic state leader, questioned about his government's policies of war and aggression, commonly answers using the words "enemy," "danger," "security," and "need." The answers are accepted by the citizenry of the militaristic country, who assume that the state leader has some privileged information, but for the lack of which he would not make such astonishing proposals. The popularity of the state leader then, commonly, increases: the people wish to show solidarity with their leader against the supposed threat. The leader, then, with a stronger base of national confidence, can withhold all specifics of a situation and introduce new information that, in fact, he has invented. The less he tells the citizenry, the more popular he becomes. Facts destroy the characterization "enemy" on which the leader so strongly relies.

Such is the situation in Combaria. A dissenter here is rarely listened to, for the stakes have escalated from country versus country to homeland versus enemy to good versus evil.

Talking to one in agreement with the message of the state, I again expressed my displeasure with my government.

"Oh," he said, surprised. "There is much you don't know."

I questioned him. "What don't I know?"

He was evasive at first, but gradually I was able to make him speak. "You don't realize that there are things you cannot and should not know," he said. "There is much that we don't know, things too terrible to even think about, things that make me afraid to even think what they might be."

"But what," I asked, "can we fear more than that which we do not know? Wouldn't discovering these things be much less fearful? At least, then, we would know what to fear."

The government supporter smiled. He was my friend, even though we did not agree. "Friend," he said, "I'm glad I'm not you. I would be fearful all the time."

a new use for literature

Recent events in Combaria suggest that no one even knows who is in charge here, who is responsible for civic policy. One man can say, "Last week I ran the country." Can any of his fellow citizens in good faith dispute him? But what does it take, in fact, to govern? Certainly there are no special talents required. In fact, only one thing is necessary to a leader: the ability to keep everyone else busy at once. For this reason, the most efficient leader would be someone who could convince the entire populace, all at once, to read a very large book. It would not need to be a well-written book, only one that would keep the interest of a reader and be bereft of political content. Perhaps a television show might suffice: the long, extended saga of family triumph and woe, set in a distant land, in a time long ago. But a book would keep the populace busy for a longer time.

After finishing the book, people would start to grow angry. "Why did we read this?" they might say. "Who has been running the country while we've been reading?" The leader, having the talent of keeping people busy, would immediately turn the tables. "Don't you see how this book is important?" he would reply. Half of the nation would then turn to writing books themselves about the importance of the book they had all read. The other half could easily be persuaded to research the subject further, or even to reread the book, on the supposition that they would get the point if they read it again. The leader, still unnamed, would see his term continue.

after the law

One day enforcers of the law began to arrest each other. Why they began doing this no one knows for sure, although there were two prevalent theories. One theory ran that enforcers had come to the point of seeing their own authority as the most lawless act in the land. Another idea went around that the enforcers were engaged in an elaborate pretense and that they actually wanted to convince criminals that no law now existed, that criminals could get away with anything now. "Soon," proponents of this second idea warned, "they will cast off their mock chains and have their biggest roundup ever."

The problems were enormous. How was one to live? If the first theory were correct, law was now illegal and no one was safe, and the best way to live was to become an outlaw. But if the latter were true, becoming an outlaw would be a sure path to torment.

Neither theory has yet been verified. Thus, they've both become true. We live in peril here in this place where the law is at once absolute and absent.

the public eye

One day a man with very good ideas decided that the problems of the world should be handled correctly and committed himself to public service. He worked very hard. Finally, after years of struggle, addresses to small groups, and countless planning sessions and nights of little sleep, he began to have a measure of success. He decided to seek a major office. On the day his first widely distributed publicity photo was to be shot, he sported a fresh haircut and new clothes. It was an excellent portrait, and soon was seen on buttons, posters, TV ads, T-shirts, billboards, and magazine covers. He was a handsome man and the picture itself earned him countless endorsements and, eventually, votes. He was elected. His smile became the symbol of the hope of the populace.

But around the time his popularity peaked, another picture began to circulate: a picture of an innocent child lost somewhere in the world. Soon the child's picture was seen everywhere the candidate's had been. Even more places: on milk cartons, donut boxes, public transit tickets, cans of shaving cream, packs of cigarettes. Soon two images were familiar to everyone: the officeholder's and that of the child lost. Had the child been kidnapped? Murdered? No one knew. But of two things everyone was certain: the child was absolutely blameless and the child was gone.

The newly elected man had been popular, but now was the flipside of a coin, the other side of which had the permanent luster of a new minting. One could not see this new side without also being aware of the dark obverse, where the man's face still beamed from out of clouds. Remaining affixed, the smile that once stood for hope now laughed at another's despair and pain. On the street, people spat at him. Even after he left the public sphere, they never let him forget, for the child had met a terrible death, was broken and dissolved by violence to the smallest possible units, passed into the water supply and was consumed daily as coffee, juice, iced tea, cocktails. People drank and delicate fists reconstituted in their stomachs.

a message from the president

The President sent a message to a woman who was successful in the field of trade. She was to come immediately to see him and tell absolutely no one—not her closest relative—of her charge. The message took the woman completely by surprise. At first she stalled for time to think, going about her business in a normal fashion, letting no one even close to her secret. She was proud of having been recognized and summoned, but why the secrecy? How would she be able to simply follow the instruction without attracting attention? What would she tell her husband, her family? A person cannot just leave work and home without explanation. But it was her President who called. She finally fabricated a set of lies to tell the people she saw each day, the people she was closest to. Thus, it began.

Arriving at the iron gate surrounding the presidential mansion, she realized she had no idea how one was supposed to see the President. In the excitement and confusion, she had never asked for instructions. Nor had any been offered. The presidential mansion was heavily guarded, and her phone calls reached secretaries who thought her a crank. "It must be more clandestine than I first imagined," she reasoned, so she took a room in the capital city and waited to be approached. She never was. It was two weeks since she had left her job and her family.

Then, when she had almost given up hope of ever fulfilling her call, contact was reestablished. Brought through the forbidding gate to the stately mansion, she was escorted through a series of chambers and briefed by top officials, including undermembers of the President's advisory staff. No precaution was overlooked as she was asked repeatedly about the minutest details of her former life. Soon, a season had gone by. The woman had not yet met the President, but as time went by she was more and more eager to do so. She realized that, in the end, she would have no one else left.

on the danger of not knowing

How do we know what goes on outside our country? Or even within?

One night, late, an old movie on television is interrupted by a special report. There has been a coup. Details are sketchy, but what is definitely known is that there has been an attempted takeover. A factory worker rubs the sleepiness from his eyes as the report quickly ends and the screen returns to black and white.

The next day, he asks others at the factory if they have heard anything. None have. He tells his fellow workers all he knows, which is very little, but as his words meet each astonished face he wonders if he was dreaming. But no, the graveness of the newsman's tone had alerted him; he had listened closely to the sparse available details; he had rubbed his eyes to make sure he had not been half asleep.

But no more details come. The next regular news broadcast is aired with no mention of the special report, and no mention is ever made again. The man seeks out every bit of information in newspapers and on radio, knowing them to be more reliable than television. But what is reliability now? He cannot even trust what he saw with his own eyes reported as truth. His own reports are treated skeptically. Nothing, judging by all evidence following the initial alert, seems to have changed, and no one seems to notice what a lonely factory worker knows to be true: that the entire basis of cognizance is now different. He can no longer do his job after a time, needing to devote more energy to uncovering information. Others work and when they come home in the evening turn on the television to see what is new in the world. The former factory worker has theories they would all call crazy. No one seems to know what he does—except, perhaps, his enemies, who would believe everything he told them even while denying it to the last.

on the danger of knowing

I heard a story about a scientist. It seems to ring true. She was commissioned by the government to investigate the problem of alleged pollution disseminated by government-supported and -regulated industries. She spent years in northern wildernesses, taking soil samples, filling small vials with lake water, picking dead fish off the water's surface, noting observations, returning to the lab, charting, returning to the field to confirm her findings. Her charge had been to determine the truth, to glean causes from certain previously noted effects and to report on these effects, the extent of which, she found, was yet to be recognized. Her report was received by the government with thanks.

Soon the scientist began to notice that spokespersons for the government were quoting her data with glaring omissions. The omissions changed the interpretations a layperson would make from her findings, while the scientist's own interpretations remained unmentioned. Instead of the problem being represented with the severity of a situation needing regulation, facts were presented that argued for a lessening of existing government controls. Her own words and figures, not misquoted but edited, made her one of the leading supporters of the policies she had discovered to be so in need of change.

The scientist was enraged. She wrote a statement intended to reveal the liberties taken with her research. She called a press conference, so that she could make public the true facts as she saw them, facts that would make clear the hazard she had spent so much time thoroughly documenting.

"From the facts that I've detailed," she concluded, "only one determination is possible: that the situation is more extreme—horrendous might be an even better word to use—than has been made public. And this leads me to one final comment." She paused to collect herself before making the strong direct accusation, then spoke: "My government's primary function, as I have seen it, from top to bottom, is as an apparatus for circulating untruths and suppressing dissent."

She had expected a reaction of shock from her audience, especially in response to this last statement, but when she looked up from her prepared text she perceived no response. She asked if they had heard and understood what she had said, and if there were any questions. There were none, and the room was soon cleared as the people made their way to other engagements. The scientist was left to wonder: is there a language strong enough to convey what I know, or has that too been sabotaged?

In the capital city lies the tomb of the unknown soldier, or rather the many, almost countless tombs of the unknown soldiers. There is one unknown soldier's grave for each war the country has fought, with the exception of the country's great Civil War, when, to the great dismay of the head of the now-defunct Ministry of Symbolism, all the dead were identified. A tour is in order. Here is the grave of the unknown soldier of the Revolution. Next to it is the grave of the unknown soldier of the counterrevolution of a few years later, of which little is known. Next follow, to the right and left, the unknown soldiers who died in the various battles fought to protect our country's long-standing early policy of isolationism. After a time the policy was reconsidered, and those countries that had previously attempted friendly relations but were now unfriendly toward our country were, in turn, attacked. The graves of the unknown soldiers of these conflicts lie just over the far ridge.

Atop the ridge is one of the most famous monuments, the grave of the unknown soldier who died for some reason now forgotten. The circumstances of his death, the particular war or conflict, were once chiseled into the stone marker at the grave, but weather has worn the stone and it is now unreadable. He (if it is a he, for this too is unknown) is the unknown soldier (if this person was a soldier—no one can be absolutely sure of the person's occupation) from the unknown war (if, in fact, it was a war that was responsible for this person's demise—it is conceivable that the person's death had nothing to do with war). It is possible too that there is no body there, which would make the grave not a grave at all, but something unknown. All that is sure is the enormous marker beside the faded stone, erected much later, one would guess, on which the word "unknown" is carved, in granite, so that it, at least, will remain forever. Let us move on, there is much more to see: the unknown soldiers of the world wars, of the economic fights of the early part of the century, of the latter-day territorial battles. One can spend all day trying to discern reasons for the unknown and still not get anywhere.

But as we move on, listen. I have a theory. Keep walking, pretend you have already forgotten the enigmatic monument. I believe it contains a surveillance camera, with which much is found out about those who pause long, internally debating what might be inside. There are those, after all, who have a certain investment in the unknown.

the power of accident (if that's what it is)

A glitch is our greatest fear. It could cost us all our money, which we no longer hide in tangible places like mattresses or the chest in the attic. It could cost us our reputations, which are no longer held in the hearts of our fellows or in the memory of our kind deeds. Glitches erase memory. And perhaps worse (though what could be worse than having your selfless contributions forgotten?), glitches kill: not metaphorically, but emphatically and without redress or even explanation. Twenty-eight people were killed yesterday by a glitch. You may have known or heard about them. And this number only counts one incident on one day, for glitches absorb most self-evidence, making accurate estimates impossible.

Don't even think about this. I'm sorry to have even brought it up, for unlike some other problems, there is no solution to or prevention of glitches. The forces that rule us do so, for the most part, benevolently, and are necessary. We can only believe this. Put them out of your mind, continue on with your life. Don't let all the random possibilities of your own physical and emotional ruin surface as you lie in bed tonight. Don't think of who controls you, who could destroy you as easily as a mouse cursor skitters across a terminal screen. You'll need your sleep and energy tomorrow. You have problems enough already.

author's commentary

On Truth and Lie in "From Combaria"

Let those who use words cheap, who use us cheap
Take themselves out of the way
Let them not talk of what is good for the city
—Charles Olson, *Maximus,* "Letter 3"

I think there is a politics to the so-called Fiction versus Nonfiction debate, and the politics has to do with the complexities of language. Simply stated, it seems to me that most of those who suppose there is a wholly separable "nonfiction," and generally all those who speak of "creative nonfiction," are discounting the complexities and difficulties of language and the ways in which narratives are *always* constructed things.

For someone of my political generation, for whom adulthood coincided with the coming to power in the United States of political conservatives (I graduated high school the same year Ronald Reagan was elected to his first term as president), the ability to recognize the seams in narrative—those points where the stories are stitched together into something coherent, but whose elisions point to something excluded—has always seemed a necessary skill. Ketchup would otherwise be too easily accepted as a vegetable; mining the harbors of Nicaragua too easily accepted as a necessary measure for American security and, besides, nothing we had anything to do with.[1] To my mind, any literary artist whose work does not exist in the light of a certain skepticism about the uses and misuses of language to some extent participates in the processes of mystification by which the powerful use us, through the stories they tell, for their own ends.

Practicing such skepticism has been called deconstruction, but can as easily simply be called reading, and is as much in the tradition of Franz Kafka and George Orwell (and many other language-minded writer-skeptics from decades past) as it is of Jacques Derrida. I began "From Combaria" in 1985, when the CIA openly advertised the presence of recruiters on the campus of the University of Colorado, Boulder, where I had just begun an MA in Creative Writing. So it was occasioned by a "nonfictional" event, to be sure. But the pieces are also conditioned by reflections on the nature of language and the paradoxes involved in any purported statement of truth—the recognition that the liar speaks in the same way. "All Cretans are liars," "I am a Cretan," goes a great illustrative paradox on this subject.[2] The form of narrative art that best conveys this hesitant, paradoxical, problematic, slippery *donné* of language, to my mind, is not whatever might be meant by "creative nonfiction" (I honestly don't know), but instead "fiction" or, at minimum, a

ted pelton

discourse that acknowledges the great difficulties involved in any act of affirmation or representation.

There are such works by authors in a narrative tradition that does not explicitly call itself fiction. Maxine Hong Kingston and Wole Soyinka are two writers who come to mind who accept the mantle of memoirist without recklessly supposing that this makes language a stable medium. Kingston's *Woman Warrior* is so powerful a text precisely because the writer is in a constant state of questioning the stories that have forever surrounded and astounded her, stories whose suspect authenticity was destabilizing for her as a youth growing up in fact-stabilizing America, but whose richness she comes to accept and train herself as an adept within. They have used her, she uses them back, and all the time I know as her reader that she is well skilled as a swordswoman against the encroachments of power. If she ran for public office, I would vote for her in a heartbeat. Whenever Kingston or Soyinka or any of the other great old artificers[3] of Literature speak, I drop all that I am doing to listen.

TED PELTON'S most recent book is the novel *Malcolm & Jack* (Spuyten Duyvil, 2006). He has received an NEA Fiction Fellowship and, in 2000, founded Starcherone Books, of which he remains Director. He is also an Associate Professor of English at Medaille College of Buffalo, New York.

pelton notes

1. For those of you too young to remember, or whose memories have kindly allowed you to forget, these are references to two of the less shining moments in the Reagan presidency. In 1981, Reagan appointees at the U.S. Department of Agriculture reasoned that money could be trimmed from federal programs for school lunches by designating condiments such as ketchup and relish as vegetables; Reagan budget director David Stockman was also linked to the decision, reversed after too much negative publicity. In 1984, the United States secretly mined Nicaraguan harbors, though we had an extant Treaty of Friendship, Commerce, and Navigation with Nicaragua. Sub-

the art of friction

sequently found to be in violation of international law by the World Court at The Hague in 1985, the United States declared the prosecution political and contrary to law and fact, and refused to pay damages. Reagan claimed the mines had been planted by Nicaraguan rebels (despite evidence of CIA involvement) and called the entire affair "Much ado about nothing."

These events are cited not so much because they are notable in themselves as because they have become something of a model for the way conservative American administrations have lied and gotten caught in lies for nearly three decades, culminating in the disaster of U.S. involvement in Iraq.

2. Cf. Douglas Hofstaeder, *Godel, Escher, Bach*, "Epimenides Was a Cretan Who Made One Immortal Statement: 'All Cretans Are Liars.'"

3. I have here in my head the echo of Stephen Daedalus's last journal entry, closing *The Portrait of an Artist as a Young Man*: "Old father, old artificer, stand me now and ever in good stead," and Joyce is as good a figure to end on as any in defending one's craft as a maker of fictions.

A few years ago, when I was married and living uneasily in Florida, I believed that there was, in a town twelve miles away, a little restaurant with green upholstery—a certain green—that served the best breakfast. This restaurant, which I thought existed at a bend in the road near some railroad tracks, had that sheerly impossible quality we sometimes ascribe to material things, often to restaurants, sometimes to whole cities we can't seem to get back to. If we could only get there again, we think, our lives would be saved, or a deep, nagging mystery solved at last. Surely you've heard people go on this way, rhapsodically, about an armchair they sat in once on a Thursday when they were twelve, or about the smell of sausage in an English pub on a rainy day in March 1957. Some apparently trivial things appear to contain the sublime, and there's no explaining this to anyone—nor any getting over it. Even Proust wore out his friends, trying.

Still, in my mind's eye was that bend in the road, the railroad tracks, and the breakfast house of my dreams. I drove to the town one day, with a friend who puts up with such eccentricities, and found no restaurant there at all, of course, though I'd gotten the bend in the road right, and the railroad tracks.

"Maybe you dreamed it," said my friend warily.

"Maybe," I said, trying to tamp down the little fear that's been with me since childhood—a fear that, though I seem to get along okay in the world, I'm secretly mad as a hatter.

Then I moved out to the West. And sure enough, that particular shade of green, though not the restaurant, was everywhere: a green somewhere between duck-egg and a Granny Smith apple—only denser, richer, a color never found in nature. Sometimes I'd find it in the mud porch of a turn-of-the-century farmhouse, or on the wall of a new friend's bathroom. It had been there all along, in the paintings of Kandinsky and Chagall, and on the occasional umbrella. It was on a T-shirt I wore until I stained it on the day I ate the best oyster of my life and fell in love when I shouldn't have.

This green is not military, not forest-service. Nor is it the color of small imported Spanish olives or the giant ones stuffed with garlic, though God knows

I love olives. Their green has its own pleasures, akin to those of oysters—shiny, subtle harbingers of the primitive, which is why, the day I fell in love when I shouldn't have, I asked for three in my martini. At the time I wondered why the waiter seemed taken aback; the request seemed perfectly natural, no big deal.

We must get beyond, or away from, olives. My green is the color of old shutters in photographs of French country houses, of the floors and even the vats of a tortilla factory in Puerto Vallarta three months before I fell in love when I shouldn't have. It is a color you cannot find in the narrow color strips they give away in paint stores, where the delusional come searching, aching, for the shade of green they've been waiting for all their lives. Chalky, dusky, somewhere between mint and the color of 1950s tile in the kitchen of the house my husband and I bought.

The owner of the paint store looked grieved, as if I'd asked him if there really was a God. "I can't help you," he said mournfully. "That green doesn't exist except in pictures."

Of course not. It can't be found outside, this green—not exactly, though it wants to be, in a way that haunts the edges of almost knowing. It has nothing to do with gardens or gardening, a hobby I'd taken up when my husband and I moved out West—not because I wanted to but because the house we bought had a garden so beautiful it would have been criminal to mow it down. But our garden wasn't that green. Not the green of pear tree leaves nor the green of the rhododendron; not even the greeny-gray of certain aromatic sages that can make you weep for a smell lost from childhood; not even the triple-dark green of a trout stream under cloud cover. Here again, oysters and olives come to mind—along with that feeling of succumbing to something that laps away at the safe edges of your life. I was thirty-six and living in Florida when I fell in love with green, but forty and in another state entirely the day I fell in love when I shouldn't have.

I've asked a psychologist if there is a connection between unmanageable desire and a dream of a green restaurant. She laughed but did not explain her laughter. Is this part of treatment?

Just before I left Florida, I took my friend who puts up with such eccentricities to a tiny inland town under a canopy of oaks and kudzu where a hundred psychics lived and worked. We had made no appointment, but in the town's general store a bulletin board announced the telephone number of the day's psychic "on call." So it came to pass that a woman named Eunice told me what I already knew: that I was "leaving the state," as she put it, and damn glad to be; that I would not miss it one bit.

Then she went on. She said she saw me with my hands in the dirt, and she didn't mean that metaphorically. "You're going to be a gardener," she said.

"Not possible," I said. "I don't garden, not interested."

"Your work will take a turn toward the metaphysical."

"God forbid," I said. "I don't even know what that means."

"You will be lucky in love," she said. "But it won't look like luck for a long time."

We sat a moment in silence.

"Go," she said. "I see a long journey." And then she laughed, and sent me out into her yard, into dazzling uncertainty.

author's commentary

To essai or not to essai?

What I find most mysterious about the writing process—at least my own—is how little I think about questions of genre, when first I begin. But students often want to know *how to tell* if something should be fiction or that other thing, the one known by many names, none of them terribly satisfactory. I personally like the word "essay," considered dry by some, but coming from the French word "essai," as in a trial, a progress, an experiment.

In my experience, genre is not the question that matters when the fire of a particular piece is beginning to burn. I personally try *not* to ask "what are you?" for as long as I can stand. My job, when I begin to draft something, is to overcome my own self-consciousness, and this means keeping my balance on a sort of tightrope over the abyss of definite answers. That is, I am trying to keep from nagging myself about what's been successful for other people, or worked in the past for me, or what objections an editor might raise. If I fall off the tightrope, or out of the partial trance of good concentration, this place where rhythm and image are the reigning deities, I might not get back to the place where the surprises wait, this other, deliciously darker abyss—of stories, true and not.

In any case, my stories and essays don't often announce their forms right away, and I have more luck if I don't push it. Such questions will sort themselves out eventually. I *can* say that literary nonfiction, or the personal essay, tends to bloom out of my own personal experience—usually some kind of journey or small adventure I've had that seems, on the surface, quite mundane, but nonetheless irksome, suggesting it has some unsettling news or mystery yet to divulge. If I get this feeling, I try, as my freshman composition teacher, years ago, once advised, to simply "tell what happened"—only this way will something else show up. Again, the tightrope: if I look to the side, or down, in hopes of seeing the true subject directly, I'll fall off for sure.

A short story, on the other hand, usually comes to full term if it is based on something about which I have only a handful of facts: the fragment of a story from someone else's life, an anecdote that drifted past years ago, and has had time to gestate without my even knowing it was there. Again, note the high percentage of not-knowing, even a certain willful ignorance. This, in my experience, is the only way the material will keep growing—I'm sure it is based on some dreadful neurosis. But as Robin Williams, playing a shrink in a movie, once said to an ex-smoker who kept lifting a ghost-cigarette to his mouth, "For God's sake, just *be* who you are."

This is harder than it seems.

MARJORIE SANDOR is the author of three books, most recently the linked short story collection *Portrait of My Mother, Who Posed Nude in Wartime* (Sarabande Books, 2003), for which she won the 2004 National Jewish Book Award in Fiction. Her essay collection, *The Night Gardener* (October 1999, The Lyons Press), won an Oregon Book Award in Creative Nonfiction in 2000. Her essays and stories have appeared in such publications as *The New York Times Magazine, The Georgia Review,* and *The Southern Review,* and have been anthologized in *The Best American Short Stories 1985* and *1988, Best of Beacon 1999, The Pushcart Prize XIII,* and elsewhere. In 1998 she received a Rona Jaffe Foundation Award for fiction. She lives in Corvallis, Oregon, and teaches fiction-writing and literature at Oregon State University.

Our Day with Jerry Springer

davis schneiderman

Upon arriving at my first tenure-track position, assistant professor of English at a Midwest liberal arts college, which would allow me to teach both creative writing and literature, with equal emphasis on each, I immediately began to survey the landscape of my 300-level postmodernism class. Adding a "graphic content" warning to my syllabus, I asked this new class to jump eyes-first into Jean Genet's *Funeral Rites,* an X-rated romp through wartime Paris with characters engaged in sex fantasies with Hitler, before moving into William S. Burroughs's *The Wild Boys,* an equally unsettling study of reality films, revolutionary communes, and runaway bodily processes. Bolstered by the works of postmodern theorists ranging from precursor Friedrich Nietzsche to post-everything Jean Baudrillard, some students were confused, some appalled, and some energized. Yet all of our discussions—despite my best efforts during our weekly session in a respectable third-floor seminar room—remained completely and utterly "academic."

Schooled in that 1990s belief in the viability of cultural studies, I hoped a completely voluntary outing to the *Jerry Springer Show*—a program renowned for its universal trashiness—would cause the three orders of simulacra and the cultural logic of late capitalism to lean, in some small way, against the heavy side of that "reality" fulcrum. I didn't go so far as to show movies such as *The Matrix* to teach the "world" as a relative cultural construction. That seemed like the easy way out, and surprisingly, the students were largely convinced a priori of the postmodern condition; they were so excited by it all that we routinely pushed past our designated ending time, lost in rapt academic discussion. *It was too easy.* I began to suspect that within the recesses of their outward enthusiasm lurked the same sarcastic detachment from postmodernism as postmodernism projected onto everything else.

Then came September 11th.

Discussing a post-attack cover of *The Village Voice*—a postcard of the Twin Towers superimposed perfectly on the Manhattan skyline—several students told me the *only* reality of the attacks for them was that their cell phone calls were temporarily blocked. No one denied that the buildings had collapsed or that people had died; it all just seemed, somehow, "fake." After all, this was Generation X mixed with Generation Y spiked with acute awareness of things like Prozac and post-irony. They *knowingly* swam in endlessly crashing waves of simulation. "God is dead" was *really* old news that Nine Inch Nails *used* to sing about, and I was just some nihilistic charlatan, my snake oil fermenting on the shelf because it couldn't compete with the high-sugar varieties of pop culture.

I hoped that the field trip would underscore this very postmodern problem of viewing postmodernism as so entirely "constructed" that its critiques proved useless. Sure, it is easy enough for academics to either condemn or condone all cultural studies "texts" (including TV programs *and* wars) as part of the great sucking sound of American culture, but because we couldn't go to somewhere such as "ground zero" in New York City to convince ourselves of what about the terrorist attack was real, we went to the *Jerry Springer Show* to find out what about our "reality" was not.

———————

Our bus dropped us in front of the NBC Tower in Chicago, local home to the network, the *Jerry Springer Show,* and its kissing cousin, the *Jenny Jones Show.* We were soon pressed into a large audience warm-up room filled with fold-ing chairs, vending machines, and a few TVs tuned to the same news channel. We watched as a talking head announced a bus hijacking in Tennessee that everyone assumed was another terrorist attack. The susurrus of joking, excited voices quieted to a low whisper, as the absurdity of our situation—waiting for a trash culture oracle to wave shiny objects in front of us—became overly ap-parent. Before long, though, the endless chatter restarted and we were led into the studio . . .

Given a choice of seating either on- or off-camera, I chose the former. A gi-ant industrial fan controlled the rear of the stage; rimmed around the tops of the walls, green paint mimicked moldy tarnish on windows that peered into nowhere. I suddenly felt very small, not like a "hip" new professor at all, but more like a victim, trapped in a basement with other bad children not so much younger than myself, waiting for something to happen. And so began the vid-eotape: This edition of Springer's "Too Hot for TV" endlessly detailed glittery undergarments dropping to the floor, flailing arms and legs smacking the faces of relatives and lovers, holiday turkeys and cranberry sauce flying violently across the set. No matter the image, the shrill voices of Springer's past guests screamed over the cacophony of every repetitive moment, drowning out our increasingly uncomfortable laughter.

Soon the producer, Todd, laden with headphones and electronic equipment, expounded on the importance of chanting "Jerry! Jerry!," as well as "reacting" to absolutely everything that would soon happen onstage. It would be our responsibility to scream, to yell, and to follow his lead. If I tell you to jump, Todd seemed to say, you not only ask "how high?" but also continue to bounce up and down until we cut to commercial. Todd enforced the rules of his regime with exaggerated glances and hand gestures, so we practiced our clapping and chanting as Jerry Springer emerged for his warm-up of stale jokes ("I don't like cocaine; I just like the way it smells"). After he suggested that his program could provide a respite from the "war on terror," it seemed clear that Springer saw himself as a counterpoint to the concurrent events in Kabul and Kandahar. He offered his show as valid cultural contributor not because of what it *does*, but because of what it *deliberately* does not.

Todd encouraged us to chant "pregnant whore"—repeatedly—every time one of the show's four expectant mothers unloaded her particular secret. One young woman in my group appeared to chant with supercharged glee, screaming noticeably louder than Todd's hand signals demanded. Even the reticent members of my group thrust their arms into the air. On the stage, an African American woman told her boyfriend that her unborn baby's father was really a white transvestite. As the transvestite almost came to blows with an audience heckler, I wondered if our guerrilla analysis mission had turned the students into postmillennial Patty Hearsts. That is, until I realized that my hands were also thrown high into the air, that I was screaming and laughing, that I was fixated on the floating overhead camera that always seemed to turn its eye *on me*. As my voice immediately became hoarse with shame (hadn't I spent years in academia combating this sort of thing?), Todd gave me a sly smile, followed by a slight upward wave of his hand.

I decided that my only response could be to silently lip-synch the chants of "Jerry! Jerry!" and "pregnant whore," but I was interrupted from this hasty plan by a pregnant stripper wending through the crowd. Clearly, my decision to seat us on-camera proved to have been precipitous as the stripper quickly snaked from the floor to the lap of one of my students. They yelled obscenities at each other while the entire audience screamed and hollered as if attending a cockfight. I made ineffectual movements of discomfort as the stripper flashed her breasts in what seemed like slow motion, and I felt my heart plummet down into the vibrating floor. How had everything gotten out of control so quickly, so completely, I wondered—"mouthing" my lines in a completely ineffectual protest?

I had only wanted to bring the students out of the classroom comfort zone and into the experience of the screen; I had only wanted to test our ability to know for certain what was "fake." But now we were complicit, I realized, as four of my students questioned the guests. One student's query about sexually transmitted diseases received chants of "Go to Oprah," while the more standard-issue insults drew hoots and applause. After Jerry's "Final Thought" bled into an agonizing forty seconds of clapping, I told the student who had gotten the surprise peep show that he did *not* have to sign the release form Todd would soon wave at him—a form that I was half convinced would spell the end of my short teaching career. He gave me a perfectly exaggerated look: why would he not want to be on television?

Our return to the northern suburbs was much quieter than our morning descent; we joked briefly about the Springer spectacle, and then became quiet, each of us lost in the realization, perhaps, that what distinguished reality from performance was not so much our ability to critically analyze, but our distance from the event under inspection. A colleague later asked me what possible relevance the field trip could have to an English class. I went through my standard explanation of how cultural studies issues relate to what we think of as "texts," highlighting the media's effect on cultural perception—but I couldn't forget that I was defending an event at which I had shouted slurs at pregnant women.

Sure, Springer was a setup, part of a cynical regime of flippant popular culture, but within ten minutes of arrival at the set, we could no longer remain "above it all." The "simulation" of Springer became "real" for us—and we were thrown into confusion about not only this, but everything. Would we go back to our cozy classroom and continue hypothesizing that the world was full of specters and simulations?

No one in the group expected *such* a radical jolt out of our comfort zones. We spoke about the experience like addicts in a twelve-step program; we wrote about the program on our online bulletin board. The *Jerry Springer Show* had killed the class's ability to jump headfirst into a "text," but we were only pantomiming an autopsy. Instead of questioning the validity of postmodernism from a postmodern position, the class seemed to question the ability of postmodernism to keep them safe from what they thought could be their "essential" selves—screaming and clapping audience members. Our ultimate response began with one student's idea to produce a *Po-Mo Talk Show* as the final class project, arguing that our experience, both enlightening and shameful, begged for a sort of public, Robert Downey Jr.–style detoxification. We would re-create the conditions of our madness in hopes of finding a cure.

The students orchestrated two skits: a patient of Sigmund Freud would "cheat" on him with radical thinkers Gilles Deleuze and Félix Guattari; an Oprah-like book-of-the-month club would be interrupted by a group of Burroughs's "wild boys." We fretted for weeks until the night of our performance, staging and restaging our own talk show experience. The class, once masters of ironic distance, slowly deconstructed the conditions of the *Jerry Springer Show* that had elicited their frenzied participation. Finally, *our* audience of college students watched with rapt attention as we deliberately burped and gurgled our way through an hour of parody, videotape, and group chants—lip-synching not a single word.

In the meantime, our episode of Springer ran. To my great surprise, the entire program was *not* focused on the obedient performance of our group, and not once could we be seen chanting "pregnant whore." The focal point of our entire semester experience became something else in the projection, and while we still puzzled over our own complicity in allowing the spectacle to proceed, we understood how easy our academic shields could turn us into a phalanx of

the art of friction

riot police. Separation from the critical moment allowed us a perspective from which to become "ourselves" again—as well as a vantage point from which to see "ourselves" as illusory. Our proximity to the event gave it life, but our distance from its projection forced it back into that mélange of white noise that my students seemed to perceive, even before taking my class, on a genetic level. The post-Springer difference, however, is that we could no longer recombine with such abandon. We journeyed into the television screen as the audience, but we came out as the actors—which made us realize that perhaps, in all of our confident analyses, we had been acting all along.

author's commentary

Cultural theorist Henri d'Mescan, in his 1978 essay "A Stegosaurus Ate My Tongue," roars at the impotency of human communication: "Consider the invention of the alphabet, the muttering sickness, the evolution of the voice box—nothing but the marionette strings of some unseen genetic puppeteer. The random scribbles of the human hand" (*End-Times Literary Supplement*, December 10, 1978, 142).

In other words, the biggest fiction is the category of nonfiction. Tired old "real life" becomes an abstraction once fixed in tangible form. It is no more "real" than the most faithful virtual-reality simulator, not because certain events don't "happen" or "occur" or "exist" or "etc." in the most ontological or phenomenological sense, but because like music, or art, or film, words are *merely* interpretation. Writers (and readers) in America (and not elsewhere) cling desperately to the fiction of nonfiction, lost, like disoriented atoms in a dying comet, amid proclamations of the fourth genre's unassailable truth.

Concurrently, the editorial mechanism of the human ego, and its obnoxious subset—the authorial ego—rises through the entry point of each automatic comma and deliberate semicolon, liberated, if you will, from the flat of the primitive backbrain to the center of the Times New Roman big top. As writers, we ooze onto the page, ready to create a world from strands of treated pulp.

Unsurprisingly, the container of the word—the "font"—derives from the

Middle French *fonte* (think: fondue): a melting together in both the casting of type and the smelting of external occurrence with internal transmission. In the space of the "font," the real and the unreal meet, dance, make love, break up. There are tears and remonstrations, angry rejections, feelings of betrayal, but nevertheless, the self-aggrandizing spirit of the word paints everything in rosy, or at least tolerable, retrospection.

For this *Jerry Springer* outing, our class willed the camera's attention to the smallest facial pores, the tiniest tremble of our lips twisted in some hideous slur, the shake of our arms in thrall to the ugly spectacle. Still, we were ultimately disappointed at our own complicity, our utter ineffectuality, when displayed for mere seconds in the program's final cut. We appear on the screen *as if we were there*, but our participation merely eliminates the *may-have-been* in the overwhelming blather of the *this-now-is*—at least for the time it takes you, dear reader, free from the burden of lost verisimilitude, to entirely reject the useless dinosaur.

DAVIS SCHNEIDERMAN is the author of, most recently, *Multifesto: A Henri d'Mescan Reader*, and, with Carlos Hernandez, he has coauthored *Abecedarium*. He is the chair of American Studies at Lake Forest College in Lake Forest, Illinois.

When I was about eleven, I bought a red lipstick for my mother. She was mad about it. She wore it constantly. It burned like solder, seared like acid, jabbed and stung like needles. She didn't care. When I was a little girl my mother always wore red lipstick. "You have to suffer to be beautiful," she said. It was months before she learned that it stung because it was rancid. I was sort of intrigued by the idea that I might have poisoned her, and almost wished the result had been fatal.

Red lips have nothing to do with fashion. Red lips, and the idea of red lips, never totally fade away. They are their own reality. They are implicitly understood like laughing good-time girls with phosphorescent blonde hair.

Red lips are magical, trashy, classy, decadent, and gothic.

Some women who have bright red lips: Madonna, Joni Mitchell, Annie Lennox, Carly Simon, Debbie Harry, Josephine Baker, Billie Holiday, Carmen Miranda, Kate Bush, Boy George, Siouxsie Sioux, Grace Jones, Patsy Cline, Tina Turner, Rickie Lee Jones, Anita Baker, Maria Callas, Donna Summer, Betty Boop, Ingrid Bergman, Isabella Rossellini, Joan Blondell, Mabel Norman, Catherine Deneuve, Grace Kelly, Jean Harlow, Betty Grable, Lucille Ball, Susan Hayward, Ginger Rogers, Michelle Pfeiffer, Sade, Norma Shearer, Lauren Bacall, Louise Brooks, Geena Davis, Faye Dunaway, Glenn Close, Joan Chen, Sigourney Weaver, Andie McDowell, Meryl Streep, Natalie Wood, Juliette Binoche, Uma Thurman, Talisa Soto, Lana Turner, Daryl Hannah, Lisa Bonet, Kim Basinger, Sonia Braga, Ellen Barkin, Claudette Colbert, Cybill Shepherd, Amanda Donohoe, Theresa Russell, Vivien Leigh, Marlene Dietrich, Greta Garbo, Nastassja Kinski, Bette Davis, Jane Fonda, Melanie Griffith, Isabelle Adjani, Joan Bennett, Annette Bening, Annabella Sciorra, Helena Bonham Carter, Hedy Lamarr, Dorothy Lamour, Cathy Moriarty, Gloria Swanson, Jennifer Jones, Ann Sheridan, Clara Bow, Elizabeth Taylor, Farrah Fawcett, Barbara Carrera, Anjelica Huston, Judy Garland, Lena Olin, Ava Gardner, Rita Hayworth, Charlotte

Rampling, Carole Lombard, Mae West, Tim Curry, Joel Grey, Diana Vreeland, Lauren Hutton, Iman, Circe, Princess Caroline, Norma Kamali, Carolina Herrera, Diane von Furstenberg, Lolita, Madame Bovary, Anna Karenina, Eva Perón, Coretta Scott King, Benazir Bhutto, Joan Rivers, Joan Collins, Sandra Bernhard, Zelda Fitzgerald, Empress Josephine, Paloma Picasso, and others.

We had this crummy painted pink cabinet in our bathroom. In one of the drawers were at least thirty or forty gold and silver tubes of lipsticks. It was magical to open them and see the magnificent array of shades from pale pink, through oranges and roses and magentas, to the bright reds and deep wines. I wasn't allowed to play with them, put them on my lips, or even open them, so doing so was a surreptitious activity, on the level of masturbation.

History of lips:
Cleopatra. Around 69–30 B.C., the lipstick of choice for her and other chic women of ancient Egypt was a reddish-brown clay, colored by iron oxide. It was used to tint both lips and cheeks. Sometime later in Italy, Poppea, wife of the wicked emperor Nero, experimented with ochres, circa A.D. 37–68.

According to Robert Salvatore, beauty director for Max Factor and founder of Hollywood's Max Factor Museum of Beauty, ladies of high fashion in fifteenth-century Italy had a cosmetic array of almost modern magnitude, including color palettes for the lips. Their use persisted regardless of economic conditions and social attitudes.

When I was very young, like around three or four, or maybe five, there were certain times I was allowed to play with my mother's lipstick. She'd supervise, though, so that I wouldn't press too hard, or go too far and paint more than my lips, so I wouldn't be tempted, because the stick of cerise smelled so good, to bite off a chunk and chew it. All of which I did when she wasn't around.

Elizabethans stained their lips with crushed roses, geranium petals, and blossoms.

In 1770, the British Parliament passed an act providing that women found guilty of seducing men into matrimony by cosmetic means should be tried for witchcraft.

In time, the use of lipstick ceased being a crime, but continued to be seen as a sign of moral turpitude. Proper Victorian women were expected to wear no makeup at all, though many would secretly moisten crepe paper flowers—whose dye came off when wet—and use that to give their lips a carnation-colored glow. Lower-class women—Jack the Ripper's victims for example—painted themselves with garish abandon and looked to contemporaries like the trollops they were.

I practiced my reading skills on a still-packaged lipstick of my mother's:

> Now there's a lipstick that gives you the best of all possible worlds: a luscious, memorable mouth plus dramatic color fidelity and staying power. The breakthrough formula glides on micro-layers of pure color. So each shade starts true and stays true. In any light. And along with the dazzling color, True Lipstick lets you enjoy hours of true comfort. Feels lightweight, never sticky. Won't feather or stain. True Lipstick in twenty irresistible shades. You'll want more than one. Everything a great lipstick should be.

Before my father came home from work each day, my mother always brushed her hair and put on some bright lipstick, as if that habitual act, and that neat façade, could cover up the domestic disorder and disarray of everything else in our house.

As I got older I recognized that the act of putting on lipstick was not merely to look neat. It had something to do with sexuality, and not only being attractive, but being attractive in a certain sexual way. I watched for clues. I watched my mother's lips. I watched my father's eyes. I wasn't sure of anything. In those days I looked for sexual clues everywhere—suddenly the universe was about sex. Yet I didn't know very much at all. It was all there to be explored, discovered. Now I realize that maybe my mother expected the lipstick to work some magic on my father. I think the results never came up to her expectations.

At the turn of the century there weren't many commercial preparations for the lips. Gibson girls chewed their lips to make them red, or sucked on hot cinnamon drops.

In 1890, the Butterick Company came out with a book titled *Beauty*. One preparation it recommended involved a liquid, really a combination of cold cream and something called "alloxa," that was applied to the lips with a soft brush, usually made from a squirrel's tail. It was said to have a curious effect. It bloomed, or colored, into a very nice pink.

Theatrical rouge, a vermilion compound of bright red mercuric sulfide, was definitely injurious to the skin, and quite garish-looking.

One day when I got home from school, my father was already home. His thick dark chest hair curled over his ribbed, white undershirt, and his long, thin bare legs sticking out of the wide openings in his funny boxer shorts made him seem very vulnerable. He looked like those birds, flamingos, or herons, whose long legs seem too thin to hold up their bodies. Mother's black curly hair was a wild mess, and she was screaming at him, waving one of his white shirts around like a flag. Dad hadn't gone to work at all that day, and didn't go the next day either. I thought I'd get to stay home too, as if it were a special holiday or some special family thing, even though the atmosphere was far from happy. I was surprised when Mom told me, in a firm, clipped way, to get ready to catch the bus. I felt hurt and left out, and thought about it all day. That incident brought up the underlying feeling of some secret stuff between them that probably had to do with something sexual, and that had absolutely nothing to do with me.

Eventually I locked the bathroom door and opened the painted-over metal wall-hamper. I was assailed by a mixture of Mother's perfumes, and some strong, musty, oily smell that I recognized immediately as Dad's, an odor that was his even when he'd just bathed. I threw everything, my father's shorts and shirts, my small underthings, and pajamas, my mother's shriveled bras and French-cut bikini bottoms, out on the white, not-too-clean octagon-tiled bathroom floor, not knowing what I was looking for, my heart pounding up in my throat, my fingers trembling. Years later, I'd feel the same sensation when going through my husband's pockets to find some evidence of infidelity. I studied underpants closely, and spotted weird stains, like dried blood, on one or two of my mother's. As I was putting things back, sickened by the close smell of all the dirty clothes cooped up in the hamper, I noticed a reddish smear on the stiff, curly collar of my father's white shirt with the thin green stripes. I studied it carefully. It was dark in the center, blurry at the edges. Still, it was very faint. It could have been from my mother; it was a similar shade of red. I put my lips on it instinctively, pretending that the stain came from them. I did it so lightly I just faintly felt the soft nap of the fine, well-washed cotton rub across my lips.

Movies: In the beginning, only theatrical people wore what is called lipstick. The Leichner Co., of Germany, produced theatrical makeup in the form of boxed, individually wrapped crayonlike grease sticks with sharp points. That's where the word "lipstick" comes from. Max Factor, a Russian immigrant whose background included a smattering of opera and theater, had, by the early 1900s, come to California to become the Hollywood distributor of Leichner products.

Then, around 1909, Factor began creating his own improved lip products for film stars. The existing red lipsticks, on black-and-white film, looked jet-black. So Factor created a brown lipstick with bluish undertones, which looked softer on film.

Factor applied much of the makeup himself. Actresses' mouths bore his thumbprints: two on the top lip and one on the bottom. The outside corners of the lips were covered with foundation. The lip shape was bee-stung—to make you look puckered. Think Clara Bow. That was chic and romantic.

When Factor's lipsticks, in shades of red, became available to the public, women emulated what they saw on the silver screen. You looked as if you were always ready for a kiss.

When my parents weren't home, I'd try on lipstick in the living room, because one wall was a mirror, and you could see yourself close-up. I liked the way different shades, pinkish, orange-ish, changed the tone of my skin, and transformed the colors in my hazel eyes, even brought out tones in my hair, sometimes verging on reddish, sometimes browner, or black. I liked looking at myself really close-up. I looked different that way. I couldn't see my face as a whole, or my body at all. But delicate blue veins were visible on the sides of my forehead. My eyelashes looked huge, and almost as if they were two colors, black near where they emerged from the lids, and reddish at their tips. I could see all the shades in my eyes that weren't ordinarily visible: a line of green around the circle of translucent amber, and then a brownish-green star shooting out from another green circle around the pupil. These were subtleties I looked forward to having some lover notice and appreciate someday.

I'd open the tube carefully, first winding the tube of color all the way out, just to revel in its hue, and its unused glister, thinking about how good it would feel to run a fingernail along the fresh oily surface. Then I'd roll it back in till just a bit stuck out. I had to concentrate to get the color to follow the lines of my upper lip, which I always did first, the center of one side and out, then the center of the other side and out. Then I'd press my lips together, and some would come off on my bottom lip. This I would darken with the lipstick. Then I'd rub my lips together once more, enjoying the moist, oily sensation. I'd study how this color looked for a while. Then I'd blot my lips on a tissue, as my mother did, creating a more matte look.

I'd repeat this process with at least three shades, ultimately wiping the last one off too, because I wasn't allowed to wear lipstick yet. By the time I'd tried on a few colors, the lipstick felt thick and greasy, and I felt as if my lips were being smothered, as if they couldn't breathe properly—the way my feet felt when I kept on my rubber rain shoes all day in school. But before I removed the last color, I'd get as close to the mirror as I could, trying to see how it would look or feel to kiss me. Somehow this was very exciting. I'm not sure if it was from imagining being kissed, or from me, turning myself on. Maybe I was turned on imagining myself turning someone on.

After I'd wiped off all those layers of lipstick with tissues, my lips were stained pink, and swollen. An entire area around my lips was also pink, and somewhat raw. It always surprised me that neither my mother nor my father seemed to notice.

In 1920, Clara Bow started doing less of a pucker and more of a cupid's bow. In the Thirties, Joan Crawford rejected the kewpie doll mouth and used a lip brush to spread the color all the way out to the sides of her lips, creating a sort of bow-and-arrow effect. Later her mouth resembled a large scarlet gash.

One place I, and all my friends, secretly put on lipstick was at the movies on Saturday afternoons. We'd stand outside and smoke, then go inside and put on lipstick in the ladies room. Most of us had practiced enough so that we could do it smoothly and look cool. Sometimes some boys from the neighborhood, or from our class, would show up. Mostly the boys sat together and the girls sat together. Once in a while one of the boys would sit near one of us, and eventually put his arm around her. We'd watch jealously to see whether they were still facing forward, looking at the movie.

One day Marc Ratner came over to me. He was wearing his brown leather jacket with some kind of fur collar. He had thick lips and a wide smile. He followed me to my seat, his hands stuck awkwardly in his belt, and sat down beside me. The theater smelled of Lysol and popcorn. We said nothing to each other. I faced forward, not daring to look at him, my hands in my lap. I was conscious of nothing but his warm body and his breathing beside me. My heart was beating as fast as a sparrow's, somewhere high in my chest. After what seemed like a half hour, he put his arm around the back of the seat and left it there. Five minutes later it dropped onto my shoulder, where it lay draped as if it had fallen there by accident. I moved only my eyes to the side to sneak a glance. Marc was looking straight ahead, seemingly absorbed in the film. When I didn't take his arm away, his hand slowly drooped close to my breast. I remained perfectly and absolutely still, waiting to see what would happen, my stillness conferring permission. When the movie was over, and the lights came on, there'd be a feeling of disappointment somehow. We'd look at the credits for a moment, then leave. The boys would slowly form their group, and so would the girls. Sometimes, if there was time, we'd smoke another cigarette, and then go wipe the lipstick off with toilet tissue.

Premier cosmetic figures began cropping up all over the place: Helena Rubinstein, Elizabeth Arden, Mrs. C. J. Walker. Men gradually came in and took over the firms. Men like Charles Revson and Max Factor created a closer alignment between the cosmetics and pharmaceutical industries.

What the Americans developed, the French adopted and made their own. Even expatriates from America living in Paris at that time were very conscious of ruby red French lips. In an interview, Ernest Hemingway once said, "You know, I can remember a long time ago seeing a girl on a street in Paris and wanting to go over and kiss her just because she had so much damn red lipstick caked on. I wanted to get that lipstick smeared all over my lips, just so I could see what it felt like."

At a time when all of us in our grade still weren't allowed to wear lipstick, Doris Gottschalk brazenly wore a greasy pink we sometimes, when we talked about her, called Penis Pink. She also bleached her dirty-blonde hair in the front and pulled her hair up behind her ear on only one side. Because of this she was considered a promiscuous and sexually active girl who, by her trampy looks, invited sexual overtures. The guys loved her and hated her. We girls feared her. I was jealous. She made being bad seem exciting. I wished I had the courage to do the same. I think she turned us all on.

Anatomy and anthropology: Lips aren't really a body part, they're a border. "Lips are the transitional skin between the skin on the rest of the face, and the mucous membrane that coats the inside of the mouth," says dermatologist Ronald A. Katz. "The lips have more sensory receptors than other tissues, so they react more to stimulation."

"The color red enhances the blood flow beneath the skin, whose appearance naturally reddens during sexual excitement," notes Rutgers University anthropologist Lionel Tiger. "When other kinds of primates exhibit display behavior, their sexual presentation is clear. The females' genital regions swell and redden during ovulation. Human primates cover their sexual organs because that part of the anatomy is so powerful." Tiger theorizes that that is how the mouth became the analogue for women's genitals. And reddening the mouth is an elaborate, complex way of exaggerating our primatology. "And hot red lipstick is," he adds, "extremely attractive. It's a highly evocative color."

It's not that I was ever really allowed to wear lipstick, but one day when I put it on before leaving the house, no one told me to take it off. No one even noticed. We all gathered in Lissie's house because her parents were out for the evening. We sat around on the living room carpet and on the couches and chairs, the boys and girls singling each other out until we were a large group of couples. When I think about it now it seems odd that the guys and girls got together only for whatever sexual activity we had then—we might never see that particular boy again, or we might find ourselves with someone else next time we got together for this peer group sex activity.

When the vampire in the video we were watching bit into the woman's neck, she went limp, as if with uncontrollable weakness and desire. When the vampire raised his head, his long white canines were visible, and his lips were bright red and dripping.

Darrell's neck smelled of Old Spice. When I touched his pompadour, it was stiff, but touching his hair still sent a chill through me. I ran my fingers up and down the shaved hair at the back of his neck. His smooth arms goosefleshed. We were both on the cigarette-smelling beige carpet, leaning against a leather La-Z-Boy. The room was dark, but I could hear breathing, sighs, and small smacking sounds of lips breaking contact. Darrell's mouth smelled of beer and garlic, and was repugnant and attractive at the same time. He bent over and kissed my earlobe. Our hands were linked and sweaty. Everything was magnified, like when I used to look at myself closely in the mirror. I felt each bone and vein and his skin and every blood vessel in Darrell's hand. His hands seemed to feel me in the utmost detail, including my breath and heartbeat and circulation. He puts his mouth near mine and I feel a tingle around my entire face even though our lips haven't yet touched. When our lips meet, they begin to glow. They grow enormous, and spread into each other. Darrell's tongue feels alive and strong, like a fish making its way around the shoals of my teeth and tongue. Our pressed-together mouths radiate their own moisture, heat, and light, and expand more, until they are our entire bodies. Slowly, our mouths become the room, then the world, and eventually, the universe.

lynda schor

Truth/Lies

I'm into the absolute truth of whatever it is I'm writing, its integrity, and the truth of its form. I'm a postmodernist, which means I think about truth a lot, but haven't come to any unwavering conclusions about it. I call everything I write "fiction," no matter how genre-bending, or how close to autobiography, it is because I'm interested in connections and meanings and form rather than verisimilitude. The author Frederick Busch says, "All fiction lies. All artful fiction lies in order to tell some truth." And the author John Dufresne has written a fiction-writing manual called *The Lie That Tells the Truth.*

In the story "Lips," I was playing with collage. I love using texts in my stories, and I enjoy satirizing styles of texts such as informational articles, art reviews, self-help pieces, food reviews, etc., each of which has its own kind of style and tone. "Lips" began with a factual article I liked about makeup, and it took a few years before I thought of a way to use it. In "Lips," I like the way the fictional text is different from the facts, and I like the ways that the two different styles of texts relate. The sections that seem like an article about makeup almost make the fictional sections sound true. Which they are. Which they are not.

Some of my stories have been so autobiographical that I even used my own name for the narrator—yet there has always been some separation between me and the character me. The real me, and whatever is autobiographical, have always been subservient to the form and the meaning I am creating, so it wouldn't occur to me to call any of these "true" stories memoirs.

The memoirs I like best *(The Kiss, Running with Scissors, The Liar's Club, This Boy's Life)* are more like novels. They work well in every way, including their forms. I don't ask myself whether everything in them is exactly the way it happened, nor do I care. I can't imagine that some details aren't exaggerated, and I can't imagine that anyone can recall the details of dialogue. I loved Lucy Grealy's *Autobiography of a Face,* because in it she explores the complex ideas of external beauty along with the story of her jaw cancer. *The*

Glass Castle, a beautiful memoir by Jeannette Walls, is always surprising, with its wonderful characters, great dialogue, and all the scary complexities it brings up about families and relationships. Yet it should have ended sooner. Thinking more about "truth," rather than form, the author seems to have felt a need to let us readers know how things turned out—up to the moment of publication.

I care a lot about truth. That's why the idea of an organization like The Smoking Gun (the one that outted James Frey and led to his crucifixion) lurking around the edges of fiction and memoir scares the shit out of me, though it brought up some fascinating issues about truth and lies in fiction and memoir. Some ugly things about the publishing world were exposed, one of which is the promotion of authors and our secrets, rather than the promotion of our art and our novels. We need The Smoking Gun, and organizations like it, not to police our art for exaggerations and incorrect facts, but to help us ferret out the lies and misdeeds of our current administration (and others, past and future) so that we can continue to have a country we are free to be artists in.

LYNDA SCHOR is the author of *The Body Parts Shop,* a collection of stories. She lives in New York City.

1505 Bluebell Ave.
Boulder, CO 80302[1]

I. butterfly of the positive force

Birds and roosters were making a racket and the big volcano was already loom-ing in front of the sun when he crawled from under the mosquito netting and stumbled out to the balcony. Green on green on still another green, tapestried with flowers yellow and red and pink and white, was what he saw as he looked out across thatch and palm, terraced rice paddies and over the ravine to the tas-seled line of jungle against the dawn stained blue. That reminded him of a Kupa Kupa Barong fluttering by the day before, you don't see them much, "butterfly of the positive force," shiny sky blue panels on black wings. There and gone. The invisible visible. Maybe it meant the positive force would predominate today.

His wife was already out watching the dawn.[2] For her the dawn was always a positive force, but he wasn't always sure whether dawn meant one more hello or one more goodbye. She was younger than him. And healthier.[3]

Midrash

JULIA FREY
julia frey

1. Asked to write something about this unpublished story, I have decided to write a commentary, or midrash, in the form of text notes. I was with Ron in Bali when he began it and witnessed the events that provoked it. As a biographer, I'm in a paradoxical position. I feel impelled to be as flat-footed and factual as possible, but since it was my life, too, I'm a thoroughly unreliable narrator. Ron, an admittedly autobiographical writer, knew the risk he was taking when he married a biographer. Ambivalent, he both wanted me to write his biography and worried that I wouldn't tell it his way. You're right, Ron. I'm telling it my own way.

Ron and I began living together in 1980. We bought the Bluebell Avenue house together in 1986. Ron explained to his mother, "That's much more serious than getting married." We finally married in 1992, when we knew he had some kind of illness, though we didn't know what. We figured if I was his wife, I could at least get to him in a hospital. A month or so after we married, he was finally diagnosed with a

"It's going to be hot," she turned her face away from the sun.

"You were talking in your sleep again."

"What did I say?"

"Help."

Her positive force rose with the sun. But at night the negative force arose and in the morning he could see the two struggling in her face. He was the opposite, for him the mysterious night was friendlier.

---

rare muscle disorder called "inclusion body myositis." IBM killed off his muscle cells one by one. Ron was told that he could expect to be completely incapacitated, in a wheelchair within four years. We dealt with this news very pragmatically. The first evening when we got back from the doctor's, we sat down and made a list of all the trips we'd ever wanted to take, in order of difficulty, most difficult first. We knew he'd get weaker and weaker, but no one really knew how fast the malady would progress, and at first we were afraid to actually take the risk of traveling to places without sophisticated health care. When, in 1996, against all predictions, he was still walking, we decided the hell with it, and took off. We started with Galápagos, las Amazonas, and Macchu Picchu. China, Bali, and India came the next summer.

The fact that Ron never decided to publish this story seems significant. I'm guessing as to his motivations, but when he wrote it, we both thought he might be dead within a year. As time passed, and he did not die as scheduled, the emotional intensity he expresses in the story may have seemed exaggerated to him. Contrary to his hip persona. He survived beyond all expectations, until 2004.

The story signals a sea change. In his last stories ("Running on Empty," "Never," "77," "The Cat": published posthumously in *Golden Handcuffs Review* no. 4, Fall 2004), his writing became more and more about his feelings, how they kept making cracks in his macho mask.

The Bluebell Avenue address limits composition dates: We traveled to Bali in July 1997. He began taking notes for this story while we were there, and continued working on it in September 1997, in his Bluebell study. He did the images and revised it over some time. He must have considered it finished before we left the Bluebell address in July 2000. In any case, he did not work on it again. The original manuscript, with final corrections, is in the Harry Ransom Center at the University of Texas, Austin.

2. As Bali is less than ten degrees south of the equator, the days and nights begin at six o'clock, year-round.

3. By the time we got to Bali from three weeks traveling alone in China, we were both pretty tired. We considered the two weeks in Bali as R & R.

ronald sukenick and julia frey

He took his cane and preceded her down the long flight of steps to the thatch-covered breakfast terrace. It was a cheap little place amid the paddies, the hotel, something between a hotel and a homestay, no hot water, no glass or even screening in the windows, not enough electric light to read.[4] They'd picked it from a guide book almost at random. The guests, mostly from New Zealand or Indonesia, looked like they were on budget or knew about it. The others usually arrived when they were finishing breakfast. Banana, pineapple, mango, papaya, mangosteen, jackfruit . . .

Alone on the terrace, they watched the sarong-clad workers coming out to the paddies to tend the irrigation system of dirt dikes, then talked with Wayan or Putu about going to the cremation ceremony. After which she went to town with her friend Madi and he went back up to his sketch pad on the balcony and summoned up the positive force, helped by a brilliantly yellow-bellied Sun Bird sucking at an equally brilliant red hibiscus. But ink was the only thing he'd brought, black ink, charcoal, white chalk, white paint, all he wanted was black and white. Because white was invisible. And black was invisible.[5]

When he was done sketching he found himself staring at the vaguely waving palms in the pool compound where guests were already splashing around. This trip may not be being a success he thought. Then he remembered that the point of the trip was to stop thinking and it would certainly be a failure if he didn't.

He went down to bargain with Wayan or Putu about the price of transport to the cremation. There were around four men working at the hotel and as far as

---

4. The Penestanan Bungalows, near Ubud, was listed in a guidebook I was leafing through in a Singapore bookstore. A series of bungalows and a main house with four bedrooms. We were upstairs, where the view was. Mosquito netting, cold water, twenty-watt bulbs. Total simplicity, magically lovely. Pool, garden, breakfast hut overlooking the rice paddies. Little altars everywhere. Spectacular, but difficult to get to. Ron had to maneuver a sometimes slippery mud trail between rice paddies, plus several flights of steps, to get down to the garden, then up to our room.

5. In Bali he only had notebooks and pens. Shortly after that, as his malady progressed, he could hardly hold a pencil, but he made drawings by moving his finger over a screen that created computer images of the lines he sketched with his finger. Black-and-white images.

he could make out they were all named Wayan or Putu. They were all very nice and did their best to be helpful.[6] When they didn't understand something in English their standard response was "Yes." Accompanied by laughter. It could get confusing. As in "Will it be rainy or sunny today?" "Yes." Immediately followed by "You have program this afternoon? You need car? I make special price."

It took a half hour of bargaining to agree on a price for transport. Everything he said was translated into Balinese and discussed vigorously by everyone before an answer was funneled back in English.

After all that, next day, the car didn't appear when it was supposed to. But the delay gave him a chance to say goodbye to Madi, the American woman he and his wife had met around the pool. She was very sweet and had a beautiful figure in a bathing suit. Wayan and Putu had a crush on her. She was a rock climber and seemed to spend all her nonworking time traveling, even managing to use her work as an opportunity for travel.[7] He liked wanderlusting women, he guessed they corresponded to something in himself. He didn't know whether it was the need for escape or the need for discovery.

The car was an hour late. They missed half the ceremony, but the ceremony was held under a brutal midday sun that made him feel lucky to have missed

---

6. The Balinese were remarkably sweet and gentle. The one time we ran into any discomfort with Wayan and Putu was when we wanted to go to the cremation. Cremations were a big tourist attraction and they had already scheduled all the cars, trucks, and bicycles anybody could round up to take tourists to see it. They didn't know what to do because they wanted to be nice, to try to accommodate us. Putu insisted Ron borrow his "dress sarong" to wear to the cremation.

7. I found Madi stunning. By unlikely coincidence, she too came from Boulder, Colorado, where she had been teaching third grade when a broken heart made her decide to ask for a teaching exchange in Taiwan. About forty years old, she was unmarried, a fanatic hiker and skier, who also taught Outward Bound courses. When we met her in Bali, she was vacationing after her first year in Taiwan. Later in Boulder, we had her to dinner and found it hard to find anything to talk about. It was as if all the "town-gown" stereotypes and hostilities had papered over the openness and real affection we had felt for each other in Bali. A year after that, we saw her again at a pottery sale. She looked stressed and gray, ten years older. I remember wondering if she didn't recognize us, because we also looked so different, or if she chose not to respond to our inquiring glances.

ronald sukenick and julia frey

half the ceremony. What he saw of it though, the burning of the body topped by the life-size effigy of the *nandi*, the sacred bull, intrigued him because he didn't see any signs of grief, and nobody seemed to mind the intrusion of crowds of tourists.[8] Maybe there was an up side to death that he was missing.

He interrupted Wayan or Putu, who was looking toward the volcano and singing to himself while Putu or Wayan was down near the pool sweeping up the fragrant many-colored debris of blossoms that had fallen in the night. He asked him about the absence of grief over death and his answer, long and sincere, amounted to something like "Yes." From what he could gather it was the communal nature of life here that buffered the concussion of death. Death was like a tear in the net that needed to mend rather than an ending. On the contrary, it was the start of a voyage. Wayan or Putu had treated his inquiry as a child's question almost, as if grownups wouldn't be thinking about such things. So there he was, thinking again.

Or to think in a different way? Without the self as factor? What would that be like? If you could die and remain part of the intangible thinking network? Thinking without thinking?

Painting as thinking without thinking?

II. black butterflies of bali

The cremation. They had to walk an unexpectedly long way under a very hot sun, then stand around a long time, so his legs were tired by the end of the ceremony. His health wasn't so bad, except he'd always heard the legs were first

---

8. Somebody's grandmother had died in the wrong season for cremations, so they had buried her for a few months, as I understood it, until she could be cremated. On this day, her disinterred body was on a high pyre covered with logs and brush, with the papier-mâché Nandi perched on top. The Balinese family and friends of the deceased sat in the shade on palm mats, as if at a huge picnic. In rows, facing the pyre, all dressed to the nines in indigo batik, singing, chanting, and eating. We tourists, respectfully dressed in sarongs from the waist down, stood on the sunny side and watched the whole thing burn. I was particularly struck, as the pyre collapsed, to see a blackened elbow pop out of the embers.

9. When we went to Asia in 1997, Ron could still walk, slowly and carefully, using

to go and his were going.[9] Abruptly, as they left the site, he fell on his behind in the dust, had to be pulled embarrassingly to his feet by strangers. Then, their transport again late, there was the long walk to find it, now in the absence of the slow funeral procession, cars and motorcycles whipping along the narrow shoulderless road. Vehicles cannonballed by an inch from his elbow. He knew he had to be very cautious not to take another tumble, this time toward the road, which, at the wrong demisecond, would launch him rocketing into the last unknown. So forewarned a few stumbles but no tumble. That was the good side to the bad side.

He caught sight of the big golden-pink water bird bulleting by the balcony, color of women's underwear, S-shaped neck retracted, arrowing like a missile toward some invisible target. It was so fast he never got more than a glimpse of it and so couldn't identify it reliably.

Hibiscus, frangipani, jasmine, bougainvillea . . . Odd the flowers were so colorful while the basic Bali butterfly was black, big buggers too, five-inch wingspan some. They looked like butterflies in mourning, so he guessed he'd come to the right place, he caught himself thinking.

"What was that nightmare about 'help'?" he asked her.

"Someone was trying to rob me."[10]

"Of what?"

"Don't know. Saw the golden bird again."[11]

---

a cane. "I have to exercise the few muscle cells I have left," he used to say. He hated watching his body slowly frittering away on him. There was no cure for IBM. Or as Ron said, it had the advantage of having no disgusting treatments. The malady itself didn't make him suffer. But he got very tired and had a tendency to fall down unexpectedly. And he was too weak to get up again by himself, so if he had the bad luck to be alone when he fell, he was stranded, like a turtle on its back. The inexorable decline with no hope of a cure depressed him. There was nothing positive to look forward to.

10. It seems obvious now that Ron was being stolen from me. He was being stolen from himself. I repressed it frantically when I was awake, but I talked in my sleep.

11. I think I was the first to fall in love with this bird. "I saw the most beautiful bird again," I would say, and run in from the balcony to get Ron. That thing was so darn fast. It was always going so fast you could barely glimpse it. We lived on our balcony

193

"When?"

"Just before. Don't you think this is like a lost paradise?"

He didn't answer. He didn't want to discuss abstractions. Abstraction leads to death, is a kind of death. Painting was not abstract, even abstract painting, it was the thing itself. He was in repose here, he didn't care how you labeled it, escape, evasion, denial, whatever. He wanted to sit here and stare at palm trees. Madi was always trying to get them to do things, they made exciting excursion plans, but in the end they never did any of them.

Why was she dreaming of being robbed?

Oddly, talking with people around the pool the way you do, he discovered a man approximately his age who used to live in the same town he did in the States. Even knew someone in common.

"I'm afraid he's died though."

"Dead? How?"

"Just a few weeks ago."

"Sudden?"

"No, he was expecting it."

"Expecting how?"

"Diagnosed a year ago."

"He was young."

"Yes, I've started reading the obits. Five close deaths in recent months."

"What brings you here?" the other guest asked.

"Getting away from it."

"As if you can get away from it."

He decided he would go into town and indulge himself in possibly a mangosteen *lassi*. Or maybe a jackfruit *lassi* in the café with the lotus pool.[12]

---

most of the two weeks in Bali, in part because it was so hard for Ron to get up and down the steps.

12. That was the year we had five friends die before summer. By Christmas it was seven. The Lotus Pond Restaurant was beautiful, so beautiful it didn't matter if you could get better and cheaper lassi elsewhere. Lassi, made of fruit and yoghurt, was the only food in Bali that either of us liked much. Maybe it was because the food in China was so amazing. Balinese food seemed boring by comparison.

III. the golden bird of bali

He couldn't find the golden bird in any of the bird books. It wasn't quite gold anyway, it was a sort of golden pink.[13] No description was quite right. That was the bad side. The good side was he'd have to keep looking. Keep wondering. That was why he'd dropped his bird watching hobby some years ago, he found that once he established an ID for a bird it became a lot less wonderful. It was good knowing stuff but there was a down side to it.

He looked out over the rice paddies and thought the thought of leaving was sad.[14] Maybe they should have come to a less gorgeous place, ugly even. But that was just a thought, the kind of thought he'd resolved not to have. He wondered what Madi thought about when she was scaling cliff faces. Probably nothing. He should have been a rock climber. It was a way of moving beyond yourself, she said.[15]

Bali was filled with starving stray dogs, dying in the streets. He didn't like to think about them but he did. Part of the down side of paradise, there must be others. The garbage in ditches and streams. If he hung around long enough he'd probably find out, he had that kind of mind. And wished he hadn't.

He heard drums in the distance, went out on the balcony and with binoculars spotted the banners of a procession going down the curving road into

---

13. We saw the bird several times a day. It always flew past our balcony at great speed, zapping across the rice paddies. Living on our balcony, we gazed out onto Bali without really participating in it at all. It was mostly speculation.

14. I loved looking at the endless terraces of the rice paddies. They were serene and restful. The actual labor of building and shifting the small mud dikes that controlled the irrigation ditches was constant and appeared to take great skill. We sat for hours watching the men and women with their sarongs hitched thigh-high, wading through the mud, using their feet for the actual dike maneuvers, like a strong but delicate dance.

15. Madi and I hung out together while Ron was writing. Taking long walks, we talked about the meditative nature of rock climbing. Since it takes all your concentration not to fall off the rock face, you don't dare lose focus for even a moment, or it might be your last. When you finish the climb, you feel exhilarated, as if you've emptied your head of all the static that usually keeps you from paying attention to the present. While you are climbing, you live only in that instant.

ronald sukenick and julia frey

town. Women with headdresses doubling their height, constructions of fruits, rice cakes, flowers, splendorous colors. A palanquin giving Sang Hyang Widhi a lift to a neighboring temple, or rather one of his representatives. Because God is unknowable.[16] How do you know how to deal with the unknowable?

IV. balistic

"I found it, the bird. In a bird book in the bookstore in Ubud. It's a Cinnamon Bittern."[17]

"The pigeon is holed," his wife said. "What now?"

"Now?" He used to check them off on his bird list. Checked, stored, and ignored. Maybe he should make it an offering. The Balinese were constantly making offerings to their gods, and judging from the number of offerings strewn around they must have gods for everything. He would come across them all the time, tiny, exquisite compositions of woven leaf, bright-colored blossoms, bits of food, laid at household shrines but also at portals, paths, stairways, whatever. Offerings to invisible spirits, or at least he couldn't see them. Was the golden bird a spirit? What kind of offering could he make?

By accident he discovered why Wayan was late to drive them to the cremation was he was double dipping. Something Putu said clued him. He'd arranged to give someone else a ride to it first, so his excuse of a flat was as flat as the imaginary tire. When he mentioned this angrily to the usually gentle Wayan there was a flash of nastiness that startled him because he realized that he had no idea who he was dealing with in these people, that they were mostly invisible. Maybe he didn't want to know.[18]

---

16. As is death. Ron's preoccupation was constant as he watched it approaching; he wanted to face it, but it is faceless.

17. I was the one who actually found it in the bird book. Ron had said he didn't want to know—it would steal the magic. And, as he observes, it did.

18. I had a different take on this. I felt we had pushed them by not accepting "no" when they said they had no car. Then when they tried to help us out by coming back for us, we got mad because they were late. But I agreed with Ron it would be impossible to live in Bali because we were permanently excluded from the culture—it was inconceivable to imagine being integrated into the Balinese community.

Or need to. Several days later he was talking to Putu about transport to the airport on the way to Yogjakarta.

"Cost is twenty thousand rupaya."

"I thought you said thirty." They had previously bargained over it for twenty minutes.

"No, twenty now."

"Why twenty now?" He suddenly felt he was bargaining in reverse.

"Yes."

"Okay, twenty."

"Wayan take you."

"I don't want to go with Wayan."

"Is okay."

"I don't trust him."

A laugh. "Yes. Is okay?"

"Twenty?"

"Okay?"

"Okay."

Because it occurred to him that this was some roundabout complicated reparation that Putu had arranged for the flat tire. Just how this had gone round and round and come out here maybe he didn't need to know. Maybe he needed to make an offering to the god of bargaining instead.

So Wayan was Wayan and Putu was Putu. More or less.

When it came to it, he gave Wayan a good "extra," maybe that was his offering. Wayan pocketed it, responding, "You need program this afternoon?"

Happy natives.[19]

V. yogja

Borobodur was hellish in the heat. At ten in the morning it was already too hot. Used to the small domestic temples of Bali, the huge pile of carved stone

---

19. Trying to make up for our discomfort by giving us a reduction on the next trip seemed to me to be logical behavior, a way of meeting conflicting demands, consistent with this peaceful, deeply religious world.

seemed oppressive to them even if the sculpted tales of Buddha were sublime low relief comic strips. Scripture in stone was not the same as being part of the script in Bali, where there was always some sign of the spirit around some superstition or procession or ceremony appearing as mysteriously as a wave out of the sea. But then Bali was Bali even if it was Indonesia. This was just Indonesia.[20]

In a café in Yogja where he was getting a massage to alleviate back strain from climbing Borobodur, she accumulated an Indonesian young man. It was something he took for granted by now, the way men appeared around her. He found him at their table after his massage, a short dark type with movements surprisingly feminine, tossing his long thick hair about as if he had a contract with visibility. An artist, in fact, he knew by coincidence some of their painter friends in Amsterdam, where he'd lived.

"I have long hair to show I am against," he said. He looked like Wayan and Putu but came on like a hippie. Try and put those two images together, he thought. He couldn't. He thought if he could he might get a good take on the state of the spirit in the Third World. As a schizzy mirror for his own.

When they got back to Bali a few days later she told him she remembered what they were trying to steal.

"Yes?"

"The kite."

They saw the golden bird again. At night the forest rainfall was like applause.

VI. kites

He'd seen a Vermilion Flowerpecker that afternoon, its redness was startling. The kite was black, in the shape of a crow. A birthday present. There were lots

---

20. Yogja is on Java, the main island of Indonesia, which, except for Bali, is Muslim. My principal memory of Yogja was the suffocating exhaust fumes and chaotic traffic, dominated by motor scooters, often ridden by women whose hair and shoulders were piously covered with white scarves.

of kites in Bali, fantastic shapes and bright colors hovering in the blue, but black was what he needed. A somber bird, a soaring kite.[21] Black as a slate.

"How would you feel if you were God and you had already thought of everything?" she asked.

"God doesn't have to think."

"Wouldn't you like to know what's going to happen?" she asked.

"At my age I don't know that I want to know."

"I admit I still have a foot in the future."

"That's the up side to the down side," he suddenly knew it, "I can dispense with the future." An image flashed in his mind from when he'd been walking through the paddies the other day. A woman in a sarong, topless, perfect breasts, arms lifted to the hair she was washing, absolutely still as he watched.

At just the right moment, on Bali things happen that way if you let them, there and gone a Kupa Kupa Barong, blue sky on black night. For the few instants it was visible he offered total attention, as offerings go it was all he had to offer. He wondered whether it always had been or if there were something better. He wondered how it compared to rock climbing.

Yes.

VII. on location

Here in Bali there had been a long, ugly colonial history. In the not so distant past the conquering forces of Europe marched in and after several defeats managed to overcome the native warriors. The Dutch were relentless. There was

---

21. Ron's sixty-fifth birthday was in Ubud, July 14, 1997. I gave him a Balinese crow kite for his birthday. Ron always said he identified with crows; if he was a bird, he'd be a crow. He liked the way they were glossy and black. He said they were very smart. And sociable, holding "meetings," as he called them, all talking at once. But even as I bought the black kite in the market with Madi, I thought it looked pretty dark, pretty depressing. I could have chosen a blue bird kite. But Ron was a crow. He said so. You don't change those things just because they're depressing. It would almost be disloyal. The actual kite is in Ron's archives at the Harry Ransom Humanities Research Center, University of Texas, Austin.

money to be made. Nothing else made any difference. There was no difference in anything else. There was wealth and there was more wealth. And beyond that there was still more wealth.

When defeat was imminent the Balinese had a disturbing habit, disturbing even to the Dutch. They would march out of their fortifications in richest regalia, men, women, and children, and deliver themselves to wholesale self-slaughter. First the soldiers and courtiers would come out and deliberately expose themselves to enemy fire. Then the women and children would do the same, the women taking knives to anyone who wasn't finished off, and the king would be the last to go. It reminded him of a trance dancer they'd seen in Ubud walking through fire, the man's eyes fixed on something they couldn't see or understand. The Dutch couldn't understand. How could they understand what was invisible? That things they couldn't see were more important than things they could?

It was a beautiful day in Bali. He could almost see the invisible becoming visible.

RONALD SUKENICK (1932–2004) was on the cutting edge of American fiction and publishing for four decades. Winner of an American Book Award for Lifetime Achievement and the American Academy of Arts and Letters' prestigious Morton Dauwen Zabel Award, he was the author of twelve works of fiction and criticism, including *98.6* and *Mosaic Man*. He was founder and publisher of *American Book Review*.

JULIA FREY, Ronald Sukenick's widow, is the author of *Toulouse-Lautrec, a Life*. She is currently writing a memoir of her life with Sukenick.

She's tugging on her backpack straps. "Please don't make me go."

"Honey, you've gotta. I'm sorry."

"Please. I really don't feel good."

"I know. If you feel worse, call me and I'll come get you, okay? Just try going for a little while, for me, okay? Please?" I can't believe I'm begging her now.

She looks down at her shoes. Pink Barbie sneakers with sparkly laces. "Okay."

I hate this. I hate this even more than I hated going myself.

I don't remember very much before kindergarten, and what I do remember doesn't really matter. I puked all over myself in my Christian elementary school when we watched *The Neverending Story*. I can't remember if I was sick or not, but I just threw up. I had to sit half-naked under a blanket while my mom made the thirty-minute commute to pick me up.

Kindergarten was a little better. I learned the alphabet and colored a lot. One day we made footprints on long sheets of black paper by covering the soles of our feet in white paint. I stepped on my teacher's foot; she was wearing black shoes. She didn't seem angry at all but I was embarrassed.

Each teacher in our grade taught us about a different continent on "Around the World" day. Mrs. Jackson gave us an elephant stamp on our paper passports underneath "Africa" written in bold letters. She put black makeup all over her face and wore a long swath of colorful fabric wrapped around her body. All this came back to me in my African American Studies class freshman year. I was trying to think if I'd ever had a black teacher before and suddenly I remembered Mrs. Jackson, all dressed up in blackface like it was no big deal. She was old then. She could be dead now.

Fifth grade was a mean, gray-haired woman who chided us for our lack of artistic skills and made us draw fruit for hours. I dotted my i's with stars and she circled all of them with red pen. She taught us about the proportions of faces and told us never to draw elbows like macaroni noodles. She swore in front of us. I wonder now if she was going through a divorce, the death of a child. She was so unhappy. It was something I couldn't understand at the age of ten, like flirting. Like showing Marcos Garcia how to do long division and having Sabrina Maloy chase me home after school, calling me a fat bitch for talking to her boyfriend.

Sixth grade meant babysitting for the twin toddlers of my half-time teacher. I can't believe I babysat when I was eleven. I should have had a babysitter.

Middle school brought the dry dog-bark laugh of my literature professor, Ms. Alvarez, a woman with wide eyes and short brown hair. We read *The True Confessions of Charlotte Doyle* in her class. During our presentations on the book we served hard tack and tea, just like Charlotte ate and drank for months.

I cried when I learned I was pregnant. Just held my belly and cried. For myself and for whoever was with me. My boyfriend didn't want a baby. He didn't care that I wanted the baby, but he didn't want it. I was older and he was too spoiled, still a child himself. Running around on his parents' dime, driving fast on empty freeways, and dancing with me on the beach. He loved me but he couldn't stay. He gave us some money—plenty of money, actually—kissed me on the forehead, and drove off. We still talk sometimes, usually late at night on the phone. He always sounds far away.

"How is she?"

"She's good. She's sleeping now."

"Does she look like me?"

"Yeah, in her eyes, a little bit. She got your chin." I can hear him smile.

"Do you need anything?"

"We're fine."

I realize I'm lucky. We're both lucky.

"Are you gay?"

Eighth grade was strange.

"Are you going out with Scott?"

It's like everybody turned crazy.

"Are you a goth?"

I wore blue jeans and green sweaters. My periods were out of control—sometimes, I bled all over my jeans, even if I was wearing a tampon and a pad. I stuck out. I spent a lot of time staring at the poster in the guidance counselor's office with all the blue fish swimming to the left and the one red fish swimming to the right. "Go against the flow!" I was the one who had male friends but not boyfriends, good grades but fat thighs, a belief in God but, strangely, I was absent at any of the local churches.

Scott was in my literature class but we never talked to each other. He ate lunch with the popular kids and dated a busty brunette named Lindy. He was tiny, probably not even five feet tall yet, and thin as paper. Translucent, almost. He wore Old Navy jeans and Tommy Hilfiger T-shirts that looked two sizes too big for him. His hair was matted down against his head with large dollops of styling gel. Scott held his pen at a funny angle and bit his lip when he was thinking hard. I'd watched him for a while, wanted to say something to him, but could never think of anything. One day we were in the library together, sitting at the same table, when he looked up from his notes and asked me if Medusa was the goddess of war.

"No, that's Athena," I told him.

"Oh, yeah. That's right. I get her confused with Ares."

"He's the god of war."

"Yeah."

"I think you'd like this." I pulled out a hefty book of mythology that I'd picked up from a pagan shop called Moonshadow. I spent most of my allowance there on silver jewelry and books about magick.

"*Magick of the Gods and Goddesses?*" He flipped through the pages with a furrowed brow. "Are you a witch?" He was serious. Not like the other kids, who asked just to make fun of me, to get more fodder for their jokes.

I nodded.

While I was pregnant, I drank tea made from raspberry leaves and burned blue candles for protection. I walked by the ocean and listened to the water like it was a voice. At night, I counted the stars and clasped the amulet around my throat while I prayed. I burned sage and hummed as I walked in stars around my apartment. I would close my eyes, breathe deeply, and imagine my entire body as a concave mirror—everything would bounce off of me, nothing could touch me.

The questions never made any sense. When people are asking you things all the time that you can't answer, you start to get a little irritated. Make things up. When they asked about me and Scott, we'd give it our best in tones too sultry for thirteen-year-olds: "It's only casual sex," we'd say, often in unison. When they asked if I was a lesbian or a witch or a Satanist, I would tell them no, slowly and calmly, hoping that they would see how stupid they were being. But no one ever seemed to get that the questions were stupid. No one saw when poking and prodding stopped being funny.

Scott broke up with Lindy. We ate lunch alone together in the supply room. Somebody spit on Scott on the bus. He said he didn't really care, but we started to think maybe we should do something. We were at my house eating popcorn and drinking Diet Cokes one afternoon when he suggested we get back at them.

"How?" I asked.

"I dunno, something subtle, like . . ."

"Blaming them for cheating?" I smirked. The only thing we had over them was brains and the trust of our teachers. "They don't care what we do."

"They don't have to know it's us."

We chewed in silence for a minute.

"You can look up their library records, right?" We both volunteered at the same branch of the local library. We often spent hours tucked away in a back room scanning books to be sent out to other branches. Whoever thought it was a good idea to leave teenagers unsupervised with access to the library database was very naïve.

"Yeah," he said, "but I can't change the amount of fines they owe or anything, I don't have the password."

"No, no, you don't need to do that. You just need to open up their account and check out books to them."

"Oh," he smiled. "Check out the books, right, and then they never return them?"

"But not just any books." Scott grinned at me and I continued, "Only certain books. Like, books on witchcraft or homosexuality or teen pregnancy or something."

We thought we were so devious. We checked out books that they never returned. We poured honey into their lockers—surprisingly easy, we found, if you waited 'til after school and fiddled with the lock like it was stuck while the other person squeezed ten-cent honey sticks through the vents. There must have been cameras. Someone saw, I'm sure, but no one said anything.

It was another restless afternoon in March when we were at Scott's house. I never remember having any homework. We always finished it at school. His mother had fixed us a plate of baby carrots and low-fat peanut butter. His house was boring, always so clean. Pale-colored carpet and softly ticking clocks. White appliances. The day before, Katie Kovak, the only eighth-grade girl with D-cup breasts, asked me if I believed in Satan because she saw me playing with my tarot cards on the bus. She told all of her friends that I was a Satanist and they gasped and crossed themselves when I walked by.

"We could egg her house," I suggested.

"That's too easy."

"I should put a spell on her."

"What kind of spell?"

"One that would make her tits deflate." We laughed.

"You know, the problem is she'd probably like that."

I got up from the table and looked at Scott, who was drawing shapes in the peanut butter with his carrot. "Come on, let's go buy eggs."

"Why? We're not gonna throw them at her house in broad daylight, are we?"

"Do you think I'm that dumb? Come on."

We walked to the mini-mart at the corner and bought a dozen eggs. I started walking to Katie's house and Scott stopped behind me, digging his hands into his sweatshirt pockets.

"This is a bad idea, Zoe."

"Trust me. Please."

He followed, slowly. When we were at the end of Katie's block, I sat down on the curb and took out my memo pad. Slowly, in my neatest handwriting, I wrote:

> Katie,
> We were going to throw these eggs at your house, but we thought we'd leave them here instead so you could make yourself an omelet. Enjoy!
> Yours truly,
> Athena and Ares

Scott laughed. "What the hell? What does that mean?"

I took my hair down out of its tightly wrapped bun and used the elastic band to attach the note to the eggs. I handed the package to Scott. "Run," I told him. "Leave it in her mailbox."

Scott wasn't much of a jock, but he could run like hell. He tore ass down to her mailbox and back and when he reached me, breathless, he grabbed my hand and dragged me home, stumbling along after him.

Scott came to visit me when Athena was just a baby. I was living in an apartment near the ocean. Scott was still so skinny, but taller. His face had filled out. We hadn't seen each other in a long time.

"She's beautiful," he said. "She's so beautiful." We drank orange juice out on the patio and watched the sun sink into the water. He asked me what I was going to do with her.

"I don't know," I said, bouncing her on my lap. "What do you think we should do, baby?" She laughed and laughed as I bounced her higher. I looked at Scott. "I think we're going to take over the world."

We didn't do very much after Katie and the eggs. Sometimes Scott would give me a look and we'd roll our eyes, but other than that, we extracted revenge the only way that thirteen-year-olds could—in knowing that someday we would be something, and the other people wouldn't. In high school, the people we didn't like had less time for us. We had Gay-Straight Alliance meetings when they had cheerleading practice. They scored touchdowns on the football field and during halftime, we'd march across it, instruments in arms.

I took classes with juniors and seniors. Sometimes it was better because they didn't know me. I was quiet. I tried to be quiet. When I was a freshman, someone in my junior biology class wrote "bitch" on a handout I distributed for an oral presentation. I honestly didn't know why and I was so baffled by it, hurt by this anonymous student's aggression. I did all group work alone. Sometimes pretty girls would try to be nice to me if they thought I would help them. They offered pot or invitations to parties at their houses. Boys were the strangest. They made me nervous. I was always the butt of their silent jokes. I never believed anything they said to me. I always assumed they never asked for what they really wanted.

I never had any classes with David Borgen. He was in lower math, science, and English classes, but gym was the same for everybody. We were doing laps around the track and he lazily jogged along in his loosely laced white sneakers, a silver chain bouncing up and down against his chest with each stride. I was walking, staring straight ahead, when he slowed down next to me. I set the muscles in my face and tensed my arms. It wasn't him, it was just my natural reaction when anyone like him tried to talk to me.

"Hey."

I glanced at him and looked forward again. "Hi." Braced myself for the punch line, the joke. Something about my thighs. Thunderthighs. My ass. Jiggling. What? Say it.

"I think we should go out sometime."

"What?" My cheeks flushed red. Hell of a joke. What an asshole. Wanted to punch him. Why is he doing this?

"I'm a pretty nice guy. Really." Two years ago, he joked that I ate one of the lesser planets in his solar system diorama (it was made of a blue peanut M&M and had fallen to the ground) and that I had broken some of the cracked floor tiles in the science classroom by walking on them.

"I don't think so." I tried to keep my voice even.

"You sure?"

"Yeah, David. I don't really think we have anything in common."

"All right, all right. I get it. Whatever." He trotted off, head down, not looking back. What a joke. What a weird fucking joke.

He hadn't done anything. Wasn't rude. Didn't heckle me with his friends. I felt embarrassed all the same, the subject of some joke he'd tell later. How he asked out the fat girl one time. How she got out of breath just telling him no.

People always felt compelled to say something about us. We looked funny. I was big and round with bright red hair and she was a tiny bird with black feathers around her face.

In grocery stores, gray-haired women would bend down into Athena's face and coo, "Aren't you a precious one?"

She'd hide behind my knees, afraid. I'd smile. "She's shy."

"She must take after her father with that pretty black hair," said one woman, glancing at my red curls and freckles, then at my bare left hand. A tongue clucks. She was nice, so she smiled and walked away. The mean ones always had more questions. I'd pretend to be thoroughly engaged in testing the ripeness of a melon when they'd ask Athena where her daddy was—"Chicago," she said, which was more or less the truth as I knew it—or if we went to Holy Cross.

"No," I'd say.

"Oh, First Presbyterian?"

"No," I'd say again, giving a warm smile. "We're witches."

They'd open their eyes wide and put a hand to their lips. As if on cue, Athena would wiggle her nose at them and run off to find a bag of gummy worms. Later, in the parking lot, Athena would pick out the green worms one by one as I put our bags in the trunk.

"Baby, promise me something."

"What, Mommy?"

"Don't ever let those ladies bother you."

She'd pause as she bit off the head of a worm. "I think they're funny."

"Why's that?"

"They smell like shoes."

In math class, we were working on algebra problems in small groups when Jerry Smart, a short boy with a square face, locked his index and middle finger in an oval and said, "Look, it's you!" Then he stuck his tongue through the gap and squeezed his fingers tight. "Leggo!" he yelled, muffled. "Leggo uh me!" I told him to stop it, that it wasn't funny. I turned hot and red, grossed out that someone would pretend I was squeezing his tongue in my vagina.

I told my math teacher I'd been sexually harassed and stood there, red-faced and holding back tears as Jerry pleaded, "I was just kidding!" I could feel the blood burning in my ears. Just kidding, just kidding. Just kidding when he raped some girl four years later, or so I heard through a friend. I wonder if his friends scared her like they tried to scare me. Girls crowded me in the locker room, asking me why I'd lie about Jerry, why I'd be such a bitch.

"Why are you trying to get him in trouble?"

"Are you jealous because he's dating Alyssa?"

"You know he was just joking."

I did what I thought was right.

I don't even remember her name now, she was small and blonde with bangs that she moved from her face with a single finger. She looked out of the corners of her eyes when she spoke, never looking directly at me.

"You are being really unfair. He, like, didn't do anything to you." She lowered her voice and brought her face in close to mine. "Do you want everyone to hate you?"

I'm an old lady now. Memories of school have poured out of my head like water. I've just got the drips left and they're drying up fast. I've got a baby and I don't want to send her there, to run the gauntlets and walk the planks. I named her

209

Athena. I thought it might help her. She always says, "More, Mommy, more!" She can't do things too many times without them getting too easy for her, too boring. I just think she'll die there, no matter where "there" is. Some private hippie satellite school for the arts, a prep school, a magnet school, an alternative school, it's all school. It's all gonna hurt her in some way, eventually. Athena's different. Smart. What else is there to do but teach here now, here, about all the things they will make her unlearn later?

author's commentary

Nonfiction Divination

My editor at HarperCollins told me that in a marketing meeting, they had discussed the possibility of marketing my memoir as a fictional novel.

"It has to do with shelving," she told me. "There's no youth nonfiction section in most bookstores, so they were afraid it might get lost in the shuffle. . . . It would just be easier if it was labeled as fiction. More people would see it, so more people would buy it."

"But," she told me, "I said they couldn't do that. I mean, they could say Stephen King wrote it and they would sell more copies, but it wouldn't be true. You wrote it and it's true."

The authenticity of memoirs has been a topic of hot debate with the recent outing of J. T. Leroy (found to be a hoax created by Laura Albert) and James Frey, who got a severe tongue-lashing by America's book club ringleader, Oprah Winfrey. When teenagers e-mail me or Instant Message me, they often ask, "Is it really true? Did you really do all of that?"

I tell them Yes, I really led a wild and exciting life at age fifteen (although more exciting lives have been lived), but what I really want to ask is, *Does it matter?*

Does it matter if I made it up or if it's true? In a media culture saturated with "reality" television, shocking documentaries, and twenty-four-hour news channels, it's no surprise that people are addicted to authentic experiences—or at least the idea of them. For readers, it's important to know whether an author is merely transcribing some event or if she is creating something brand-new, something that has never happened to her before.

The truth probably lies somewhere in the middle. Some writers are capable of inventing entirely new universes for their readers, filled with strange creatures and unearthly scenarios. But even those books have some basis in real life—at some point, the emotions and words of the characters have probably been felt or heard by the author. It's not so different for the rest of us. We're piecing together what we know with what we can imagine.

"Pagan Baby" is my own personal understanding of fictional nonfiction. Some of the characters described were people I knew growing up, and some events actually happened, but other parts are imagined. As a young writer, I often feel like I'm practicing a form of nonfiction divination—although I haven't ever been a thirty-year-old single mother, I might become one someday. I can project myself into that situation. In a way, it *is* nonfiction, it just hasn't happened yet.

ZOE TROPE is the pseudonym of a fat redheaded girl who published her high school memoir, *Please Don't Kill the Freshman,* when she was seventeen years old. She intends to graduate from Oberlin College with a B.A. in Art History in 2008. Her writing has been published in anthologies, magazines, and newspapers, including but not limited to: *Northwest Edge III: The End of Reality, Sixteen: Stories about That Sweet & Bitter Birthday, Curve Magazine, New Moon Magazine, The Oregonian,* and Pindeldyboz.com. Trope loves three things relentlessly: her boyfriend Matt, the movie *Rushmore,* and Portland, Oregon. Sometimes, she answers e-mail that is sent to ztrope@gmail.com.

There is a woman who is a tailor. She lives in Green River, Utah, and makes her livelihood performing alterations, taking a few inches here, letting out a few inches there, basting in hems then finishing them with a feather stitch.

While hiking in the San Rafael Swell, this woman was raped, thrown down face-first on the sand. She never saw the face of her assailant. What she knew was this, that in that act of violence she lost her voice. She was unable to cry for help. He left her violated and raw.

The woman returned home and told no one of her experience. Instead, she grabbed a large spool of red thread, a pair of scissors, and returned to the Swell.

The woman cut pieces of thread and placed them delicately on the desert. Six inches. Three inches. Twelve inches. They appeared as a loose-stitched seam upon the land. She saw them as bloodlines, remembering the fetishes of Zuni she had held that draw the heart down. She recalled rabbit, lizard, and rattle-snake. She continued to cut lines in memory of animals she had known, seen, and spent time with in these redrock canyons: deer, mountain lion, flicker, and raven. And on one occasion, she recalled watching a black bear amble down Crack Canyon. For this creature, she left a line of red thread three feet long. She cut one-inch threads for frogs and left them inside potholes to wriggle in the rain when the basins would inevitably fill.

Time and space shift; it is fall. The woman is now walking along the banks of the Colorado River. She takes her spool of red thread, ties one end to a juniper and then begins walking with the river, following each bend, each curve, her red thread trailing behind her for miles, stitching together what she has lost.

It is spring. The woman is standing in the deep heat of the desert beside a large boulder known by locals as "the birthing rock." Tiny feet the size of her index finger are etched on stone. Ten toes of hope point to figures of women bearing down, legs spread, with the heads of children coming forth. She recognizes them as two beings seen as one, repeatedly.

The woman picks up an obsidian chip that has been worked by ancient hands; the flaked edge is razor sharp. She holds it between her fingers like a pencil, opens her left hand and traces her own lifeline from beginning to end. The crescent moon below her thumb turns red. She places her palm on the boulder and screams. In the midst of the politics before us, I think of the woman in the San Rafael Swell and her spool of red thread basting memories back into the land.

Emily Dickinson writes, "Life is a spell so exquisite that everything conspires to break it."

How can we not respond?

author's commentary

"Bloodlines" was written in the summer of 1995 in response to a bad Utah wilderness bill that was introduced in the United States Congress. It was part of a larger collection called *Testimony—Writers of the West Speak on Behalf of Utah Wilderness,* edited by Stephen Trimble and me.

Discouraged over the lack of response from our Utah delegation led by Representative James Hansen and Senator Orrin Hatch, who were ignoring the fact that over 80 percent of Utahans wanted more wilderness not less, Steve and I decided to cast a wider net of influence in support of these public lands. We sent a letter to American writers who cared about wildlands, particularly those in Utah. The response was immediate and moving. Within three weeks, we had over twenty essays, poems, and stories written on behalf of these precious desert lands in the redrock canyons of southern Utah. Writers from Poet Laureate Mark Strand to former congresswoman Karen Shepherd to Scott Momaday to Mardy Murie to Rick Bass contributed.

We created a small "chapbook" and distributed it among Congress members with the help of the Southern Utah Wilderness Alliance, a scrappy and smart grassroots environmental organization based in Salt Lake City. With their help, we were able to garner the support of Representative Maurice Hinchey from New York and Congressman Bruce Vento from Minnesota, both great advocates of wilderness, to write a letter to their colleagues urging them to read this little book and vote against this incomplete wilderness bill, which would only protect 1.8 million acres of Utah wilderness in contrast to the citizens' proposal setting aside 5.7 million acres. Senator Russ Feingold supported *Testimony* in the Senate and sent it to his colleagues with a convincing cover letter.

At a press conference, reporters from the *Washington Post* asked Steve and me why we were wasting our time with this, didn't we know how much paper gets floated up on the Hill? It would never get read. Steve turned to the reporter and said very calmly, "Writing is always an act of faith."

The bill was defeated in the House of Representatives and in March 1996, Democratic senators led a filibuster. What was needed was words. Senator Bill Bradley stood on the Senate floor and said, "With all due respect, Senator Hatch, these wildlands do not just belong to Utah, they belong to all of us." He then said he would like to read the words from one of his constituents, John McPhee, on why these lands matter. *Testimony* was read, then entered into the *Congressional Record*. The bill was defeated.

On September 18, 1996, President Bill Clinton created the Grand-Staircase National Monument protecting over 2 million acres within America's Redrock Wilderness.

"Bloodlines" represents my contribution to this effort. I wanted to write a story that would create the emotional landscape of abuse, a metaphor that speaks to the idea that the body of the land is our own.

TERRY TEMPEST WILLIAMS is a writer concerned with issues of social justice in relationship to culture and landscape. Her books include *Refuge—An Unnatural History of Family and Place, An Unspoken Hunger, Leap,* and most recently, *The Open Space of Democracy.* She is the recipient of both a Guggenheim Fellowship and a Lannan Literary Award in creative nonfiction. She divides her time between Castle Valley, Utah, and Moose, Wyoming.

Afterword

*Writing Workshops in San Miguel de Allende with Beverly Donofrio (Memoir)
and Kaylie Jones (Fiction)*

Before our workshops, Beverly and I exchanged e-mails for about a month. We hadn't seen each other in a long time and this written conversation turned into one of the best writing workshops I've ever taught.

BEVERLY DONOFRIO: We met when we were unpublished hopeful writers at graduate school at Columbia University together, almost twenty-five years ago now. Although you were over a decade younger than I, we immediately hit it off, saw a kindred soul in each other. So, we started out at the same graduate school in the same workshop; we were inspired by the same teacher, Richard Price, yet when you wrote your story, *A Soldier's Daughter Never Cries,* you called it fiction. When I wrote my story, *Riding in Cars with Boys,* I called it memoir. What do you think the difference between autobiographical fiction and memoir really is? What did you gain or lose by considering or calling your book fiction?

KAYLIE JONES: Frankly, I never felt I really had a choice but to write fiction. I grew up in a fiction-writing household. My dad was a fiction writer, and growing up around him was a strange and fascinating experience. My brother and I were always competing for attention with the characters in his books. At dinner, he'd talk about these characters of his as if they were real people who lived with him in his "office," as he called his private writing space upstairs. I remember an ongoing battle he had with himself for weeks, when, toward the end of his life, he was trying to finish *Whistle,* the last book of his WWII trilogy. One of his main characters, Bobby Prell, had been badly wounded in combat, in the legs, and the government was waiting to see if he was going to lose his legs or not before awarding him the Congressional Medal of Honor. According to my dad, they never awarded the medal to "cripples." For weeks this went on, with him agonizing over Bobby Prell's legs, as if my dad himself had no control whatsoever over what was going to happen. This was very exciting indeed. One day, he came down from his office and said, "Everything's going to be okay! Bobby Prell's legs are beginning to heal! He isn't going to lose them after all and he's going to get his medal." And we had a celebration.

It was in this atmosphere that I learned about writing, and the discipline of writing. Listening to my dad and his writer friends discuss books, and discuss characters in books, the line between fiction and fact already seemed to me totally arbitrary, totally blurred. For me personally, when I went to Columbia at twenty-one, I realized that writing a memoir would involve not only a certain loyalty to facts, but also an understanding of those facts—I certainly didn't have that kind of memory, or understanding of my life, when I began to try to write *A Soldier's Daughter Never Cries*. Eventually, I became interested in the notion of writing a "faux memoir," which is why I started the novel out with a paragraph about how the narrator's memories are tinted certain colors, which do not correspond to anyone else's memories of those same events. I was hoping to establish the unreliability of the narrator's memories, the solipsism with which a child views the world.

The second reason I chose fiction instead of memoir is that I felt freed from having to be loyal to facts. I became loyal to the story's needs instead. This is the first thing I tell my fiction-writing students: Let go of the facts, your first loyalty is to the story's needs. If you dissected *A Soldier's Daughter Never Cries* scene by scene, not one single scene would hold up under the scrutiny of history. Every detail is changed to fit the story. So instead of a photograph of a time and place, you end up with a kind of abstract representation of a time and place.

You were a hero to me back then (I never told you). You were so young and beautiful and full of life, on your own in your early thirties, with a teenage son to raise. And you'd done it all by yourself. I was right out of college, way overprotected, scared to death of being in New York City on my own. I was living free in my mom's Park Avenue apartment. I never told you this either, but when I used to come visit you in your apartment in Alphabet City, I'd take a cab and then walk the last few blocks, as if I'd taken the subway! It seemed to me you already had a great deal of understanding of your life, and could see the forks in the road and the roads not taken, so to speak. The only great loss I'd ever suffered was my father's death when I was sixteen. While this left me completely bereft, from you I learned that it was possible not only to survive life's injustices, but to survive them without being a victim. Better to fight back, that's what I learned from you.

Reading your memoirs—and other excellent memoirs—I sense that careful thought went into the structuring, the decision of when to offer up what bit of information. So that memoir becomes an exploration of the author's life choices, an organizing of facts according to some kind of profound hindsight. Chekhov says that good fiction calls for "total objectivity," which is meant to allow the reader to draw his or her own conclusions. In memoir, the writer is allowed to draw conclusions for us. I may still have a memoir in me. We'll see.

Do you disagree with my definition of the differences between fiction and memoir? Why did you choose memoir instead of fiction? As I recall, you weren't at all sure, when you began Columbia, which way you wanted to go with your book.

BD: I think there can be significant differences between fiction and memoir but not so much between autobiographical fiction and memoir. I have an ex-friend who was forty during the time of life he wrote about in his memoir, but he said he was thirty, because being younger and making all those stupid mistakes made him more sympathetic. Memoir writers, too, must serve the story. I draw the line at changing actual facts, at least I believe I do, but I may be fooling myself, because like many writers, I've been a fabricator since I could complete a sentence. Remember how we had *two* pathological liars among the twenty students in our class at Columbia? I definitely change sequencing all the time, make incidents that may have occurred in a span of three years happen in one afternoon. I think all memoirists do this, otherwise you would not be able to make a story. I considered myself a fiction writer all the way through selling the proposal for *Riding*. It wasn't until I met with my editor for the first time at dinner and said, "My novel," and he said, "Novel? I didn't buy a novel. I bought a memoir," that I became a memoirist. But I think it was a blessing. Outrageous things happen to me. My life is eventful. I have always loved telling my stories.

And it's true that as a memoir writer I get to say exactly what I think. That may be what I love most about writing memoir.

You know, I think I suspected you took cabs to my apartment. You reminded me of the time we were out one evening and walked over to my apartment on Twelfth Street and Avenue A. There were a few abandoned buildings and one was used as a crack house with a guard standing at the door. As we walked past, he lifted his shirt to display a meat cleaver tucked inside his belt. You grabbed my arm, "Oh, my God, Beverly," you said. "Did you see that?" The guard had never showed *me* his meat cleaver, and I remember thinking that you were at much greater risk walking around the city at night. You were pretty, young, and projected a vulnerability I'd turned into a hard crust long before. So, in a way what you admired in me, the toughness of a fighter, made me a survivor, for sure, but it also made me defended and cut off from certain emotions, including fear.

I remember writing a story in Richard Price's class, all of it true, about a woman who has a date to meet up with her boyfriend on Valentine's Day, runs into an old friend and his pregnant wife on the street, ends up in a ménage à trois, and completely blows off her boyfriend, who is waiting for her with champagne in a bucket of ice. We discussed the piece in class. It was a fiction-writing class and I called the piece fiction. Richard asked, "Why did she do that?" and I had no answer. This was shocking to me that I understood myself so little, and that I couldn't even make up an answer. I'd simply written the story because I thought it was interesting, and I'd thought that "interesting" had been enough. It was that story, my increasing inability to "feel" things, as well as some deep sadness at the time, that caused me to enter psychotherapy, intensely, twice a week. How, I asked myself, can I ever be a writer if I don't understand my own actions, motivations, neuroses? I was in psychotherapy through all of graduate school and for three years later. Five years altogether, and it is no accident that at the same moment I graduated therapy I was awarded a contract to write *Riding*.

So, your observation that writing memoir becomes an exploration of the author's life choices is true. It's a cliché but I've always subscribed to the maxim that the only life worth living is the examined life. Memoir requires one to do exactly that. Both of my memoirs have brought me through pain to understanding and some forgiveness, both of myself and others.

My memory of you and your work back then was first of all that you were determined, focused, disciplined, and a tireless writer. I probably never told you at the time but I was filled with admiration for your stamina and your grit. I, on the other hand, was blocked most of the time and spending half of my days in bed imagining bricks falling on my head. I also remember that you were in deep pain from the loss of your father, and that you were processing that loss in your work. If I remember correctly, your first book, *As Soon as It Rains,* was mostly about the loss of your father. And that same theme resonates in your second book, *Quite the Other Way,* which took place in Russia. So, I imagine writing fiction is also a way to process one's life, and of expressing one's obsessions.

KJ: So, it looks like they are the same, or very similar—at least in the context of *A Soldier's Daughter Never Cries* and *Riding in Cars with Boys.* In my last two novels, I believe I moved further away from autobiographical fiction, in the sense that there are substantial differences between my characters and myself. Nevertheless, we share many experiences that I've re-created and reinterpreted for the novels.

Do you remember the day we walked home from Columbia at 116th and Broadway, all the way to your apartment on Avenue A and Twelfth Street? It was the very first warm spring day. Five men—*five*—exposed themselves to us along the way. That has never happened to me in that number, before or since. What do you think that said about us at the time?

When you showed the movie of *Riding* to my six-year-old daughter Eyrna and her friends last summer in San Miguel, she kept running into the kitchen where we were sitting and talking to ask you, "Did that really happen like that?" And mostly, your response was, "Oh, no, that's just Hollywood." At one point she ran in and asked, "Was your daddy really that mean to you?" The answer you gave her, in a deep, emphatic voice, was, "Oh, no-o. He was much meaner."

What I wanted Eyrna to understand, emphatically, was your real-life success. Which, in the film, was completely excluded. That did not make me happy, because yours is in fact a great success story. You went to college, you went to graduate school. You wrote two wonderful books. I'd like to know how you felt about the movie of your book. And why do you think Hollywood felt it necessary to take away the film-Beverly's success?

BD: I'm so glad you asked that question. But first I want to say that I completely forgot about all those men exposing themselves until you reminded me this past summer. And that tells you a lot about how fallible memory is. I wonder why I forgot it. I do remember that you were a knockout. Good thing we didn't make a practice of walking together all that much.

It was a crying shame they didn't include the fact that I went to college in that movie. For personal reasons but also because I think it would have been a better movie had Beverly gone to college. My greatest motivation when I was writing *Riding* was to tell other working-class girls, other young women who got pregnant, kids who had made a big mistake and felt like their life was ruined because of it, that their life didn't have to be ruined, that you get other chances, that you can realize your dreams. The voice I used in the book yearned between the lines, "If only I could go to college, if only I could go to college." My parents hadn't graduated high school and had no great ambitions for their children, in fact, quite the opposite. They were afraid they'd lose their children if we went beyond them. I hated it in the movie when the father was so disappointed his daughter was pregnant because he'd had such great ambitions for her. My parents wanted me to get married, have a bunch of kids in wedlock, and live next door. Having ambition was actually rebellious. When I told my mother sophomore year about my high college plans (this scene is in the book), she said, "Get real. Take typing. Get a *good* job when you graduate." So the fact that the essence of my book, the essence of my experience, was eviscerated from the movie just killed me. It was a ruined opportunity to send an inspirational message to millions of kids. And as I said, I believe, objectively, that the movie would have been much improved had the very dark second act been given the grace of some hope in its final moments by rewarding Beverly for all her struggles by throwing her the bone of a college acceptance letter in the mailbox.

You know how people in certain primitive cultures believe that if you take their picture it robs their soul? That's kind of how I feel about that movie. I can't say for certain why Hollywood decided against college. It could be that Jim Brooks, the producer and the artistic vision behind the movie, didn't understand what was so hugely affirming about the college experience. I'm not sure he even graduated college, and he is one of the most successful men in the industry. Besides, he never set out to duplicate the book. He told the screenwriter, Morgan Upton Ward, from the get-go that he must make the movie his own, but the truth is Morgan never got to make the movie his own, he got to make the movie Jim wanted to make—about a relationship between a mother and son, an imperfect relationship between two people who are basically stuck with each other, but love each other anyway. And this was his right. Movies do not have to be fair representations of the books from which they are adapted.

The truth is that if I were given the choice between having no movie made or this movie, I'd choose this movie. For a Hollywood film it takes big risks, it talks about difficult subjects and is not a comfortable film to watch. It is flawed, but in many ways it's a good movie. The process was immensely interesting to watch and be involved in; I sold lots of books; and it has opened doors in my career.

This brings me to my question to you. You told me that Eyrna was excited to meet me because I was the first person she'd ever met to have had a movie made of her life. And you said, "But Eyrna, I, your own mother, had a movie made of my life." And she said, "But it wasn't true." I, however, know that the characters in the book and in the movie were at least based on your family and on you. I may be wrong but it seems that I read somewhere at the time that [Ismail] Merchant and [James] Ivory were attracted to the story because it was about expatriates in Paris during those years, and specifically about your father, James Jones, who is an icon. Back when I saw the movie, I'd thought that I'd remembered you telling me that your father had said things his character actually says in the movie. When the girl has a series of backseat flings with crude boys, and goes to the father for help, because she really doesn't know why she did it, he tells her, "Backseats and drive-ins and beaches are no place to have sex, baby. Especially the beach. Ugh, I hate that sand . . . listen, be smart about this now. They'll figure you're easy and keep on trying with you. Just say no

221

beverly donofrio and kaylie jones

till you find someone you really like. When you find someone you really like, come talk to me." Are you content not to claim that movie as being about your life? In general, I'm very curious to know what you think of the movie and how you'd characterize your movie-making experience. And don't you find it really strange that we've both had movies made of our lives?

KJ: Hah! I just asked Eyrna if she remembered saying that, and she said I misquoted her. Her correction: "Mom, what I said is, 'your movie isn't *all* true.'" This is getting seriously confusing.

I don't claim the movie wasn't autobiographical. I claim that it was fictionalized. Many things happened close to the way I wrote them, or maybe they didn't. I can't remember! I absolutely loved Kris Kristofferson. He reminded me in person so much of my dad that it was scary. My dad and I did have a conversation like that, not exactly that conversation, but close enough. It was shortly before he died. What struck me years later was that he knew he was dying, and was trying to squeeze in as much good advice and information about life as he could in the short amount of time left to him. He didn't hedge, because he knew he was running out of time. When I was sixteen, he seemed a little brutal to me, but honest. I didn't understand why he would allow me to have boyfriends, or drink, or smoke pot, unlike other parents. Now I see that he was trying to protect and guide me before I was left on my own. Later in life, I saw how much he helped me, and I try to be as honest with my daughter as my father was with me. Not as brutal, because as far as I know, I have all the time in the world. Anyway, that was what I was trying to show in the novel. The strangest thing about the making of the movie was this: James Ivory always saw it as a memoir. He copied, and I mean exactly, the furniture, paintings, silver, lamps, rugs that are still in my mother's house on Long Island, mostly Louis XIII furniture they brought back from Paris when we returned to the States in 1975. When James Ivory had this stuff made in Paris, and put on the set there, and sent me photographs (I was about to give birth to Eyrna and couldn't go), I almost fainted. He so exactly reproduced our home, but then certain things weren't right, were out of place, or the wrong color, that it felt like one of those weird dreams when you're in your own bedroom, you open the door and you're in the Sahara or something. Just too weird. Even weirder when my husband and I took five-week-old Eyrna down to the set in Wilmington, North Carolina. We walked into a house on the water and there was all the furniture from my own childhood home!

Funny thing, my best childhood friend, Jamie Bruce, who directs movies and TV shows, called me after he saw the movie. He was speechless. The only thing he could articulate was "Your dad was sleeping on the wrong side of the bed." That's how weird it felt to him, and he was only a guest in our house. And yet. And yet, I never considered the book a memoir. I suppose I expected James Ivory to visually make it all up. But he wanted the film to be an exact replication of my Paris home in the Sixties and Seventies, correct in every detail, and I didn't disabuse him of this notion. I just kind of went along, accepting, almost with surprise, that he and Ismail Merchant, the producer, saw it as a very slightly veiled memoir and intended to market it that way. I guess I realized at that moment, in retrospect, how much of the truth really was in that book. And then here came the problem: the public expected some kind of "roman à clef," a "Daddy Dearest" story, a spilling of the dirt. There was none of that in the film. Secondly, it was not a biography of a famous writer, but a child's view of life growing up in a foreign country with a famous writer father, and the adoption of a French child into that family. I think it made a good story. I still do.

And yes, my friend Beverly, I think it is extraordinarily strange that we both had movies made of our lives—or at least of two people extremely similar to ourselves who lived parallel lives to ours. I think it's even stranger that we both went to Wesleyan at the same time (though we never met there, we probably passed each other a million times) and then to Columbia, where we became good friends. And how about my visit to San Miguel, which I planned before I knew you had moved there? Coincidence is God's way of staying anonymous.

What's next for you now? Are you planning to write a novel?

BD: How surreal that you wrote a novel and the movie people went nuts duplicating the physical world exactly, while I wrote a memoir and the movie people simply used it and the photos I gave them as inspiration for their own visions. But then Merchant and Ivory are not exactly Hollywood.

223

beverly donofrio and kaylie jones

You said earlier that your last two books were not autobiographical. I am sorry to say of your five books, I missed reading your fourth, but I did read your fifth, *Speak Now*. It definitely is not your life, and the plot is completely made up. It seems to me that many novelists write about themselves in their first or their first few books to process their experience. Eventually their demons are exorcised and that need evaporates. I think that's happened to me, too. In fact, I've begun two novels, one historical and another vaguely autobiographical but with a plot. I hope I really do finish them. The only fiction I ever sold is a kid's book about a mouse. And I wrote that one because my therapist told me I had a fiction block, that I was afraid of my audience, and that I might not be so intimidated if I broke the ice by writing for children. The theory is that my fiction block began when I was twelve and wrote a pretend letter to my best friend. I wrote it as though it was from a boy we both had a crush on. My father found it. When I said I made it up, he accused me of lying, slapped my face, and sent me to my room saying, "No daughter of mine . . ." Condemned for my first work of fiction, placed under suspicion for being a lying little hussy for the rest of my adolescent life. I take this as a challenge. I *must* write a novel.

And what about you? What next?

KJ: A few years ago, I got really mad at a writer I admire when he wrote a *New York Times* column on writing saying that he didn't trust any writer who complained that writing a novel was hard work. He just infuriated me. Not only do I find writing a novel hard work, I find it psychologically challenging. It takes over my life. I become obsessed with the book, at the expense of my family. I'm extremely grateful to be able to do it, I'll tell you that. Writing and teaching writing are a great life. I don't have to take a whole lot of shit from anyone. I get to go places like San Miguel de Allende!

When I'm in the process of writing a novel, I'm living in an alternate reality. I love it so much—the book, the process—that reality interferes. Now I have a seven-year-old daughter and a kind, supportive, loving husband. They need me. My little girl needs me. I grew up with a writer who let nothing and no one step in the way of his work. It was his life's passion. While I was writing *Speak Now,* one day, my daughter came home from nursery school with her babysitter, and came running to me as I sat at my computer, and I angrily pushed her away. The look of devastation on her face said it all, and I realized that I care more about her than I do about anything in the world. So I turned off the computer, and learned to meditate for twenty minutes after I finish writing for the day, and before I see her. I finished *Speak Now* and decided to take a break from novels. Now I'm writing short stories and articles. I have a novel in my head, but I'm resisting starting it. Eyrna will only be little once. Soon, before I know it, she'll be away, having her own life, and I'll have all the time in the world. I'm trying to teach myself to be less obsessed, less driven by my work. I'm gearing up to start this new book, but I'm not quite there yet. I even have a working title, *The Anger Meridian*. This comes from my Salvadoran massage therapist, who says that when you wake up at 4 A.M., it's very hard to go back to sleep, because that's the anger meridian. For years I'd wake up at 4 A.M. and have no idea why, and not be able to go back to sleep. Now I often sleep through the night. I guess I'm getting better!

BD: Better? You're great! I was not such an attentive mother as you, and still I had the idea that I could not truly write until my son went off to college. And because I believed this was true, that's pretty much what happened. I admire your absolute will to write. Writing is not easy, novel or memoir, and that kind of will and desire is what it takes. I am *so* happy to have the opportunity to teach writing with you in San Miguel. I think we'll learn a few things ourselves.

after the workshops

We had the memoir and fiction students write several exercises together, as a group. The most interesting results came from their two-page scenes in which they described a person experiencing his/her first major betrayal. The writers read their work aloud to the entire group. It was almost impossible to discern the fiction pieces from the memoirs; however, all the memoirs were in first person, while only about half the fiction pieces were in first person. We found that beginning writers seem to need to mine the ore of personal experience, to write about what they know, as Beverly pointed out in our conversation. When forced to write about painful experiences, the writers, while balking at first, produced their best work.

It also became clear to us that the same rules of good writing apply to both genres. A writer can't convince a reader of anything by insisting upon it with generalities, or by judging the situation for the reader. Only specific details, delivered with an even neutrality, capture the imagination and compassion of the reader, who wants to make up his/her own mind about a situation, even in memoir. Images are what grasp the reader's attention, and that was true all the way back to the *Iliad*.

BEVERLY DONOFRIO'S best-selling memoir *Riding in Cars with Boys* has been translated into fifteen languages. It was made into a well-loved motion picture, starring Drew Barrymore and directed by Penny Marshall. Donofrio was a producer. Donofrio's second memoir, *Looking for Mary, or the Blessed Mother and Me,* was about her search for faith through the Virgin Mary.

KAYLIE JONES was born in Paris, France, and attended French schools until she returned with her family to the United States in 1974. Her father was the novelist James Jones. Her third novel, *A Soldier's Daughter Never Cries* (Bantam, 1990), won a New York Public Library Young Adult Fiction Award. The novel was adapted as a Merchant-Ivory film directed by James Ivory and starring Kris Kristofferson, Leelee Sobieski, Barbara Hershey, and Jesse Bradford in September 1998. Her novels have been translated into many languages, including French, Dutch, German, Japanese, Italian, and Spanish.